PRAISE FROM ...

"Even great for adults!
My daughter (11) and I loved planning our trip with this book! It ended up being the only book we carried as we toured the Eternal City. The information was great with wonderful tidbits to keep the interest level high. We home school so this was our field trip, and this book was invaluable. Our copy has been our notebook and is full of written notes, highlighting, post-it notes, and drawings. We wouldn't part with it for anything!"
—**Williamsburg, VA**

"This book added enormously to our visit, particularly in Galleria Borghese and St. Peter's, not necessarily places I would expect a 12-year old to enjoy. The book made them great fun. It was not my first time around St. Peter's, but I saw things I had passed by before. The general advice is spot on."
—**Dublin, Ireland**

"I'm overjoyed! It's exactly what we were looking for."
—**California**

"**RWK was wonderful, and we weren't with kids!** The best guidebook we had, it gave good tips on how to see the highlights without suffering museum fatigue."
—**Australia**

"This book was an invaluable source of helpful hints…even our well-seasoned traveling companion was impressed. [It] was our family's lifesaver!"
—**Pennsylvania, with four children, aged 10 and under**

"I just wanted to pass on our thoughts after using your book as our main planning tool. Your book was excellent! Each of the tours was the perfect length, and the notes scattered throughout allowed us to appear very knowledgeable to our kids (and sometimes also to those of other people nearby!) We loved our visit and especially loved that the kids enjoyed it as much as they did—due, in no small part to your book."
—**Web Comment**

"[RWK] is a work of art—and not just a work of art but something truly useful."
—**Professor, Department of Classical Studies, Loyola University Chicago**

"DEFINITELY buy RWK. It is simplified, but not dumbed down. The short biographies of key Romans are a brilliant way to connect kids (and

adults) to the highlights of Roman history. It is full of kid-friendly tips on timing, food, etc."
—**Wyoming**

"I am blown away. I just wish I could find one like it for every city we're visiting."
—**New York**

"Many thanks for your book…the games and ideas will be brilliant to keep our almost 4 & 8 year old kids amused without them really even realizing it! Some grateful parents!"
—**Glasgow, Scotland**

"This guide book is the best guide book I've ever read for families with young children. It's wholeheartedly recommended!"
—**Web comment**

"I highly recommend [RWK]…I would be lost without it. It's small and filled with fun itineraries and great tips! Better than the other five books I have combined."
—**Web comment**

"**Must-have book for families in Rome!**
I was amazed. [It] is great for kids of all ages, and that includes moms, dads, and grandparents. Loved the format."
—**Florida**

"It is really excellent. With the book you can be as flexible as you like, especially important with younger children."
—**California**

"**Don't leave home without this book.** RWK is just as important for your trip to Rome as obtaining your passport. It has everything you need to discover the delights of Rome at your own pace and the pace of children. I have lived in Italy, on and off, for over 30 years. As I read this excellent book I found new and interesting things to see and to do."
—**Claudesplace.com**

"Thank you, thank you, thank you!"
—**Web comment**

"Pasquesi's wonderful book was an incredibly useful resource in planning the details of our day."
—**Publisher, Italiakids.com**

"I'm enjoying [the guide] a lot more than the regular travel books!"
—**Professor, Purdue University, The American Academy in Rome**

ROME WITH KIDS
AN INSIDER'S GUIDE

J.M. PASQUESI

SOLOROMA

Rome with Kids: An Insider's Guide
Published by Solo Roma Inc.
1850 North Clark Street, Suite 2806
Chicago, Illinois 60614

For more information, please visit www.romewithkids.com

Second Edition 2014
First Edition 2008, reprinted with updates 2009, 2011
©2008 by J.M. Pasquesi, all rights reserved

Publisher's Cataloging-in-Publication
(Provided by Quality Books, Inc.)

Pasquesi, J. M. (Joan Marie)
    Rome with kids : an insider's guide / J.M. Pasquesi.
    p. cm.
    Includes bibliographical references and index.
    LCCN 2006932154

    1. Rome (Italy)--Guidebooks. 2. Children--Travel--Italy--
    Rome--Guidebooks.   I. Title.

DG416.P377 2007   914.5'630493
                         QBI06-600545

    ISBN-13: 978-0-9773093-1-3
    ISBN-10: 0977-309-312

Illustrations by Patrick O. McKenna and Giancarlo Pasquesi
Maps, floor plans, and cover design by Best Design Chicago, Inc.
Maps, photos, illustrations © J.M. Pasquesi, all rights reserved

Stay updated!
Web site: romewithkids.com
Twitter: Rome_with_Kids
Instagram: SoloRoma

Published by Solo Roma Books, Inc.

10 9 8 7 6 5 4 3 2 1

CONTENTS

Acknowledgments 9
Preface 11
How to Use This Book 13
    Know Your Romans 14
    Know Your Family Crests 22
    Know Your Kids 22

PART ONE: ANCIENT ROME 25
Map of the Area 26

Chapter One: THE FORUM & CAPITOLINE HILL 27
Legendary twins raised by a she-wolf, a "talking" statue, the belly button of Rome, an ancient board game, and a secret passage are among the finds at Piazza Campidoglio, the Capitoline Museums, the Tabularium and the Roman Forum.
What's Around? 46

Chapter Two: THE COLOSSEUM & PALATINE HILL 51
An ancient schoolroom, gladiators, prehistoric huts, a sacrificial altar, and a surprising view over Circus Maximus await your discovery along with the Arches of Constantine and Titus, the Palatine Museum and the fascinating excavations under San Clemente.
What's Around? 59

Chapter Three: THE MOUTH OF TRUTH 62
A hand-biting ancient lie-detector, a broken, half-sunk bridge and Rome's tiny Tiberina Island are explored along with the wide-open space of Circus Maximus, the Palatine Bridge, S. Maria in Cosmedin and the Temple of Hercules.
What's Around? 68
LET'S EAT! Capitoline Hill and Surrounding Area 69

PART TWO: MEDIEVAL & RENAISSANCE ROME **73**
Map of the Area 74

Chapter Four: THE CAMPO DEI FIORI ZONE........................**75**
The Figure of Death, skeletons, a surprising trick garden, and a vibrant open-air market make for great fun while exploring the Farnese Palace, Galleria Spada and scenic Via Giulia.
What's Around? *82*

Chapter Five: PIAZZA NAVONA TO THE PANTHEON **84**
A towering obelisk, a gigantic fountain and a huge hole in a roof are among the big things in this zone with a stone zoo. Look for a horse, a lion, a fish, a baby elephant, and an ancient Egyptian cat while you take in the excavation of Domitian's Stadium, a church full of Caravaggio masterpieces and charming S. Maria Sopra Minerva.
What's Around? *94*
LET'S EAT! Campo, Navona and the Pantheon 98

PART THREE: BAROQUE & MODERN ROME.....................**105**
Map of the Area 106

Chapter Six: THE TREVI FOUNTAIN **107**
Throw a coin in the Trevi, find its drinking fountain, read Marcus Aurelius' storytelling column, find an ancient sundial and navigate your way to the President's Palace where you may even watch the changing of the guard.
What's Around? *111*

Chapter Seven: SPANISH STEPS LOOP..................................**113**
A house of monsters, Galileo's prison, a misfired cannonball, pedal-karts and a sinking boat keep energy high around Piazza del Popolo, Piazza di Spagna, the Pincio gardens and S. Maria del Popolo.
What's Around? *121*

Chapter Eight: THE VIA VENETO ZONE................................**124**
Bone-covered walls, a spectacular sea god, a sleeping saint and classic American burgers can be found around the "Bone Church" of S. Maria della Concezione and Triton's Fountain.
What's Around? *128*

Chapter Nine: GALLERIA BORGHESE **130**
Unwind, rent bikes or paddle-boats, or take in the scenery in this expansive, leafy park with a zoo, gardens, a pond, fountains and show-stopping art in its Galleria Borghese.
What's Around? *137*
LET'S EAT! Trevi to the Spanish Steps..139

PART FOUR: PAPAL ROME......................................**143**
Map of the Area 144

Chapter Ten: ST. PETER'S & THE BORGO..........................**145**
Climbing to the top of the Cupola, figuring out an optical illusion, finding Michelangelo's signature, exploring a fortress, playing in Castel Sant'Angelo's park, and spying the pope's escape route score high on kids' sightseeing lists.
What's Around? *161*

Chapter Eleven: SISTINE CHAPEL & VATICAN MUSEUMS...**163**
Spotting Michelangelo, searching for the skin of Saint Bartholemew, and inspecting amazing Egyptian mummies make the Sistine Chapel, the Egyptian Museum and the Pio-Clementino Museum fun for everyone.
What's Around? *173*
LET'S EAT! In and Around the Borgo 173

PART FIVE: DAY TRIPS AND MORE................................177

EXTRAS IN ROME...**177**
EXTRAS OUTSIDE ROME **190**
FURTHER AFIELD—POMPEII **194**
USEFUL INFORMATION
  Books, Computers, Internet Cafés, Mail, Shops, Transportation...**196**
WHERE TO STAY...**202**
WHERE TO EAT...**213**
ROME ON THE WEB **231**
SOURCES **233**
INDEX 235

A child's drawing of the colosseum.

ACKNOWLEDGMENTS

I thank my husband David, first and foremost, for introducing me to Rome and sharing his enthusiasm for the city and the Italian language with me many years ago. Among many others to whom I owe thanks for their support, editing, advice and inspiration: Margaret Costello, John Makowski, Melinda M. Marshall, Anne Moore, Patricia Pasquesi, and the Rome Tourist Board team. This book could not have been written without David, Giancarlo and Luca Pasquesi. They have been with me every step of the way, each sharing my passion for Rome and contributing to the book in more ways than can be mentioned here.

To David

PREFACE

Rome with children is fun. Scrambling around ruins, climbing hills and searching for gladiators in wide-open valleys and piazzas is a blast. Whether spelunking the dark recesses of excavated church basements or catching the sun-lit spray of a crashing fountain, kids can feel the vibrant pulse of this world-class, hands-on city. And to fuel all the activity there's pizza, pasta and plenty of gelato—a kid's dream cuisine.

Rome is largely an outdoor, interactive museum where the stones speak. Ancient foundations and sculptures tell us who and what was important, how and where people lived. Classical ruins are ideal for touring with children because they are so accessible.

Yet because Rome's hills, valleys, piazzas and churches are— quite literally—layered with history, taking in the Eternal City can be bewildering. It can be downright frustrating, in fact, if you have to decode the sights with a bored, tired, whining child at the end of your wrist. It is my passionate wish that no one towing kids should have to stand in front of a bunch of rubble and figure out what to make of it.

With over twenty years of traveling to and living in Rome with my own children, I've set out to share not only *what* you should see but also *how* you should see it. I've created tours that are short in duration but long on memories. I've packaged each with timesaving tips and a number of activities and engaging stories, myths and legends. I did not set out to provide yet another guide to Rome's art or history. Instead, I've chosen to reconcile an adult's desire to become immersed in the glories of this civilization with a child's desire to run, dream, climb and explore.

To that end, I've sifted through some 3,000 years of Roman remains to focus on precisely those sights that should not be missed. You *will* see the best and most famous sights of Rome, but in a manner that will spare your children burnout and boredom. Step by step, I will guide you and your children to get the most out of each sight or set of sites. I won't take you anywhere that doesn't hook your kids first. I won't leave you anywhere without arming you with bite-sized observations, intriguing questions, compelling treasure hunts and unforgettable stories to share with your children.

KID-FRIENDLY FILMS STARRING...ROME

Roman Holiday with Audrey Hepburn and Gregory Peck (1953, NR)

Three Coins in the Fountain with Clifton Webb and Dorothy Maguire (1954, NR)

Ben-Hur with Charlton Heston and Stephen Boyd (1959, NR)

Spartacus with Kirk Douglas and Jeanne Simmons (1960, NR)

After the Fox with Peter Sellers (1966, NR)

Hudson Hawk with Bruce Willis (1991, Rated R)

Only You with Marisa Tomei (1994, Rated PG-13)

Gladiator with Russell Crowe and Joaquin Phoenix (2000, Rated R)

Ocean's 12 with George Clooney and Brad Pitt (2004, Rated PG-13)

Jumper with Hayden Christensen and Samuel L. Jackson (2008, Rated PG-13)

Angels & Demons with Tom Hanks and David Pasquesi (2009, Rated PG-13)

KID-FRIENDLY BOOKS

Pino and the Signora's Pasta, by Janet Pedersen (Ages 3-8)

Gladiator (Tough Jobs series), by Helen Greathead (Ages 7-12)

The Goose Guards, by Terry Deary (Ages 7-12)
> And other Deary Roman Tales

Ancient Rome (DK Eyewitness Books), by Simon James (Ages 9-12)

Ancient Rome and Pompeii, by Mary Pope Osborne (Ages 9-12)

See You Later, Gladiator, by Jon Scieszka (Ages 9-12)

The Enemies of Jupiter, by Caroline Lawrence (Ages 9-12)
> And other Lawrence mysteries

The Eagle of the Ninth, by Rosemary Sutcliff (Ages 9-12)
> And other Sutcliff Roman historical fictions

Tiger, Tiger, by Lynne Reid Banks (Ages 9-12)

Who Can Open Michelangelo's Seven Seals, by Thomas Brezina (Ages 9-12)

Ancient Rome: Monuments Past and Present, by R. A. Staccioli (All Ages)

Augustus Caesar's World, by Genevieve Foster (All Ages)

HOW TO USE THIS BOOK

This book gives you eleven mini-tours covering all of Rome's top sights, each packaged with a host of tips to help you wring the most out of that area. Short tours are about an hour; the longest average two to three hours—about all the time a family with young kids can handle. Families with teens can easily pack three or four tours into a single day. Go-getters with more than three days in Rome can add sights from a list of suggested extras *(see **Day Trips and More**)*. You can always customize what I've put together to suit your own schedule or preferences. Be sure to note opening hours and early closings, especially midday closings for small churches.

The ages and stages of Roman topography exist both side by side and one on top of another: the ancient kings, the Republic, the Empire, the Renaissance and the Unification each affected the city greatly. For simplicity, this book is divided into four parts, major walkable areas designated (loosely) by predominant influences: Ancient, Renaissance, Baroque and Papal. An orientation map at the beginning of each part shows at a glance the sights and restaurants that will be covered. Each chapter describes what you'll see and then tells you, upfront in **Timing and Tips**, how best to pull it off.

In today's world, tourists to Rome should expect airport-type security checks at all major monuments such as St. Peter's Basilica and the Colosseum. Currently, these tend to cause a bottleneck as visitors thread through them, but most lines move along at a pretty fast clip. For hassle-free touring, you might want to select belts, backpacks, hair accessories and other personal effects that are free of metal. Though some sites, like the Vatican, have bag checks, never count on it. And be prepared to stash a stroller unguarded. (You may wish to bring a bike lock along for this purpose.) The prepared parent will also carry enough cash to cover entrance fees and a meal to avoid unexpectedly non-functioning credit card machines and to take advantage of local, cash-only restaurants.

If you find extra time on your hands at the conclusion of a tour and your children show no signs of mutiny, check out **What's Around?** at the end of each chapter. It points you to oddities, shops, churches and museums that aren't must-sees, but are wonderful nearby additions.

At the tail end of each section, **Let's Eat!** offers suggestions on where to eat along the way, with brief descriptions of restaurants and cafés in the immediate area. Full descriptions can be found in the comprehensive **Where to Eat** listings at the back of the book.

Part Five, Day Trips and More, includes secondary sightseeing ideas in Rome and day trips to attractions beyond the city center. You'll find information such as where to rent bicycles, shop for kids and check e-mail as well as the details for **Where to Stay** and **Where to Eat.** It should be noted that all phone numbers listed include Rome's city code—06—which is considered a part of local numbers and is dialed along with the rest of the number from within the city. Those calling from outside Italy must first dial an international access code followed by Italy's country code—39. To make a call from the U.S.A./Canada, for example, first dial 011-39, then the local number.

KNOW YOUR ROMANS

Popes, patrons, emperors and artists are responsible for much of the Rome we see today. Get to know the few key players listed below who created the work and paid the bills, and you'll build a richer, more intimate understanding of Rome, because their influences are everywhere. The names of a few of these important people appear in **boldface** throughout the book to alert you to their presence. Review these thumbnail biographies, listed chronologically.

AUGUSTUS (63 BC-14 AD). Rome's first emperor, formerly known as Gaius Octavianus and called Octavian until his crowning, reigned from 27 BC to 14 AD. His great-uncle and adoptive father Julius Caesar may have been the first individual to gain control of Rome since the Republic, but Augustus held onto that power for more than 40 years—a veritable lifetime. The *Pax Romana*, the long period of peace and prosperity that his reign initiated, began in 31 BC after the famous Battle of Actium where Octavian defeated Antony and Cleopatra.

Caesar's murder taught his adopted son some important lessons. Romans wanted a Republic; Caesar had gained too much power for his people to remain comfortable with one man's rule. Shrewd and perceptive, Augustus managed to rule in Caesar's wake by making it seem as though the people were really in charge. He made a grand show of restoring the Republic, though ultimately he kept all the power for himself. Public image was Augustus' forte. One of his greatest public-relations coups was to deify Caesar, thereby making himself the son of a god.

The stability of the Empire allowed Augustus to turn his attentions to a remarkable program of civic improvement and planning. He sanctioned the restoration of some 82 temples and several aqueducts as well as the construction of the first Pantheon, the Baths of Agrippa and the Temple of Mars Ultor (Avenger) in the Imperial Forums, the Theater of Marcellus, the Ara Pacis (the altar of peace celebrating his *Pax Romana*) and the Forum of Augustus. In the Roman Forum, he built the temple to Divus Iulius (Divine Julius) as well as the Arch of Augustus and a temple to Apollo. According to the ancient historian Suetonius, Augustus claimed he found the city brick and left it marble. This was no exaggeration.

The literary Golden Age of Rome also came to pass during Augustus' reign, with the flourishing of Horace, Virgil, Livy and Ovid. In fact, we have Augustus to thank for Virgil's brilliant *Aeneid*. Augustus commissioned the heroic epic to give Rome what the elite Greeks had: impressive foundation myths that recounted a glorious past and foretold future greatness, like Homer's *Odyssey*.

NERO (37-68 AD). Born Lucius Domitius Ahenobarbus, Rome's nefarious emperor (54-68 AD) later changed his name to Nero Claudius Caesar Drusus Germanicus. Emperor Claudius became Nero's stepfather when he married Nero's mother, the diabolical Agrippina. She poisoned Claudius to secure the throne for her son.

Seneca educated Nero, but the young man retained none of the learned man's virtues. Nero murdered most of his family, including his mother, two of his wives and later, fittingly, killed himself. In fact, Nero killed so many people in such torturous ways that suicide became a popular fad, an easy way out of the pain and suffering that awaited unfortunates tapped by his guards. If he didn't kill you, his prison made you wish he had. Seneca was among those who opted for suicide.

Nero became one of the vilest emperors in Roman history, known widely for his persecution of the Christians, including St. Peter. Many were wrapped in batting and used as human torches to light the night games at his circus, near what is now St. Peter's Basilica. It was small consolation that they usually suffocated before they burned. These foul acts, along with his incestuous relationships and greed for power, sparked the Roman term "Caesar Madness."

In the plus column, Nero loved the arts, and it was this love that spurred the Silver Age of Roman literature, best characterized by the writings of Petronius. Nero fancied himself an artist and an actor, too, and went on a long tour to Greece where he performed in the theaters and even participated in chariot games.

After a great fire reduced Rome to rubble, Nero built a grand palace that spanned nearly half the city. Many thought Nero burned the city in order to make way for his dream palace, the Golden House, or *Domus Aurea*. The scale of it was so huge that the site of his reflecting pool eventually became the site of the Colosseum. Its grand entrance featured a 120-foot statue of Nero. Gold, precious gems, ivory and pearls covered the walls and ceilings. Ancient biographer Suetonius tells us that upon moving in, the emperor declared, "Now, I can at last begin to live like a human being!" His reign ended when he took his own life, moaning (die-hard legend insists), "Dead, and so great an artist!"

HADRIAN (76-138 AD). Publius Aelius Hadrianus, who ruled from 117 to 138 AD, was Trajan's cousin once removed; Trajan adopted him as his son, which didn't hurt the young visionary's political career. Hadrian's influence is writ large in Rome—very large. His building program was second only to that of Augustus. He loved architecture and usually traveled with a full staff, like an ancient general contractor of sorts. His extensive travel (over ten years) influenced his projects both at home and abroad—he built constantly, and wherever the urge seized him. He even rebuilt London when he visited in 122 AD (a good part of far-reaching Hadrian's Wall still exists in England).

Major Hadrianic sights in Rome include Castel Sant'Angelo, originally his tomb and called Hadrian's Mausoleum; the Temple of Venus and Roma in the Forum; and the second (today's) Pantheon, which he built on the sight of an older building constructed by Marcus Agrippa. The staggeringly vast Villa Adriana warrants a day trip for those who have the time. It is a child's dream, with hundreds of acres of ruins, fountains and reflecting pools in various states of disrepair.

POPE PAUL III (1468-1549). Born at Latium into one of Rome's leading noble families, the cultivated and worldly Alessandro I Farnese lived a full, secular life—fathering three children by three different women—before taking up the cloth at the age of 51. Farnese was pope from 1534 to 1549 and initiated a key period of Church history by convening the

Council of Trent (1542), which spawned the Counter-Reformation. With Farnese behind the wheel, the Church set a plan of attack to counter Martin Luther's Protestant Reformation, which had dramatically cut away at the Church's power base.

The Counter-Reformation, which relied on dramatic means to bring people back to the Church, gave rise to commissions for bold new religious art and fresh forms of architecture with church exteriors designed to draw people in. The dramatic art form would culminate in the masterpieces of Caravaggio years later. The Church's efforts to gain more followers also spurred the creation of orders such as the Jesuits, whose missionary efforts spread the Word across the globe.

Paul III, in what was by then a no-brainer, gave Michelangelo the following Roman projects: the Campidoglio piazza, the *Last Judgment* fresco in the Sistine Chapel, the dome of St. Peter's Basilica and the Farnese Palace attic. As part of the Campidoglio project, it was he who moved the ancient statue of Marcus Aurelius to its position in the center of the piazza (from S. Giovanni in Laterano), commissioning Michelangelo to design its present pedestal. You will find the Farnese name or his papal escutcheon containing six fleurs-de-lis in these and many other places. Farnese's splendid tomb can be found in St. Peter's.

MICHELANGELO BUONARROTI (1475-1564). Artist, painter, sculptor, architect, engineer—Michelangelo is Rome's best-known and perhaps best-loved influence. His work is everywhere: overhead and underfoot, from the broad steps called the Cordonata of the Capitoline Hill to the ceiling of the Sistine Chapel. Michelangelo's long career spanned the art periods of Renaissance, High Renaissance and Mannerism. The defining piece of his early career in Rome was the *Pietà* in St. Peter's. With it, he gained the favor of and many commissions from Pope Julius II della Rovere.

The relationship between Julius and Michelangelo was fertile but tempestuous. Each seemed to dread and perhaps fear the other. Julius summoned Michelangelo from Florence to create his magnificent tomb, a vision of grand proportions. Honored, Michelangelo spent eight months in the Carrara Hills, handpicking tons of white marble, which he then paid to have shipped to Rome. But Julius refused to reimburse him, having already poured the papal funds into his war chests and into building the new St. Peter's. The pope refused even to meet with Michelangelo when he arrived. Understandably furious, the artist fled Rome, vowing never to return.

This could have been the end of the story—an ending without a Sistine Chapel ceiling fresco. But the mighty and terrible Julius forced Michelangelo to return. The artist then created the spectacular *Moses* statue in the church of St. Peter in Chains (originally *Basilica Eudoxiana*), a mere portion of that ambitious but never-finished tomb. Michelangelo did paint the Sistine Chapel, though, and how this master sculptor ended up painting the fresco is a good tale.

According to artist and historian Giorgio Vassari, Bramante was head architect for the new St. Peter's and envied Michelangelo's talents. Bramante did not want the great artist pointing out any design flaws to Julius, so he persuaded the pope that Michelangelo should be assigned to paint the Sistine Chapel ceiling. Bramante, you see, was confident the chapel would be a disaster because Michelangelo had no prior experience painting frescoes. He was sure Michelangelo would either flee or fail—either way, the great artist wouldn't be around to criticize Bramante's work. But Michelangelo didn't flee. And he certainly didn't fail.

When asked whether he thought painting or sculpting was the higher art form, the great artist replied that they both came from the same faculty but that discussing them required more time than executing them.

Vasari, who was a painter and student of Michelangelo's, wrote that of all artists in history, "The divine Michelangelo" held the palm for not one, but all three arts: sculpture, painting and architecture. He was a true Renaissance man.

Other Michelangelo highlights to see in Rome: the dome of St. Peter's Basilica, the Sistine Chapel's *Last Judgment* wall fresco, the Campidoglio piazza and the Farnese palace attic.

CARAVAGGIO (1571-1610). Renegade genius Michelangelo Merisi da Caravaggio came to Rome as a teen and created more than 25 masterpieces in seven years, including the St. Matthew cycle in San Luigi dei Francesi (his first Roman ecclesiastical commission). His darkly dramatic, often-disturbing work graces many churches, museums and private collections. Santa Maria del Popolo holds two of his most famous paintings: *Crucifixion of St. Peter* and *Conversion of St. Paul*. Among seven of his paintings in the Galleria Borghese are two self-portraits: as a youth in *Baccus* and as an adult in the equally famous biblical *David* (one of his very last paintings). Caravaggio lived a troubled and violent life, fleeing Rome in 1606 to avoid a murder charge; he was fated never to return. At 39 years of age, he fell ill and died en route to his beloved city, where he was expecting to receive a pardon.

Caravaggio's naturalistic style introduced a powerful new realism to the artistic landscape of the time. He changed the art world by depicting *real* people and almost no settings of idealized classical beauty. Like Bernini after him, Caravaggio was highly dramatic, but his subjects and backgrounds—especially religious ones—had common faces and mundane, even dingy settings: dirty feet, saints in common clothing, bloated faces. No billowy golden angels here! In the Doria Pamphilj Gallery you can view the *Magdalen* and the pivotal *Flight into Egypt* side by side and see how he used the same model, and even the same pose, to portray both the sinner Magdalen and the saintly Madonna.

When you look at Caravaggio's paintings, you feel like you're part of the scene. That's because he puts the action at eye level. Another Caravaggio technique is darkness pierced by dramatic light sources and shadows. An unseen light source is sometimes the only dramatic effect employed to represent the spiritual. Rays of sunlight replace the traditional disc-like halo, for example.

POPE URBAN VIII (1568-1644). Born in Florence as Maffeo Barberini, the intelligent Urban VIII was well educated at the Jesuits' college and retained a scholarly group of thinkers as his inner circle. But reason and faith in the 16th century were irreconcilable: During his 22-year papacy (1623-1644), Urban's friend Galileo  was condemned for heresy. Galileo and his telescope proved that the sun, not the earth—as was the accepted belief at the time—was the center of the universe. But doctrine is doctrine. Urban protected his friend from life in prison by allowing him to live under "house arrest." This meant that Galileo was spared a dark, dank cell and instead was condemned to life in a stately Roman villa: the Villa Medici on the Pincio, which to this day commemorates his stay with a plaque.

Urban's heraldic family symbols will become very familiar the longer you tour the city because his magnificent projects are everywhere. Thanks to his partiality to artist Bernini, most of them are legendary. The Barberini trio of bees symbolizes royal industry while the Barberini sun represents divine intelligence. The calculating Barberini cleverly replaced his family's original but less illustrious horsefly with the bees when he was appointed Cardinal. His hand is visible wherever you see his bees and suns: the boat fountain at the Spanish Steps, Triton's Fountain at Piazza Barberini, St. Peter's and of course the Barberini family palace, now home to the National Gallery of Classical Arts. In addition to a plethora of urban renewal projects, Urban fortified city walls and built a papal summer residence at Castel Gandolfo, which is still in use today.

Although Urban was celebrated for greatly enhancing Rome's public spaces, he was also considered a decadent spendthrift, leaving the church coffers nearly empty. To make cannons for the armory and supply Bernini with material for St. Peter's massive *baldacchino* (the spiral-columned canopy), Urban had tons of bronze stripped from the Pantheon's exterior, causing an outcry among the people. The destruction of such an ancient city treasure prompted the popular saying, "What the Barbarians didn't do, the Barberinis did!" But the act was not entirely without merit: Urban improved the dangerously-lacking papal armory by shrewdly mining bronze in his own backyard, saving the enormous sum of money that would have been needed to purchase and ship such heavy cargo to Rome from abroad.

POPE INNOCENT X (1574-1655). Born Giovanni Battista (Giambattista) Pamphilj to one of Rome's most powerful families, Innocent was elected to the papacy in 1644 and held office until his death in 1655. Upon his election, Innocent found the papacy in a state of near destitution caused by the excesses of his predecessor, Urban VIII. Enraged at the flagrant spending of the former  pope, Innocent actually put the Barberini family on trial. He wanted nothing to do with Urban's prized artist either, refusing at first to give Bernini even a single commission. That is, until Innocent X, whom we can thank for the beauty of today's Piazza Navona, held a competition for architects to design the piazza's central fountain. Although formally banned from entering the competition, Bernini designed and built a model anyway, and an admirer put it in the pope's path. Having seen it, Innocent could do nothing but hire the great artist.

Still, Innocent was a harsh and severe man. No one seemed to care for him, including his dominating sister-in-law, Donna Olimpia Maidalchini, a frightful woman whose influence only increased the pope's unpopularity. (Find a scary bust of her in Galleria Doria Pamphilj.) When Velázquez presented his famous, stern-faced, all-red portrait (also in the Galleria) to the volatile pope, many thought the consequences would be fatal. Instead, the insightful pope said, "You've painted me as I am." Guido Reni, another brilliant artist, certainly agreed. When he painted *St. Michael the Archangel Defeating Satan*, he gave the devil Innocent's face! The act was likely well received by the patrons of the church in which it was hung—none other than the Barberinis, Innocent's archenemies! Judge for yourself in the church of Santa Maria della Concezione on the Via Veneto.

The Pamphilj mark on Rome is ubiquitous. In Piazza Navona alone, the family funded Bernini's *Four Rivers* fountain, the lovely Pamphilj palace and Borromini's Church of S. Agnese in Agone. You can stroll the vast gardens of the Villa Pamphilj in Trastevere or visit the still privately-held art collection of the Doria Pamphilj Gallery by Piazza Venezia. The Pamphilj papal escutcheon carries a dove and three fleurs-de-lis.

GIAN LORENZO BERNINI (1598-1680). Chief architect of St. Peter's for many years, the remarkable Bernini brought the Baroque style to Rome practically single-handedly. He was a sculptor, painter, set designer, playwright and inventor in addition to being an architect. His masterpieces define many of Rome's greatest sights: the Spanish Steps, Borghese Gallery, St. Peter's, Triton's Fountain and the Piazza Navona, to name a few.

Bernini's artistic genius was to create dynamic scenes depicting peak moments of dramatic impact, with figures in the midst of the action. His sculptures beckon you to walk around and see them from all sides. This was a significant artistic departure for the time: traditionally, sculpture was viewed from the front, because it was often made to fit into a niche. Art critics thought, too, that good sculpture should reveal the block it came from—a viewer should be able to envision the marble block from which it was carved. A great sculpture, then, could roll down a hill unharmed.

When Bernini used more than one block of marble, he changed those standards. If he wanted a statue with outstretched arms, he would just make the arms separately and attach them to the main body rather than find a wide enough hunk of marble. He was so masterful at working marble that he was actually criticized for making sculptures look as if they had been molded from clay.

Bernini worked for eight popes, including Paul V (Borghese); Paul's nephew, Cardinal Scipio Borghese; and for several kings. But his greatest sponsor was Urban VIII of the Barberini family. Urban called Bernini the very day his fellow cardinals elected him to the papacy to say the artist's luck was great to have him elected as pope, but that his own luck was greater to have Bernini available for commission during his pontificate!

Incredibly, Bernini never completed anything that fully pleased him. Hard to believe when you wander the Galleria Borghese, which holds many of his most famous sculptures and even one of his very first—a small sculpture in the round—*The Goat Amalthea* feeding the infant Jupiter. Ironically, this master of the Baroque now lies interred under a simple stone pavement in Santa Maria Maggiore.

Though our goal to approach Rome with a razor-sharp focus limits us to these few major players, where appropriate we will discuss other great contributors such as Cardinal Scipio Borghese (nephew to Pope Paul V), Sixtus IV and Julius II (the della Rovere family popes) and the Medici pope Leo X. Their crests respectively are the Borghese dragon and eagle, the della Rovere oak tree and the Medici's five red balls with a single blue circle containing three fleurs-de-lis at the top.

KNOW YOUR FAMILY CRESTS

Rome is a marble zoo, chock-full of animals on buildings and fountains, over doors, adorning statues and staircases. The stone flora and fauna are family symbols that show who financed the works they adorn. They make up family heraldry, or crests; we often refer to their groupings on heraldic shields as *escutcheons*. Searching for them will add a fun scavenger-hunt element to nearly every tour you take. A Crest Quest instantly changes any museum or church into a quiet playground.

By familiarizing your kids with these crests, you can buy yourself some adult time. Maybe you are interested the long hall of 16th-century maps in the Vatican Museum, a place that can quickly render a child bleary-eyed. Throw down a challenge for kids to tally as many papal symbols as possible—skulls, bees, dragons, stars, suns, eagles, fleurs-de-lis, trees, balls—and you will initiate a game that lasts for the duration of your stay. Let them report later, over lunch or dinner. How many kinds did they find? Which is their favorite? The strangest? The most-often found? Can they remember the family names these represent?

KNOW YOUR KIDS

Plenty of play is crucial when traveling with kids, especially youngsters. Throughout this book, you'll find a variety of activities, questions, treasure hunts, counting games, mysteries and suggestions for where to let the kids run. They're all outlined in boxes or in the margin to help you get the most out of what you're seeing. Like this:

SPQR

It's on everything, from triumphal arches and water fountains to manhole covers and garbage cans. What does it mean? The letters stand for **SENATUS POPULUSQUE ROMANUS**, which means The Senate and People of Rome.

The strategy is simple: pack in as much play as possible by using the suggested activities. Pair a park visit with a tour of a confining museum. Plan on renting pedal-karts on the Pincio when you tour the Spanish Steps. Balance indoor visits with outside downtime. You get the idea.

KNOW HOW TO SKIP THE LINES

Keep in mind that you can often skip long ticket lines by simply calling ahead or booking online (for a small fee); telephone numbers and Web sites are provided. Many booking sites allow you to print your tickets at home. Simply pass the line and present your ticket(s) at the entrance. You'll save hours of waiting and avoid draining precious energy and enthusiasm. Plus, your kids will think you're a hero when you let them cut the line!

Rome is fun for everybody when you're armed with great facts, memorable stories, energetic activities and lots of places for family refueling. Pick a tour, check out the Timing and Tips box, put on your comfortable walking shoes and let's get going!

PART ONE

ANCIENT ROME

Early Rome consists of three contiguous areas: the Palatine and Capitoline hills and the valley between them, home to the glory of Ancient Rome, the Forum. The Palatine and Capitoline were two of the city's original Seven Hills—the other five are the Quirinal, Viminal, Esquiline, Aventine and Caelian. The Palatine was a secluded residential enclave; the smaller but higher Capitoline held all temples and political buildings.

When the marshy valley between these two hills was drained around 600 BC, the Forum—commerce, housing, temples and monuments—took root and flourished. This area has been the heart and soul of Rome from the Age of the Kings through the Republic and the glory years of the Empire. Even today, it offers the quintessential Roman experience.

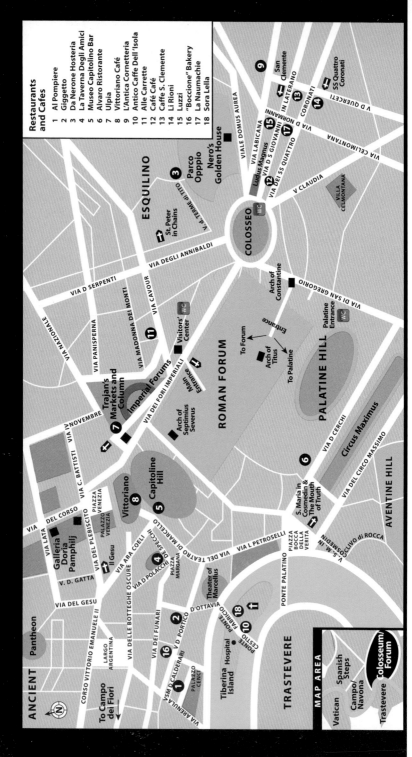

ANCIENT

Pantheon

To Campo
dei Fiori

ESQUILINO

**Restaurants
and Cafes**

1 Al Pompiere
2 Giggetto
3 Da Nerone Hosteria
4 La Taverna Degli Amici
5 Museo Capitolino Bar
6 Alvaro Ristorante
7 Ulpia
8 Vittoriano Café
9 L'Antica Cornetteria
10 Antico Caffe Dell'Isola
11 Alle Carrette
12 Café Café
13 Caffe S. Clemente
14 Li Rioni
15 Luzzi
16 "Boccione" Bakery
17 La Naumachie
18 Sora Lella

Parco
Opppio

Nero's
Golden House

San
Clemente

St. Peter
in Chains

SS Quattro
Coronati

COLOSSEO

Arch of
Constantine

Arch of
Titus

Entrance

ROMAN FORUM

PALATINE HILL

Palatine
Entrance

To Forum

To Palatine

Visitors'
Center

Trajan's
Markets and
Column

Imperial Forums

Arch of
Septimius
Severus

**Capitoline
Hill**

Vittoriano

Circus Maximus

AVENTINE HILL

S. Maria in
Cosmedin &
The Mouth
of Truth

Galleria
Doria
Pamphilj

Il Gesu

Theater of
Marcellus

Palazzo
Cenci

Tiberina
Hospital
Island

TRASTEVERE

MAP AREA

Vatican

Spanish Steps

Campo
Navona

Trastevere

**Colosseum/
Forum**

VIA DOMUS AUREA
VIALE DOMUS AUREA
VIA LABICANA
Ludus Magnus
VIA D S GIOVANNI
IN LATERANO
VIA DEI SS QUATTRO
VIA DI NORMANNI
CORONATI
V D QUERCETI
VIA CELIMONTANA

VILLA
CELIMONTANA

V CLAUDIA

Arch of
VIA DI SAN GREGORIO

VIA DEGLI ANNIBALDI

VIA CAVOUR

VIA D SERPENTI

VIA PANISPERNA

VIA MADONNA DEI MONTI

VIA NAZIONALE

VIA IV NOVEMBRE

VIA DEI FORI IMPERIALI

VIA C. BATTISTI

PIAZZA
VENEZIA

PALAZZO
VENEZIA

VIA DEL PLEBISCITO

VIA DELLE BOTTEGHE OSCURE

VIA D POLACCHI

VIA D ARA COELI

VIA DE SPECCHI

VIA DEL TEATRO DI MARCELLO

PIAZZA
MARGANA

VIA L PETROSELLI

PIAZZA
BOCCA
DELLA
VERITA

VIA D CERCHI

VIA DEL CIRCO MASSIMO

V. S. M. IN
OCLIVO di ROCCA
V. S. M. IN
MEDIN

PONTE PALATINO

PONTE
FABRICIO
PONTE
CESTIO

D'OTTAVIA
PORTICO

VIA DEI FUNARI

V D PORTICO

VIA ARENULA

VSM D CALDERARI

CORSO VITTORIO EMANUELE II

LARGO
ARGENTINA

VIA DEL GESU

V. D. GATTA

VIA LATA

DEL CORSO

THE FORUM & CAPITOLINE HILL

CAMPIDOGLIO, *Piazza del Campidoglio.* Also called **Capitoline Hill,** this is where you will find the **Capitoline museums** housed in two buildings flanking the Senate. The Palazzo dei Conservatori, the building to the right of the Senate building, is the place to purchase museum tickets.

CAPITOLINE MUSEUMS, *Piazza del Campidoglio, 1. Open 9am-8pm. Open 9am-2pm Dec. 24 and 31. Closed Mondays, Jan. 1, May 1, & Dec. 25. Information and reservations: Tel. 39-060608 or museicapitolini.org. Tickets € 9.50 + extra for exhibitions. Ages 5 and under, free. Tickets online: ticketclic.it (booking fee applies, but you can skip the line). Audio guides are € 5 each. Free coat and stroller check. Strollers are permitted in museum.* The ancient **Tabularium,** beneath the Senate building, is accessed through the museums.

THE ROMAN FORUM, *(Roman Forum/Palatine Hill archaeological area), Via della Salara Vecchia (Via dei Fori Imperiali at Via Cavour) Open daily 8:30am-7pm or until one hour before sunset. Closed January 1 & December 25. Tickets, € 12, valid for two days, include one entry to Colosseum and one to the Forum/Palatine. Tickets online: coopculture.it (booking fee applies). Print tickets at home or save to your smart phone to skip the line! Information, guided tours, and booking: Tel. 06-399-67700. Audio guides are € 5 from the Forum gift shop. Main entrance is on Via Fori Imperiali. From the Colosseum, you may enter near the Arch of Titus. Strollers are permitted, and you can follow an accessible sidewalk around a portion of the site.*

Timing and Tips

The Forum and Palatine Hill are unified. Thus, the Forum/ Palatine+Colosseum ticket allows one entrance to the Colosseum and one to the Forum/Palatine. The Forum may be entered near Capitoline Hill, as discussed here, or near the Colosseum/Palatine entrances. Touring the Forum and Palatine together is economical, but it makes for a long day, especially with small children.

See the Forum/Palatine early in the day, especially in steamy July when there is no shade from the brutal heat of the midday sun. Count on spending two hours, at most; return to the Campidoglio to beat the strongest sun and thickest crowds by ducking into the cool museums for an hour or so. You will be doing a lot of walking, especially if you include a tour of the Palatine, so take water—and maybe a few snacks for the younger kids to squeeze more time out of the visit.

An early-morning visit is infinitely more pleasant: fewer people make it easier to navigate and keep track of kids. If the kids aren't up for much museum time, take an early lunch nearby. Most restaurants open around 12:30pm. Going then will allow you to avoid the larger, later lunch crowds.

Public bathrooms are in the museum, the visitor's center and the Forum, near the Temple of Castor and Pollux and to the right of the Temple of Romulus. The museum has a stroller check.

An ideal day in Rome, especially if you have only a few days, begins with a tour of the Forum, the Capitoline Hill and its two museums, stuffed with ancient finds. Here, where Romans lived, worshiped and worked for thousands of years, you'll see where Rome began and how it evolved. The kids can run around the ruins, you can take in the museums quickly, and everyone will swoon at the splendid views.

The **ROMAN FORUM,** once a swampy, malaria-infested area between hill-cities, became the greatest symbol of power in the Roman Empire out of need: those little neighboring cities lacked a place to meet and trade. During the age of the Tarquin Kings, around 600 BC, the stagnant waters were drained into the Tiber by building a large sewer, the *Cloaca Maxima*. This single act gave rise to the Forums.

Around 45 BC, Julius Caesar began an effort to restore and improve the already-aging Forum. Cut down in his prime, the job was left to his adopted son, **Augustus**. Augustus carried out many grandiose plans and

improvements, justifying his claim to have "found the city brick and left it marble." The Forum was restored and rebuilt many times, but Augustus was responsible for making it truly splendid.

Built as extensions to the Roman Forum, the Imperial Forums of Caesar, Augustus and Trajan were separated from the original in the 20th century by the large Mussolini-built road, Via dei Fori Imperiali. Running from the Capitoline to the Colosseum *(Colosseo)*, the busy street is closed to motor traffic on Sundays, when you'll find crowds of pedestrians showing up to enjoy the privilege of strolling sans vehicles. Julius Caesar began the Imperial Forums with a temple to Venus— mother of his claimed ancestor, Aeneas. The visual reminder of a goddess in his family line provided a good deal of cachet. Caesar's adopted son Augustus added to the family's prestige by proclaiming Caesar divine, too, making himself the son of divinity.

Sadly, the Forum was ransacked in the mid-16th century and used as a quarry for precious marbles and materials needed to build great churches, St. Peter's chief among them. Pagan temples that had remained intact for centuries were destroyed in less than a month's time, despite protestations from Raphael and **Michelangelo**.

Just as the Forum was always the seat of commerce, the **Campidoglio,** situated on the smallest of the original Seven Hills— the Capitoline—has always been the city's political and religious center. Since antiquity, it held the grand temple of Jupiter and included the smaller Arx Hill, which consisted of a military station and the temple of Juno Moneta, all now gone. The gods Jupiter and Juno, equivalent to the Greek Zeus and Hera, were the protectors of Rome. It was very fitting that temples dedicated to these important figures were built on such a high and sacred place.

Romans are a people of tradition, and so the Campidoglio still functions as a political and religious hub. The temple dedicated to a mother goddess is now a church—the glorious Santa Maria in Aracoeli—dedicated to the mother of God. The ancient Tabularium still has a political function: the Senate House, built on top of it, is home to Rome's civic government.

> $$$ Cash, moola, moneta: The Juno Moneta was used as a mint, and it is from here that we get our word, "money."

THE CAPITOLINE MUSEUMS occupy the two buildings flanking the Senate. Sixtus IV della Rovere founded them in 1471, when he donated a small collection of important statues to the Roman people; the She-Wolf (*Lupa Capitolina*) and Constantine's giant head were among them. A cool third space, *Centrale Montemartini*, displays hundreds of ancient sculptures against an industrial backdrop of machinery in Rome's first electricity plant (offsite). The jewel among many highlights here, however, is the **Tabularium**—the terrace underneath Palazzo Senatorio—which affords an emperor's-eye view of the Forum, the Palatine and the Colosseum. It's a spectacular opportunity to stand on a lofty ancient building and survey the cradle of Western civilization. Also of particular interest to kids are the **Temple of Jupiter** ruins (in the museum) and the ancient debris in the courtyard: fragments of a head, hand and foot from a colossal statue of Constantine found at the Basilica Maxentius. Older children may be willing to tour the galleries (where you'll find the Capitoline café and its fantastic panoramic terrace) to check out paintings of masters like Reni, **Caravaggio** and Titian.

THE WALKING TOUR

The Forum's ancient ruins make for an exciting start to a tour of Rome, but for the fullest effect, preview them first from the 17th century **Piazza del Campidoglio**. Our tour begins on the west side of the **Victor Emanuel II Monument,** at the base of a set of flat, wide steps

known as the **Cordonata**. **Michelangelo** designed them in 1536 for the grand entrance of Charles V, Holy Roman Emperor, on the event of his coronation. Broad enough to accommodate both man and horse, the steps lead up the Capitoline Hill to the piazza, the way the great artist intended.

Before you ascend, note on your left the steep staircase of **S. Maria d'Aracoeli**. You may want to return here later to explore the church (see *Extras in Rome*) dedicated to the Mother of Christ, once the site of a pagan temple to Juno, mother of the gods. The interior is a scramble of old and new: its columns came from various Imperial edifices, including a palace. (Soccer fans will appreciate knowing that Rome's superhero, Totti, was married here in 2005.)

STAIRWAY TO HEAVEN?

Compare the ultra-steep, medieval stairs of S. Maria d'Aracoeli to the gentle, wide steps of the Cordonata. Which would you rather climb? The point has been made that the flight to the top of the pagan world is pretty easy, but the path to heaven is arduous—122 severe steps to the church!

As you climb the Cordonata, note the statue of Cola di Rienzo on your left. Di Rienzo fought to re-establish Roman sovereignty in the 1300s by taking the control of Rome away from the popes. The city was then a part of the Holy Roman Empire and many wished to return it to a Republic. Di Rienzo died on this spot.

Flanking the top of the steps are colossal statues of **Castor and Pollux,** mythological sons of Zeus who helped Rome win a major battle against the last Tarquin king and establish the Roman Republic (officially, 509 BC). The sculptures beside them are called the *Trophies of Marius.*

KIDS!

WHERE ARE THE BODIES?

The "Trophies of Marius" represent the piles of armor left behind by defeated armies. There are no people represented because the idea was that enemies were unimportant; their defeat was all that was essential.

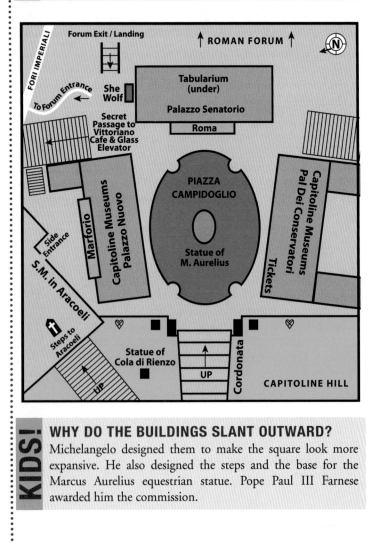

KIDS!

WHY DO THE BUILDINGS SLANT OUTWARD?

Michelangelo designed them to make the square look more expansive. He also designed the steps and the base for the Marcus Aurelius equestrian statue. Pope Paul III Farnese awarded him the commission.

Welcoming you to the piazza, in the center, is a statue of **Marcus Aurelius.** It's a copy of the original, a rare surviving equestrian, which is on display in the Exedra of the Capitoline Museum, Palazzo dei Conservatori. The statue survived only because later Romans mistook it for their beloved Emperor Constantine, who made Christianity the official religion and ended the Christian persecutions once and for all. Look for **Pope Paul III Farnese's** fleurs-de-lis on the pedestal.

Marcus Aurelius was one of Rome's most beloved emperors. Teens who have seen *Gladiator* may remember Aurelius' tormented son Commodus (the bad guy in the movie, played so brilliantly by Joaquin Phoenix). Look for a bust of crazy Commodus in the Capitoline Museums.

In the courtyard of the building to the left of the Senate look for lounging **Marforio**.

TALKING STATUES!

Marforio is one of Rome's "talking statues," on which people attached signs—usually political barbs—as an anonymous way to voice opinions that might otherwise result in the author's execution. Statues have even held debates with each other. You will likely pass a few of these characters in your journeys, but the most famous is **Pasquino**, south of Piazza Navona. Two others are nearby: **Facchino**, the porter, on Via Lata at the Corso, and **Lucrezia**, an enormous fragment sitting in front of Palazzo Venezia.

In front of the **Palazzo Senatorio**, which is the central building of the three on the piazza, you will see the **goddess Roma** flanked by two lounging river gods, Nile and Tiber. Originally a statue of Minerva, this goddess is dressed in rare porphyry, a reddish-purple marble of great value.

KIDS!

WHO'S WHO?
Clues identify each river god. See the cornucopia symbolizing the fertility of the Nile? And to which river do the legendary twins of Rome belong?

THE LEGEND OF ROMULUS AND REMUS

*T*he Trojan hero Aeneas was destined to start a master race of men. After all, his mother was the goddess Venus. Virgil beautifully crafted his story about Aeneas and the origins of Rome to connect the Romans with illustrious gods and the pedigreed Greeks. After the great battle of Troy, Aeneas fled his burning city and didn't stop until he hit the shores of Italy.

Generations later, his descendants—twins Romulus and Remus, fathered by the god Mars—were born to a beautiful Vestal named Rhea Silva. Since Vestals had to remain celibate upon pain of death, the royal twins were abandoned in the Tiber River (at Alba Longa).

From there, they floated to the banks of what is now Rome and were raised by a she-wolf. The twins were destined to rule a great city, but only one could be king, so Romulus killed Remus and founded Rome.

On the terrace left of the Senate building is the feral foster parent of Romulus and Remus, a copy of the famous bronze statue called *La Lupa Capitolina,* housed inside the museum. Originally though to be thousands of years old, the She-wolf is now dated to the Middle Ages; the twins are a Renaissance addition. Those who simply don't have time to visit the museums should stop and enjoy this replica now.

We will return to the Campidoglio, but for now, continue past the she-wolf statue and down the serpentine street leading to Via Fori Imperiali to enter the Roman Forum. Do stop on the landing first to enjoy the spectacular view: the Arch of Septimius Severus in the foreground, the  commanding Temple of Saturn to the right and way off in the distance, the great Colosseum and a series of umbrella trees dotting the Palatine Hill.

Upon entering the Forum, go right, heading toward the **Arch of Septimius Severus**, passing the long ruins of the **Basilica Aemilia** (right side) as you go. Just before the Arch, you'll come upon the fully intact **Curia (284-305 AD),** seat of the Senate since its founding by Tullus Hostilius (re-built several times, once by Caesar), where 300 senators could gather for meetings. The extra-high ceiling helped amplify all those important voices.

Trials were held in front of the Curia in a space called the **Comitium.** At its far end was a raised, semi-circular speaker's platform called the **Imperial Rostra,** where lawyers such as Cicero tried their cases.

Words are powerful—Cicero's writings often slandered Marc Antony, who had him killed and then nailed his head and troublesome right hand to the Rostra.

Rostra means ship's prow. Indeed, the Rostra was decorated with prows captured in the sea battle of Antium (338 BC). You can see a pretty spectacular rendition of it in *Ben-Hur* in the scene when the title character arrives in Rome.

If you look carefully, you will come upon a mystery: a dusty square of black marble known as the ***Lapis Niger***. Early Romans used black marble to mark sacred places. The mystery is that no one knows why this spot is so special. Steps lead to a (closed) viewing area below the stone where only the base of a statue remains. Archaic Latin writing (605 BC) on the base, called *lex sacra*, warns against profaning a sacred place. This is the oldest Latin epigraph found to date.

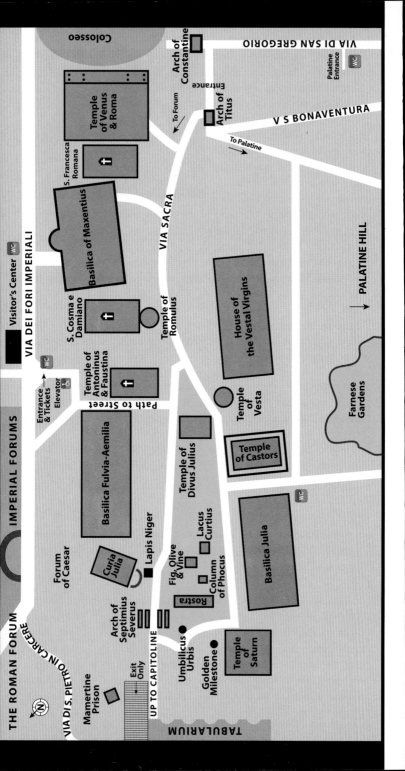

CAN YOU FIND THE LAPIS NIGER?

Standing in the middle of the road, draw an imaginary line down from the Arch of Septimius Severus and over from the Comitium. Where the lines intersect, you'll find a flat, dusty square of stone, like flooring. Rub it or wet it a little to bring up its natural black hue. The crumbled and deteriorating *Lapis Niger* is less than stunning, but it has a right to look beat up: it is the oldest relic in the Forum.

KIDS!

But what was here? It could be the tomb of Romulus, the city's first king, but most archaeologists believe it marks the place where senators murdered him. Romulus was killed, they know, next to a shrine to Vulcan called the *Vulcanal*. Since a great amount of ashes and bits of terra cotta—indications of large sacrifices—were found here, it's possible that this was the scene of the crime.

THE THREE OLDEST AREAS IN THE FORUM

The Vulcanal, or *Lapis Niger,* a shrine near the Arch of S. Severus
The Comitium, a lecture space in front of the Curia
The Cloaca Maxima, a drain on the far side of Basilica Giulia

All from the Age of the Kings, 753-509 BC

Now let's take a closer look at the grand **Arch of Septimius Severus**. Built in 203 AD to commemorate the tenth anniversary of Emperor Septimius Severus' reign, this grand structure set the standard for all triumphal arches. The enormous hulk is humbling. Imagine having never seen anything taller than a typical hut-dwelling and walking under this. Gladiators and triumphal processions led newcomers directly past

arches like this to impress and intimidate. Gladiatorial games were actually held right here before the Colosseum was built; the underground passageways and chambers are just below your feet! A staircase inside leads to four tiny chambers in its attic (*not accessible*).

SEPTIMIUS SEVERUS (193 AD) was the first African emperor. His biggest victories were over Parthia (modern-day Iran and Iraq). His son Caracalla built the famous Baths of Caracalla.

WHY IS PART OF THE INSCRIPTION MISSING?

Walk through the arch and look up at the west attic, fourth line from the top, to find holes from some removed letters. Septimius Severus had two sons, but Geta, his second, was literally erased from history. Upon their father's death, Caracalla commissioned his brother Geta's murder to gain total power. He then ordered all statues, references and traces of Geta removed from the city. Here on the arch, Caracalla replaced a reference to Geta with praise for his father, *"Optimis fortissimisque principibus"* (best and most valiant emperors).

For efficient exploring, we'll turn right, cut across the short end of the Forum, go down the length of its right side then cut over to head back up the left side in a kind of loop. This eliminates a lot of backtracking.

CAN YOU FIND THE BELLY BUTTON OF ROME?

The Umbilicus Urbis is a circular, cistern-like pit that marked the center (navel) of ancient Rome, ca. 2 BC.

WHAT A PIT!

According to Plutarch, Romulus dug this circular pit as a religious rite. Each man threw a bit of soil and the first fruits of his crop into it, and then the new city was marked out from here, the city's center. Those first Romans also believed the deep pit was a point where the living could communicate with the underworld.

Continue right to the remains of another curious structure, the **Golden Milestone,** or *Milliarium Aureum* (20 BC), near the Temple of Saturn. **Augustus** created the bronze column to mark the point from which everyone measured distances to other major cities in the Empire. The cities and their distances from Rome were written in gold letters. Around 30,000 miles of Roman roads were built courtesy of her army, hence the phrase, "All roads lead to Rome." Only the milestone's base and a small fragment remain.

Beyond the Golden Milestone, with several of its gigantic columns still standing, is the commanding **Temple of Saturn**. This huge temple was in keeping with the duality of the political and religious functions of the Forum, because it served as both temple and treasury. Turn left and head down the length of the Forum. To the right are the bare ruins of the Basilica Giulia stretching over a long tract of land.

FIND AN ANCIENT BOARD GAME
The steps on the Basilica Giulia's far (southern) end are engraved with ancient board games. Look for the gashes in the marble.

Before you reach the southernmost end of the basilica, look left for the **Column of Phocas,** the very last monument erected in the Forum (608 AD). It honors the little-known Byzantine emperor who donated the **Pantheon** to the Church. Without that donation, the Pantheon would surely have met the same fate as other ancient temples: abandoned and quarried for building materials. Instead, the Pantheon remains the most intact edifice of its era.

Immediately after the column, also on the left, is a scruffy area considered the **Heart of the Forum.** Two things help distinguish it: a symbolic grouping of plants and a depression of sorts called the *Lacus Curtius.* The devotion to these two areas reminds us that the Romans were a superstitious people who relied on ritual and symbolism for spiritual guidance and a sense of control. The grouping of fig, olive and grapevine plantings represents Italian agriculture, and they have occupied this spot for thousands of years (replanted often).

THE VALOR OF MARCUS CURTIUS

*W*hen *the ground opened and people began falling to their deaths right in the center of town, superstitious Romans thought they were being divinely punished. It was decided that the abyss would close when the Romans threw in their most prized possessions. They tried everything: money, jewels, silver, gold. Finally, a soldier named Marcus Curtius, believing that the Roman army was the city's most valued asset, rode into the abyss horse and all. The sacrifice worked, and the site now bears his name.*

At the end of the Basilica Giulia, three pretty Corinthian columns identify **The Temple of Castor and Pollux**. Remember the enormous statues of them topping Michelangelo's steps? The legendary heroes, and brothers to Helen of Troy, were seen here drinking from a nearby ancient spring.

On the left you'll find the **Temple of Julius Caesar,** dedicated in 29 BC by his adopted son, **Augustus**. The temple memorializes the spot where Caesar was cremated in 44 BC. By deifying Caesar, sly Augustus positioned himself as the son of a deity and added immeasurable prestige to the family name. Adoring fans still bring flowers to honor his memory; your kids might get a kick out of doing the same. (With no offense to mighty Caesar, this is an opportunity to take a bathroom break since facilities are discreetly off to the right).

The round, partially intact **Temple of Vesta** is easy to spot. Climb the few stairs behind it to grab a glimpse of the charming **House of the Vestal Virgins.** In summer, the Vestal statues and gardens are adorned with roses. The large chunk of remaining ruins on this side of the Forum is, in fact, part of the sprawling Vestal complex.

GROWING UP VESTAL

*V*estals had many duties, but the three most important were keeping the symbolic fire of Rome perpetually burning, holding important private wills and keeping safe the ultra-sacred relic of Rome's foundation, the Palladium. Only guesses survive as to what the mysterious Palladium was, but most scholars believe it was a tiny wooden figurine of Pallas Athena taken from Troy when Aeneas fled in search of a new home, Rome. The Virgins kept it in a secret hiding place.

When girls joined the Vestal cult, around the age of eight years, their hair was cut and hung on a lotus tree until they completed their 30-year service. Those who broke their vows of chastity were buried alive.

It's easy to lose sight of how influential women were in ancient Rome because most the intrigue involves men: builders, gladiators, dramatic artists and crazy emperors. Vestal Virgins, for instance, were at the top of the chain. Their influence could pardon a convicted criminal.

Now, cut over to the **Sacra Via** and make your way to the **Temple of Antoninus and Faustina** (141 AD), built by Emperor Antoninus Pius for his wife Faustina. The inscription dedicates it to a beloved emperor and his wife: Antoninus was the father of (adopted) Marcus Aurelius Antoninus. Remember him? His equestrian statue adorns the middle of the Capitoline Piazza, and his victories are depicted on the column of Marcus Aurelius.

KIDS! WHAT'S WITH THAT DOOR?

Why are the stairs of the temple a deadly drop from the entrance? Imagine stepping out and plummeting down. It's because the door belongs to the church, which was built when the old temple columns were still half-buried. So, the door was at ground level until the Forum was excavated.

If you've had enough of the Forum or wish to exit, take the path left of this temple up to Via di Fori Imperiali (to entrance and visitor's center with restrooms). Otherwise, let's check out one more building on its right (Colosseum) side, then turn and head back to the arch of Septimius Severus and up to the Capitoline, where, I promise, there's an immediate snack break.

KIDS! CAN YOU FIND THE SACRA VIA?

Look for bits and patches of large ancient pavers that make up the oldest road in Rome. You are following in the footsteps of great generals like Caesar and Pompey who led triumphal processions down the sacred street after major victories. Chained prisoners of war, luxurious and exotic war spoils, musicians, magnificent horses and scads of soldiers were all part of the lavish spectacle. The victorious general rode in a gilded chariot pulled by four white horses; his men followed, singing and poking fun at him with often-graphic barbs. It was all in fun, and the only heads that rolled on that day belonged to captured enemy generals who were put to death at the end of the procession.

The Temple of Romulus, now Jupiter Stator, (306-312 AD) has some very impressive bronze doors. They are nearly 1,700 years old, and the lock still works! The Temple of Romulus was thought to be dedicated to Emperor Maxentius' son, who died young—not to Romulus, Rome's first king. Temples were normally dedicated to gods, but the dedication of this one to a mortal, and only a child at that, was part of a hubristic trend in Imperial Rome.

CAN YOU TELL WHO WAS A BIG SHOT?

The marble columns flanking the magnificent bronze doors are carved from *porphyry*, a rare marble with a reddish-purple hue. You'll find porphyry in places of honor all over town: on Capitoline Hill you'll find it on Roma's dress and St. Helen's altar in S. Maria in Aracoeli. Look for more at St. Peter's Basilica. Porphyry is a sure-fire way to know that someone or something was considered important.

KIDS!

SS Cosma and Damiano is attached to the Temple of Romulus, which once served as the church's entry vestibule. The church has a glass wall that allows you to look inside the temple, should its Forum doors be closed. To get there, take the ramp left of the Temple of Antoninus and Faustina up to the Via di Fori Imperiali and go right (see *What's Around?*).

From here, especially with small children who tire easily, or in strong sun, it's best to tour the Capitoline museums.

ALTERNATIVES: If you prefer to skip the museums, continue down the Sacra Via to see the **Basilica of Maxentius** ruins, the vast **Temple of Venus & Roma**, and the **Arch of Titus** (81AD), which commemorates that emperor's sack of Jerusalem in 70AD. Bas-reliefs show Roman soldiers absconding with the seven-branched candelabrum and sacred items. From the Arch, you may head up the Palatine hill or exit the Forum to the Colosseum (both discussed in the next chapter).

CONTINUING IN THE FORUM: Keep a keen eye out for the Temple of Venus & Roma. While the Venus chamber is visible, kids love seeking out Roma's hidden hall, tucked behind it (access is on the right of the Venus). Further bonus is the stunning, expansive view of the Colosseum from this raised temple.

Red porphyry covers Roma's chamber, inlaid in the floor, rising in tall columns, and even on the remaining fragment of her dress, which sits on the dais where she once held court.

FIND ROME'S BIGGEST TEMPLE

KIDS!

Hadrian's gigantic Temple of Venus and Rome was built in 135 AD to honor Rome's two protective goddess figures: Roma and Venus, mother of Rome's legendary hero, Aeneas. The goddesses were placed back-to-back, in mirror-image sanctuaries. Visitors could worship Venus, then go around for a visit to Roma, and so can you.

ROMA AMOR. Venus is the goddess of Love (Amor), which is Roma spelled backwards! The symmetry of their temples is echoed in their names.

GIRL POWER

*Venus was an old-school goddess, but Roma was new. When subjugated cities of the Roman Empire began cults to worship the city depicted as a goddess, **Hadrian** liked the idea and brought the concept back to Rome. Powerful Roma usually has a sword or staff in one hand and an orb of worldly power in the other. Remember the **Capitoline** Roma in her rare porphyry dress? Venus, on the other hand, represented love, beauty and maternal care. She protected Rome as mother to its founder's earliest ancestor.*

TOURING THE CAPITOLINE MUSEUMS: Exit the forum by taking the steps up to the Capitoline Hill.

CAN YOU FIND THE SECRET PASSAGE?

Scramble up the steps and find the she-wolf statue. Take the short flight of steps across from it into the building at the top. Now do you see it?

Use the little-known passage to reach the terrace café of the **Victor Emanuel II monument** (see *What's Around?*) where you can recharge for your tour of the museums. The steps across from the she-wolf statue lead into a building behind the S. Maria d'Aracoeli church. Enter, turn right then follow the long corridor on your left to the VEII terrace and café. The short, maze-like quest rewards you with views in all directions and lets you avoid the arduous climb up the Vittoriano's front steps just to get here. Alternatively, there's another rooftop café inside the museums, but it's not as fun to find!

REACH FOR THE SKY!

Find the cool Glass Elevator on the Vittoriano terrace for a *Charlie and the Chocolate Factory* ride straight to the top of the monument!

When you're refreshed, return to the piazza for a quick museum tour. Once inside, head downstairs and follow the connecting gallery, really a tunnel, to midpoint where a guard sits stationed at an excavated ancient wall and street (partially intact): reward in itself. Take the few adjacent stairs up to the Tabularium level. The astounding view of the Forum will draw you, but don't miss the **Temple of Veiovis** on your immediate right, behind glass. Its massive marble steps and giant tufa stone blocks are right where they were uncovered and partially restored.

The Tabularium's expansive portico provides a knockout panorama of the ancient city. Just before your reach it, look for the huge frieze, or tablature, that once adorned this ancient archive building. It's hanging on the right.

WHO WAS EXECUTED HERE?

Look for a knife, whip, axe and skull (of an ox) on the frieze. Why? This was an archive building since the 1st century BC, but it also housed the offices of the executioner, who prepared and conducted animal sacrifices.

You've seen the jewel. Now enjoy as much of the rest of the masterpiece-packed museums as your kids will allow. Search the Conservatory's for:

- Huge *Romulus and Remus* fresco (Hall of the Horatii and Curiatii)
- Larger-than-life **marble statues of Urban VIII Barberini** (begun by **Bernini**) and **Innocent X Pamphilj**. (Hall of the Horatii and Curiatii)
- **Temple of Jupiter's (Jove)** awesome 6th century BC ruins, interactive computers, and the super-old **Marcus Aurelius equestrian** in a super-modern glass room (M. Aurelius Exedra).
- **Crazy Commodus.** For this bust, the emperor insisted he be depicted as the god Hercules—lion skin and all. (Lamiani Gallery)
- **The Lupa Capitolina,** the original bronze statue (Hall of the She-Wolf)
- Other dramatic pieces include the **Capitoline Gaul**, dying on his shield and Bernini's snake-haired bust of **Medusa**.

WHAT'S AROUND?

GALLERIA DORIA PAMPHILJ

Via del Corso, 305, just north of Piazza Venezia.
Open 9am-7pm. Closed Dec. 25, Jan. 1, and Easter.
Tel. 06-679-7323
Tickets € 11, include an audio guide. Ages 6-25, € 7.50.
Web site: dopart.it

The mid-18th century Doria Pamphilj is a stunning Roman palace near Piazza Venezia with a world-class, 17th-century art collection (think Caravaggio, Raphael, Lippi)—one of the largest collections in the world still privately owned. Descendant Jonathan Pamphilj narrates the audio guide tour of his smashing family home. The jewel of the collection is the extraordinary red portrait of the Pamphilj Pope **Innocent X** (1651) by Diego Velazquez (see *Extras in Rome*).

MAMERTINE PRISON

(S. Pietro in Carcere) Clivo Argentario 1, at the Forum (halfway down the steps from the Capitoline).
Open 9am-7pm (5pm in winter).
Tel. 06-69861
Tickets € 10. Ages 9 and under, free.

This jail-turned-teeny-chapel near the Arch of Septimius Severus was once a dank dungeon dating from the 6th century BC. Here Romans imprisoned enemies of the state, such as King Jugurtha, **St. Peter** and St. Paul. A column in its deep, dark pit is believed to be where **Nero** chained St. Peter. Those chains now reside in the church of Saint Peter in Chains (*Vincoli*). The wet floor is a result of a natural spring underneath, which was considered a miraculous production of Saint Peter.

ROMAN HOUSES UNDER PALAZZO VALENTINI

(Domus Romane), Via IV Novembre, 119A, under the Provincia di Roma building, steps from Piazza Venezia.
Open 9:30am-5pm. Closed Tuesdays, Jan. 1, May 1, & Dec. 25.
Tel. 06-32810
Tickets € 10 adults. Ages 6-25, € 8. Ages 5 and under, free.
Tickets online: ticketone.it (small fee applies). Entry is limited and by guided tour only.

Little is left to the imagination on this stunning high-tech tour of major archaeological excavations. Luxurious imperial-age homes are explored beneath glass floors and brought back to glory using advanced lighting effects. Mosaics, frescos, marble floors, ancient streets, and pools are re-created and explained by historians and experts. The tour takes about an hour and a half. Amazing!

SS. COSMA AND DAMIANO

Via dei Fori Imperiali, near the Forum entrance.
Open 9:30am-12:30pm and 3:30-6:30pm.
Nativity room open year-round, sporadic hours, small fee

View the inside of the Temple of Romulus from a glass wall in this unique church. It's part of an ancient temple first built by Vespasian in the 1st century so, technically, it's an even older building than the Pantheon. The shady cloister is a nice respite from summer heat. Look for the stone birds, lions and horses that populate its charming, moss-covered fountain in which little goldfish swim. Inside the church, search for **Barberini** bees in crests, abuzz in the coffered ceiling and hovering in the temple's dome. Check out the wonderful 6th-century mosaic (pretty old for Christian art); the apostles and Jesus are great big sheep, Jesus being the one with the flirty eyelashes. Scour the mosaic's left-hand corner for bees hovering amid the flowers, yet another clue to the church's restorer. Part of Urban's restoration deal was that he could take some of the church's ancient stone (outer east wall) to use in building his own private palace.

Off the courtyard, you'll find an entire room devoted to a first-rate Neapolitan nativity, or *presepio*, carved in Naples in the 1700s. The monumental village scene—4 x 6 x 3.5 meters—looks like Rome with ruins that look an awful lot like the Basilica of Maxentius. Miniature medieval street vendors are charming, and kids will love looking for ruins they may have just seen in the Forum. See if you can you find baby Jesus. Contrary to most nativity scenes, the infant is not in the center of the display.

SANTA MARIA IN ARA COELI
on the Capitoline (7th century)
Open daily, 9am-12:30pm and 3pm-6:30pm (5:30pm, Oct.-April).
Enter through its side door on the top of Capitoline Hill by taking a short flight of steps behind Palazzo Nuovo (the Capitoline museum left of the Senate building).

This pretty, chandelier-clad treasure is a fine example of Roman architectural spirit. Romans are architectual palimpsests; they re-use ancient foundations, columns and other elements in new structures. Even the religious function of this site has been reused, because the church—dedicated to the Mother of Christ—was once a pagan temple dedicated to the mother of the gods, Juno. The uniquely Roman interior is a scramble, too: its columns have been recycled from various Imperial edifices, including a palace. You'll even find Augustus in the apse. What is a pagan emperor doing in a Christian church? Find out in *Extras in Rome*, where the church is discussed at length.

Trajan's Column

TRAJAN'S COLUMN AND MARKETS
can be viewed from Via Fori Imperiali. Or, to enter them at Via IV Novembre, No. 94, take the steps up from the far side of Trajan's

Column and keep right.
Open 9am-7pm. 9am-2pm Dec. 24 & 31. Closed Mondays, Jan.1, May 1,
& Dec. 25.
Tel. 060608
Tickets € 9.50. Ages 5 and under, free. Audio guides, € 4. Strollers allowed.
Tickets online: ticketclic.it
Web site: mercatiditraiano.it

Ambitious Trajan was a Spaniard and Rome's first non-Italian emperor. He assumed the throne in 98 AD and ruled for nearly 20 years. He wanted a forum near the other great Roman emperors, but there was no space. His genius architect, Apollodorus of Damascus, removed a huge chunk of the Quirinal Hill (one of Rome's original seven) to accommodate this last and the largest of the Imperial Forums—larger than all the others put together. The semicircular markets, which stayed a hub of activity until an earthquake destroyed most of them in 801 AD, act as a giant shim, keeping the remaining hill from collapsing.

Weary travelers entering Rome through Trajan's magnificent Forum discovered a street teeming with vendors selling thirst-quenching drinks, savory food and supplies. Even in ruins, exploring the ancient Via Biberatica and the market's storefronts and hidden spaces still has a grand effect on today's visitors.

Hadrian succeeded his adoptive father, Trajan, in 117 AD, ruled for 20 more years and completed Trajan's honorific column, a 100-foot monument with 700 feet of PR space used to glorify the family line. The column's height is even more impressive when you know that it marks the crest of the hill Trajan had removed to accommodate his

What's Around

forum. Stand at its base and look up for a vertigo-like sensation.

The bas-reliefs, originally in color, tell of Trajan's victory against the Dacians, the proceeds of which financed his Forum. Some 2,500 figures twist around the column like a giant scroll (fitting, since two libraries flanked the column, one housing Greek scrolls and the other, Latin). A statue of Trajan crowned the column, but it was replaced in the 15th century with a statue of St. Peter facing the Vatican.

With **Augustus's** mausoleum filled to capacity, Trajan found himself out of space again! Though ancient Roman law forbade burial within the city walls, his ashes were kept in a golden urn sealed in a vault below the column (now gone). He was the first and only known emperor buried not only within the walls but also in the center of town.

IF YOU CAN'T SAY SOMETHING NICE...

*T*rajan and **Hadrian** *each ruled for nearly 20 years, back to back, during one of the most peaceful periods of the empire, The Age of the Antonines. Seems everyone fared well except that brilliant but loose-lipped architect, Apollodorus of Damascus, who designed Trajan's Forum, markets, and marvelous bridge over the Danube (depicted on the column's bas-reliefs). Apollodorus often voiced his opinion that Hadrian was an amateur architect. When Hadrian succeeded the throne, first off, he dismantled the famous bridge on grounds of protecting the border from attack. The cantankerous emperor eventually exiled and, finally, executed the irksome architect.*

VITTORIO EMANUELE II MONUMENT'S GLASS ELEVATOR

Piazza Venezia. The Elevator is located on the terrace behind the monument. Find it from the front by climbing the right staircase. Or, from Capitoline Hill, take the shortcut on page 45.

Open Mon.-Thurs. 9:30am-6:30pm, Fri.-Sun. 9:30am-7:30pm.

Tel. 06-678-0664

Tickets: €7 adults. €3.50 kids. Ages 9 and under, free.

This modern glass elevator attached to the rear exterior of the monument whisks you up to the tip-top terrace for extraordinary panoramic views in all directions. Free telescopes let you hunt for Rome's most iconic treasures. Photo ops are especially lovely at sunset. For more on the Vittoriano's museums and terraces, see the full listing in ***Extras in Rome.***

THE COLOSSEUM & PALATIN

COLOSSEUM *(Colosseo or Flavian Amphitheater)*, *72 AD. Daily, 8:30am-dusk. Closed Jan. 1 & Dec. 25. Tel. 06-399-67700. Tickets € 12, are valid for two days and include one entrance to the Roman Forum/Palatine area. Audio guides € 5.50.* Avoid long Colosseum lines: smartphones can scan barcodes in front of the site. Just pay by credit card, and show the e-ticket to enter. Other options: buy online and bring your print-at-home tix with you; use a RomaPass; or try the nearby Palatine Hill ticket booths. Tickets online: coopculture.it (booking fee applies).
Colosseum Underground and Third Ring tours. Touring under the Colosseum requires an additional ticket booked via telephone or online. Tickets € 9 per person, and highly recommended.

PALATINE HILL *(Roman Forum/Palatine archeological area), Via di S. Gregorio, 30. Daily, 8:30am-sunset; June 2, 1:30pm-7:15pm. Closed Dec. 25 and Jan. 1. Tel. 06-399-67700. Tickets € 12. Valid for two days and includes one entrance to the Colosseum. Audio guide, € 5.*

SAN CLEMENTE, *Via di S. Giovanni in Laterano, 108, Piazza San Clemente. Open Mon.-Sat., 9am-12:30 and 3-6pm, Sun. 12-6pm. Tickets € 5 for excavation under church. Web site: basilicasanclemente.com.* Tickets and entrance are located in the church postcard shop.

Timing and Tips

The Forum and Palatine Hill are unified. Thus, the Forum/Palatine+Colosseum ticket allows one entrance to the Colosseum and one to the Forum/Palatine. The main Palatine entrance and the Arch of Titus Palatine/Forum entrance are both steps from the Colosseum.

To avoid buying a second ticket, energetic families should tour the Roman Forum and Palatine Hill together, but doing so taxes the stamina and patience of many children.

Public bathrooms can be found in the Colosseum (long lines), outside the monument on the southeastern side, in the train station across from it, inside the Palatine's V. San Gregorio entrance, and in the little Palatine museum.

No trip to Rome is complete without a visit to **THE COLOSSEUM**. Rome's most popular site is always a winner with kids and, since so little remains inside, touring is lightning-fast. Touring its evocative underground level and view-commanding top ring with add an extra 1-2 hours.

The Colosseum was built over the site of **Nero's** private artificial lake, just a small part of his grandiose palace called the Golden House, or *Domus Aurea* (see **What's Around?**). It sprawled from the train station to the Palatine, covering nearly a quarter of Rome. The name *Colosseo* was likely coined after a colossal statue of Nero that once stood here.

As witness to Rome's rapid expansion, the great amphitheatre filled the citizens' desire for shows that displayed wild and exotic beasts, species made available by conquering foreign lands as far as Africa and Asia, and a reminder that Rome dominated the known world.

The grand and elaborate opening games went on for 100 days. Huge spectacles, like Trajan's games of 107 AD, had some 10,000 gladiators fight 11,000 animals. Under his reign alone (from 106-114 AD) more than 23,000 men fought in the Colosseum. That's a lot of carnage in eight years. It wasn't until 404 AD, as Christianity began to take hold of the city, that the games came to an end.

Centuries after all that carnage, the mighty amphitheater still entertains the masses with occasional concerts.

GIVE AND TAKE

*A*ncient rumor says **Nero** *fiddled while Rome burned because he ordered the great fire of 64 AD to clear a significant chunk of Rome to build his Golden House, then blamed it on Christians, a mysterious new cult thought to be up to all sorts of strange practices. When Nero died in 68 AD, Vespasian obliterated all traces of the lavish palace and rededicated the land to the people. Some of the land became vast public baths, and the drained private lake became the Colosseum, modern symbol of Rome.*

TOURING THE COLOSSEUM

Before entering, take a look at the Colosseum's 80 arches and the columns supporting each level, or arcade. The top level, without arches, has 40 windows that used to light the interior hallways.

FIND SEAT NUMBERS, COLUMNS AND SOCKETS

- Numbers carved above archways worked just like they do in stadiums today: ticket holders found their seats by matching ticket to arch. Tickets, or tesserae, were free, but there was a seating hierarchy. The best seats were reserved for the emperor and his entourage followed by vestals, senators, patrician families, Order of Knights, plebian families and, farthest away, women and slaves. Where should you sit?
- Studying Greek architecture? The Colosseum has all three orders of columns: Doric on the first level, Ionic on the second, and Corinthian on the third. Take close-up pictures for extra credit.
- Ringing the top, 240 stone brackets and square sockets held the rigging for a massive awning called the *velarium*. It provided shade for spectators during day-long battles.

Imagine the grand spectacle of the marble-faced Colosseum with a statue in every arch. Like many ancient buildings, it was quarried for precious materials. Its travertine, for example, was used for Palazzo di Venezia.

Inside the Colosseum, you can't help but notice the maze of cells where the floor should be. Wild beast hunts, or *venationes*, were tremendously popular. Animals were kept caged and hungry. Then, either the animals fought each other or humans hunted them. Gladiators and animals alike were hoisted up to the floor from those cells below it. *(See listing info for how to book the underground tour.)*

STAND IN THE MIDDLE OF THE ARENA

KIDS!

Gladiators were THE rock stars of the ancient world, so you'll get a gladiator's—or maybe a Rolling Stones'—eye view. Though they were mostly slaves or criminals, some free men chose to follow dreams of fame and glory that the games could bring. Sand is sometimes spread on the floor as an extra bonus. Kids love feeling it underfoot.

Gladiator comes from *gladius*, a short sword the fighters often used.

Arena is Latin for *sand*, which covered the floor to soak up spilled blood and prevent slipping.

Before exiting, enjoy the expansive views from the upper terrace. You can find Hadrain's gigantic Temple of Venus and Roma, the Forums, and the verdant Palatine Hill. Once outside, you can search for large *cippi* stones on the back side and Constantine's Arch around the front.

FIND THE CIPPI

Five huge travertine stones that look like gravestones (south side) are all that remains of 160 *cippi*, or boundary stones. Archeologists think they were anchors for rigging the massive sun awning. Since it unfurled like a sail, sailors worked the ropes. The often-overlooked *cippi* are a bit isolated. But that's just where you're heading next, so take a close-up look.

From the Arch of Constantine, you can enter the Palatine from it's main, Via S. Gregorio, entrance or from the Via Sacra (Arch of Titus) entrance. But, wait - not so fast. Look at Constantine's enormous creation. It is the largest existing triumphal arch in Rome, and it's made from recycled parts from earlier monuments. Roman's have always re-purposed ancient architectural elements, but here we see an ancient Roman doing it!

Now spin around and look for the flat base of the *Meta Sudante*, a giant, cone-shaped fountain especially for gladiators. Water seeped down from the top, giving the illusion that the cone was sweating, *sudante*. It survived hundreds of years, only to fall under Mussolini, who didn't feel it was important enough to keep.

Romantic and secluded, the **Palatine Hill** is the cradle of Rome, the home of her legendary founder Romulus and, almost certainly, the first of the original seven hills to be occupied. Bronze Age artifacts in the tiny Palatine Museum prove it. With half an hour, you can discover why the Palatine is often a highlight for both children and adults. It's a peaceful, green place to spread out and relax, far from the crowds and noise of modern Rome. Kids adore poking around the old palace foundations, and the commanding view of Circus Maximus (Domitian's, 86-96 AD) tops it all off.

The Palatine was a swanky residential enclave for the rich and powerful; people like Augustus and Cicero lived here in relative modesty. In fact, Augustus, who was born here, returned to the hill to live in an unpretentious palace with his wife Livia. It would not have escaped him that living on the Palatine would associate him with the legendary Romulus. It was Tiberius, though, who built the first really grandiose palace, the Domus Tiberiana (ca. 22 AD).

What made the Palatine so special? Location, location, location. It was near the river, markets, baths, circus, theaters and the political hub, yet exclusive: a finite chunk of land in a dominant position above the stinky marshes and the unwashed masses. Aristocrats like Cicero could walk to work (his was the Speaker's Platform in front of the Senate House) and then quickly retire to the hill's fresh air and tranquility. It even had its own baths and stadium, thanks to Domitian. Remember Septimius Severus' Arch in the Forum? When precious Palatine space ran out, Septimius wouldn't settle. He built an artificial extension for his palace, the Domus Severiana (southern most part of the hill).

The dark ages brought several hundred years of abandonment until **Pope Paul III's** grandson, Cardinal Alessandro II Farnese, bought the entire hill and built a splendid villa and enchanting gardens (Orti Farnesiani, ca. 1550 AD). You can still enjoy a portion of them, the first botanical gardens known in Italy.

The Palatine is full of important, albeit poorly-marked ruins. Don't get too caught up in trying to find things. Instead, enjoy the romantic, airy ruins while the kids have a ball.

TOURING PALATINE HILL

From the main entrance, turn left and ascend the hill on the gentle, serpentine path (with "House of Augustus" signs). Almost immediately, you'll encounter a shortcut on the right: a stairway that cuts directly up the hill. Either way, search out the Belvedere terrace, running along the uppermost edge. The reward for this small effort is a splendid emperor's view of Circus Maximus in the valley below and the Aventine Hill beyond.

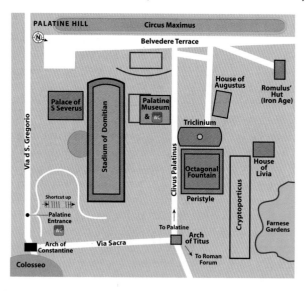

The diminutive **Museo del Palatino** is nearby in a grey building *not* in ruins. Your ticket gets you in. Dip in for a look at its Iron Age artifacts; and a pit stop, if necessary. The modern restrooms are rare in themselves!

CAN YOU FIND THESE TREASURES?

KIDS!

- A bust of notorious **Nero**
- **A Satyr.** His tail gives him away
- Prehistoric finds from the **Iron and Bronze Ages,** including a bit of original 1ˢᵗ-century masonry
- **Romulus's** house. Kids love these models of primitive dwellings that pre-date Rome's foundation (753 BC)

Make your way to the northwest end of the Belvedere ledge (right as you face the Circus) to view the Iron Age area believed to hold Romulus' hut. The walk is not a straight path; you must serpentine. **Augustus' House** is also here, so drop in and see how Rome's first emperor lived! If you wish to tour the Forum before exiting, simply follow the signs.

Especially in the hot summer months, there's only so much outdoor exploring you can do before fatigue and sunburn set in. The answer: go underground! Treat yourselves to a refreshing cool-off in Rome's stone foundations. Explore the excavations of remarkable **San Clemente,** just a few blocks from the Colosseum. Alternatively, the excavations of **Nero's Golden House** (also underground, but often closed for restoration) are just across the street (see ***What's Around?***). Both are spectacular, but San Clemente is more pleasing to kids. Either way, from behind the Colosseum, cross the street and pause to view the ruins of the gladiator barracks, or *Ludus Magnus,* on the corner of Via Labicana, before leaving the area.

TOURING SAN CLEMENTE

SAN CLEMENTE BASILICA is not just a church; it's a time machine where you can travel 2,000 years in just a few steps. Run by Irish Dominicans since 1667, it ranks as one of the most interesting churches in Rome because of the extensive excavations under it. Kids absolutely love exploring them, and you will, too.

This jewel of Roman adaptability reveals several slices of history over a single location. The fascinating excavations are well lighted and airy, unlike catacombs that may be too spooky, narrow and dark for some kids. Another plus: exploring on your own, without a confining group tour. Children especially love searching for the rushing underground spring; you can hear it before you can see it, and following the sound is fun.

To get here from the Colosseum, walk three blocks up Via d. S. Giovanni in Laterano, and take a left to Piazza San Clemente. For a quick snack before entering, Caffè San Clemente is just across the street (see ***Let's Eat***).

Inside **San Clemente,** make a beeline to the postcard shop for tickets to descend 30 feet below ground. From the 12th-century church, each level takes you further back through time. The first flight arrives at a 4th-century church, and one more staircase brings you to 2nd-century building remains that include a *Mithraeum* with an altar and schoolroom. Mithraic cults were as popular as Christianity when both were up-and-coming religions. Eventually, you'll wind up in fragments of a 1st-century building with a spring that once brought water to those inhabitants. Kids can stick their hands down an opening and feel it rushing by.

CAN YOU FIND...
One Sacrificial Altar
One Running Spring
One Ancient Schoolroom
One Irish Brogue (from the Irish Dominicans)

Speaking of school: Writing ink was made from a mixture of **squid ink, soot** and **tar!**

Older kids may enjoy one other object: a **pagan sarcophagus** (in the 4th-century church). Its bas-relief depicts the myth of *Phaedra and Hippolytus*. It seems very out of place in a Christian church, but it's another case of Roman recycling—the old sarcophagus was reused for a Christian burial.

PHAEDRA AND HIPPOLYTUS

*The tragedy of "**Phaedra and Hippolytus**" tells of a woman who falls in love with her stepson, whose only love is hunting and chastity. When he denies her, she kills herself in shame, but, for revenge, she leaves a note blaming him. Hippolytus' father falls for the note and curses his son, asking Poseidon to kill him. Poseidon sends a bull to scare Hippolytus' horse on the beach causing it to throw the boy. He suffers a fatal blow but does not die before reconciling with Dad. As happy an ending as you get in Greek mythology!*

Go-getters can take a quick detour, two blocks (uphill) to **SS Quattro Coronati** for a bit of detective work. Find its convent, ring the bell and wait for a nun to slide open a dark little window. Give her a couple of Euro and ask for the key (*chiave*, say *key-ah-vay*) to unlock a small, frescoed chapel (see ***Extras in Rome***).

WHAT'S AROUND?

NERO'S GOLDEN HOUSE

(Domus Aurea), 64 AD, Viale della Domus Aurea, Giardini di Colle Oppio.
Tel. 06-399-67700
Advance booking required. Online tickets: coopculture.it
Everyone enters in guide-led groups. Currently closed for restoration.

Many emperors were crazy with wealth, others were crazy for power, and some were crazy from being born into an incestuous line. **Nero** had a touch of all three. His murderous temperament and his bejeweled and gilded palace of outrageous decadence led Romans to coin a new phrase: "Caesar madness."

Within a year of Nero's death, most of the Golden House was pilfered, covered with earth, and built over. What remains of the sprawling palace is precious. In fact, rising damp often closes it temporarily. Excavators have uncovered around 180 rooms and continue to find more, but only a few have been open for public viewing. Teens can appreciate the outrageous proportions of what now seems to be a secret, underground lair for the likes of Austin Powers' Dr. Evil.

RAPHAEL WAS HERE

Renaissance artists like Raphael checked out fragments of Nero's frescoes (in the cryptoporticus) by lowering themselves from holes above. As proof they'd been there, they signed their names on the ceiling! Inspired by the great frescoed walls, they copied what they saw. That style is called "grotesque," because it came from this "grotto," the buried walls of Nero's palace.

In the early 1500s, the famous *Laocoön* grouping was discovered in a nearby field. It probably belonged to Nero's vast collections, and it profoundly influenced Renaissance artists. **Michelangelo** was put in charge of moving it to the Vatican holdings, and you can compare the hulking body of Laocoön with the Sistine fresco figures, both at the Vatican Museums.

Since the Golden House is subterranean, it's the perfect place to be on a hot afternoon. Use it to escape the blazing sun.

SAN PIETRO IN VINCOLI

(St. Peter in Chains), Piazza San Pietro in Vincoli, 4A (off Via Cavour).
Open daily 8am-12:30pm
and 3pm-7pm (6pm in winter).
Tel. 06-978-44950

From Via Fori Imperiali, the church is best found by walking up Via Cavour, passing a high wall and ascending a covered flight of steps called Via San Francesco di Paola (all on the right). Alternatively, the fastest route from the Colosseum is up the steps right of the metro. Go right at the top to the first street (Via Terme di Tito) and follow it to the end (a block), then turn left and go a few blocks to the church (you will veer slightly right).

Built in 422 to house the eponymous chains, its biggest draw is **Michelangelo's** celebrated *Moses*, a part of the grandiose, unfinished tomb of Pope Julius II della Rovere. Michelangelo spent eight months in the hills of Carrara handpicking the marble; stories still swirl about the pope and artist's stormy relationship.

EGO TRIPS

*H*arassed by Julius, Michelangelo walked off the job, vowing never to return to Rome, but he was forced back by the threatening pope. Popes could (and often did) kill on whim. Ironically, after all his self-aggrandizing plans, Julius II is buried in a simple tomb in St. Peter's.

Compare the powerful *Moses'* muscles, veins and latent energy with the sublime *Pietà* in St. Peter's. The *Pietà* was done early in Michelangelo's career while *Moses* was produced later, when he chose to express potential energy rather than ideal beauty. This is another example of Michelangelo's work being greatly influenced after he saw the ancient, athletic, *Laocoön* sculpture discovered during his lifetime (now at the Vatican)—seems likely when you compare the steroidal bodies.

Kids wonder about *Moses'* horns: they're an early Christian symbol of wisdom, like rays of light. Popular legend says profiles of Michelangelo and Julius are hidden in the flowing beard. Look under Moses' lip. What do you think?

CHAIN REACTION

T   *he chains that once shackled St. Peter in Rome are stored below
     the altar. In 439, Juvenal took them to Constantinople, capital of
the empire under Constantine. Empress Eudoxia placed one of them in
a basilica there and sent the other back to Rome for her daughter, wife
of Emperor Valentinian III, who gave her chain to Pope Leo I. Later,
when the second chain was returned to Rome, the two miraculously fused
themselves together.*

Colosseum underground

Palatine Hill

THE MOUTH OF TRUTH
(Bocca della Verità)

THE BOCCA DELLA VERITÀ, *on the portico of* **Santa Maria in Cosmedin** *in Piazza Bocca della Verità, between the Tiber and Circus Maximus. The church is open 9am–noon and 3–5pm daily. €.50 donation requested for Mouth of Truth photo op; €1 to view the tiny, 8th century reliquary crypt under the church altar.*

CIRCUS MAXIMUS, *now bare and abandoned, occupies the valley between the Palatine and Aventine Hills. Always open, and still staggering. Free.*

Timing and Tips

These sights, just a bit far for walking from the center of town (with kids), are best reached by cabbing directly to Piazza Bocca della Verità. It's best to save energy: take a taxi one way and walk on the return. You may skip Circus Maximus, but it seems silly not to double-team the famous site with a visit to the neighboring Mouth of Truth. Use the Circus as an active break. Children can blow off steam while you enjoy the dramatic views of the Palatine Hill above. Beware the traffic snarl running between the piazza and the river: cross with the light and keep a close eye on small kids.

PIAZZA BOCCA DELLA VERITÀ sits on the oldest ancient forum, the *Forum Boarium* (meat market). The site was once the stagnant marsh where the legendary twins Romulus and Remus were found by the she-wolf that raised them.

The *Bocca della Verità*, the curiosity for which the piazza was named, translates as the "mouth of truth," but it is actually a large, photogenic, marble disk with a human face. It served as a manhole cover for the *Cloaca Maxima*, the ancient sewer system that drained the Forums into the Tiber, but popular legend says it bites the hand of liars! The face has played a part in many films, notably *Roman Holiday* with Gregory Peck and Audrey Hepburn. It's a terrific photo op because no one can resist hamming it up when they stick their hand in and imagine it getting chopped off.

> Watch *Ben-Hur* and *Roman Holiday* to see the Circus Maximus and the Mouth of Truth in all their glory.

CIRCUS MAXIMUS is just behind Santa Maria in Cosmedin. Though there are no ruins in it, there are plenty above it. The massive Palatine Hill skyline is as impressive as the vast circus it overlooks. (Note: excavation continues on the stadium's small eastern wedge.) Still, there's plenty of history to spark kids' imaginations. Of Rome's stadiums, Circus Maximus was the largest: six football fields long. It was home to the grand spectacle of chariot racing, which was big business in Rome. Prestigious charioteers came from around the world just to race here. Racing teams had assigned colors, and almost everyone in the city pledged allegiance to a favorite team, wearing their colors proudly. Few spectators were fencesitters; people gambled on their favorites, and passions ran high. Did fights break out between loyal gangs? You bet—this is Rome!

THE WALKING TOUR

Arrive at **Santa Maria in Cosmedin** and head straight for the Mouth of Truth (*Bocca della Verità*).

TRUTH OR DARE?

Put your hand in the mouth, and have someone ask you a question. Better answer truthfully, or you could lose your hand. According to legend, the mouth was an ancient lie detector: liars had their hand "bitten" off...by a hidden guard ready to chop!

While you're here, duck into the 6th-century Santa Maria in Cosmedin to see its famous marble floors cut in striking patterns, a technique called *cosmatesque*. The church is a rare, surviving example of the simple, early Roman basilica that had no aisles.

COSMATESQUE
Any object, floor or wall decorated with geometric marble designs mixed with mosaics and colored stones or glass. Families who did this work were known as *Cosmati*.

Romantics can seek out the flower-crowned skull of St. Valentine, while explorers may wish to check out the small, ancient reliquary under the altar.

Go behind the church (around the right side) to find the vast **Circus Maximus**. Nothing remains but an enormous, patchy outline; but just by standing in it, you'll appreciate its magnitude. Look up at the Palatine Hill with its dramatic ruins of the Domus Severiana palace and the emperor's box. If you've already been to the Palatine, your kids may be able to point out where they've been.

Imagine the Circus filled with some 250,000-300,000 people. It was the largest racing stadium in the world. Ancient Rome at its peak had about a million inhabitants, so about a quarter of the city's population could fit into the Circus at any time!

KIDS!

TAKE A LAP
Most chariot races consisted of seven one-mile laps. Try running a few; many joggers use the Circus for this very purpose. How many can you take? How many does Charlton Heston take as *Ben-Hur*?

So impressive were the races and so popular the contestants that **Nero** often entered the dangerous games as charioteer for a taste of the sweet glory that winning brought.

Augustus, first to import Egyptian obelisks, put one in the center of Circus Maximus in 10 BC. Today, it adorns the Piazza del Popolo at the bottom of the Pincio.

Return to Santa Maria in Cosmedin and cross the street to the distinctive round temple, once called the Temple of Vesta, now known to be the **Temple of Hercules**.

It dates from the end of the 2nd century BC and is thought to be the oldest marble edifice in Rome. The tiny temple was very expensive because the marble had to be imported from Greece; Italians had not yet begun to quarry their own. Sometimes, on the first and third Sundays of every month, between 1-3pm, you can go inside for a peek.

The **Palatine Bridge** behind the Temple of Hercules has great views of **Tiberina Island** and the **Ponte Rotto** (Broken Bridge). For lunch, Ristorante Alvaro sits right behind the Mouth of Truth, at the Circus Maximus (facing the church, go left and take the first right one block); or, walk to charming Tiberina Island *(What's Around?)*. **Sora Lella Ristorante** is a refined choice while **Antico Caffè** is perfect for snacks. Alternatively, take the secret footpath up the Aventine Hill (find out how in *What's Around?*).

EGYPTIAN OBELISKS IN ROME:
How many can you spot?

Rome, founded in 753 BC, is ancient, but the oldest things in it are Egyptian. From 1600 BC, while Romans lived in huts on the Tiber, sophisticated Egyptians were crafting monumental obelisks. Some weigh as much as 455 tons! Thirteen of them now stand in Rome. They became popular adornments after Augustus "acquired" the first two in 30 BC and brought them to Rome via great barges. The exotic arrivals caused so much excitement, even the barges were put on display.

After centuries of deterioration, obelisks were put to new purpose by 16th-century popes who used them in their urban projects. Moving them was no small feat: St. Peter's obelisk, for instance, took nearly 1,000 men, 150 horses and dozens of cranes to position it.

1. Piazza del Popolo: Sixtus V re-erected this Egyptian obelisk from the reign of Seti I (1318-1304 BC) as he did those at St. Peter's and St. John Lateran. Look for his coat of arms (lion, tablets and sun) as well as the cross on top of each. This was the first obelisk brought to Rome by Augustus in 10 BC to adorn the Circus Maximus.

2. Piazza Navona: Red granite with 1st-century imitation-Egyptian hieroglyphics tops Bernini's *Fountain of the Four Rivers.* Innocent X moved it here from Circus Maxentius.

3. Piazza Minerva: This 6th-century BC, Egyptian red-granite obelisk rides on Bernini's clever elephant. It's the smallest obelisk in Rome and originally stood at the Temple of Isis nearby.

4. Piazza della Trinità dei Monti: From the 3rd-2nd century BC, this tops the

Spanish Steps. The hieroglyphics were added in Rome and were copied from the obelisk in nearby Piazza del Popolo.

5. Piazza dell'Esquilino: On the Via Cavour side of Santa Maria Maggiore is a twin of the one on the Quirinal Hill. Both of them originally adorned Augustus' mausoleum.

6. Piazza della Rotunda: The Pantheon square has a 13th-century BC, red granite monolith from Ramses II. This, one of Rome's smallest obelisks, also decorated the Temple of Isis.

7. Piazza di Montecitorio: One of the first two brought to Rome by Augustus, who used it as a giant sundial, it was made during the reign of Psammetichos II (595-589 BC) at Heliopolis.

8. St. John Lateran: Made in 1504-1450 BC, this is the oldest obelisk in Rome. Standing some 105.6 feet tall, the red granite monolith is also the tallest in existence. Constantius II brought it from Thebes in 357 AD and erected it in Circus Maximus.

9. Piazza del Quirinale: This piazza holds the twin of the obelisk at Santa Maria Maggiore. Neither has hieroglyphics.

10. Pincio Gardens, on the Piazza Napoleon: Hadrian had this one made in Rome to adorn the funeral monument of his beloved Antinous (2nd century AD).

11. Villa Celimontana: This residence holds the sister obelisk to the one at the Pantheon. Apparently, after it fell at the Capitoline Hill, it was put to use as a step up to S. Maria in Aracoeli.

12. Piazza dei Cinquecento: By the train station is an Egyptian obelisk only just found near S. Maria Sopra Minerva in the late 1800s.

13. Piazza San Pietro: Augustus first erected this massive structure in Alexandria. Caligula brought it to Rome in 37 AD for the Vatican Circus.

Finally, if you get to a sporting event at the Foro Italico, you'll find Mussolini's modern obelisk made from Carrara marble.

WHAT'S AROUND?

AVENTINE HILL

The pretty Aventine Hill, one of Rome's original seven, rises from the Circus Maximus. From the Bocca della Verità, take the enchanting, cobblestone walkway called called *Clivo d. Rocca* up the hill (off Via S. M. in Cosmedin). Everyone will enjoy the peaceful, secret path. At the top, turn right and enter the orange garden of Parco Savello for a rest with knockout views. End your walk with a peek through the magical keyhole of the Knights of Malta. See **Knights of Malta Keyhole** in *Extras in Rome* for more.

TIBERINA ISLAND

Kids love exploring this charming little boat-shaped island in the Tiber. Its lower level provides an unexpected open space that lets kids appreciate they're actually on an island! Plop down fore or aft and listen to the rapid waters rush by. Tom Sawyer, Italian-style.

Tiberina boasts two of Rome's oldest bridges: The Ponte Cestio to Trastevere and the Ponte Fabricio, the older of the two (62 BC). Both are still intact. In the water south (downstream) of the island, look for crumbled remains of yet another ancient bridge, the Ponte Rotto (broken bridge).

KIDS!

TIBERINA TREASURE HUNT
One broken bridge
A stairway to the island's lower "deck"
An aging serpent on a bit of old travertine wall (Hint: Walk around the point of the island nearest the Ponte Rotto to find the fragment next to a flight of steps leading to the police stationed there.)

Tiberina once held a temple dedicated to the Greek healer-god Aesculapius (293 BC), and the island's primary function is still healing, with the hospital of the **Fatebenefratelli** dominating its northern end. It is Aesculapius' serpent that forms the caduceus, the logo we all recognize today as pertaining to the medical community. The serpent climbing the fragment of old temple wall is a clue to the island's illustrious past.

TRACING A LEGEND

*T*he *Temple of Aesculapius was erected here during a great plague in the 3rd century after Romans sent an envoy to Greece seeking a cure from the cult of Aesculapius. As the ship returned to Rome, the god's sacred symbol, a serpent, left the deck and swam to Tiberina Island. Romans took this as a sign that the god wished to be honored there. The benefits of quarantining plague victims on an island seemed motivation enough.*

A little café next to the church of S. Bartolomeo on the island's main piazza offers drinks and snacks. The fresh-squeezed *limonata*, on the menu only in summer, is particularly good. If you're ready for lunch or dinner, opt for **Giggetto**, just across the bridge in the Jewish Ghetto. It's an institution of old Roman fare (see ***Let's Eat!***).

LET'S EAT!

Listed below are restaurants and cafés suitable for lunch or snacks as you tour. For full descriptions and other listings, including dinner-only establishments, see ***Where to Eat*** at the back of the book.

CAPITOLINE HILL AND THE JEWISH GHETTO

AL POMPIERE, Via Santa Maria dei Calderari, 38. On the second floor of the Cenci's grand old palace, "The Fireman" is the perfect restaurant for families. Sophisticated yet a bit worn, it's especially nice for dinner in the heart of the Jewish Ghetto. Dinner reservations recommended. Moderate.

ANTICO CAFFÈ DELL'ISOLA, Via Ponte Quattro Capi on Tiberina Island. Since 1925, this well-placed snack bar with a few outside tables has been serving homemade lemonades (*spremuta di limonata*) and coffee drinks along with an assortment of snacks.

GIGGETTO, Via del Portico d'Ottavia, 21/A. Lunch and dinner. Closed Mondays. Traditional, old Jewish-Roman cooking is presented in a casual atmosphere beside ancient ruins, near the Theater of Marcellus in the Jewish Ghetto. Giggetto is famous for its appetizer trio of fried artichokes, zucchini flowers and cod fillets (*carciofi alla giudia, fiori di zucca* and *baccalà*), the stars of Roman Jewish fare. Simple cannelloni, spaghetti and bucatini (pasta with tomato-bacon sauce) are kid-pleasers. Quality and reasonable prices.

IL BUCCIONE, *(Pasticceria Limentari)*, Via Portico d'Ottavia, 1. Closed Saturdays. This teeny shop is on every gourmand's guide to Rome. Standouts are the baked pumpkin seeds and its *Pizza Ebraica*, a bar cookie baked on sheets, like Rome's cut pizza to go. It looks like a burned mess and tastes like heaven.

LA TAVERNA DEGLI AMICI, Piazza Margana, 37. Lunch and dinner. Closed Mondays. A white-tablecloth restaurant in a picturesque little square a few blocks from the Vittoriano Monument. The service and secluded location make it great. Moderate.

MUSEO CAPITOLINO BAR, or *Caffeteria Capitolina*, Piazza Caffarelli, 4. Fast snacks and a fabulous panorama are served in the Capitoline museum cafeteria. Thirst-quenching, fresh-squeezed orange juice and outdoor terrace seating under colorful umbrellas make for a lovely break.

DA NERONE HOSTERIA, Via delle Terme di Tito, 96. Closed Sundays and the month of August. Take the steps right of the Colosseum Metro station and take a right to find this little quaint street. You'll find Da Nerone at the end of the street. The Roman food is top notch and the setting is casual. Perfect.

RISTORANTE ALVARO, Via dei Cerchi, 53. Lunch and dinner. Closed Sunday dinner and Mondays. This family-owned restaurant sits in the shadow of the *Palatine Hill and Circus Maximus*. It's a quick two-block walk from the famous *Mouth of Truth* too. Expect typical Italian fare in a warm setting. Moderate.

SORA LELLA, Via di Ponte Quattro Capi, 16. Lunch and dinner. Closed Sundays. Beloved by locals for its traditional Roman fare, this slightly upscale restaurant holds court on Tiberina Island. Reservations recommended. Moderate.

VITTORIANO CAFÉ, on the terrace of the Victor Emanuele II Monument. Get there by climbing its stairs to the museum entrance and following café signs, or enter from the Capitoline Piazza in back (easier) by taking the stairs left of the Senate building. Inside the doors, turn right, then follow the long corridor (left) to the VEII terrace and café. Views, views, views.

COLOSSEUM AREA

ALLE CARRETTE, Vicolo delle Carrette, 14 (another entrance is at Via Madonna dei Monte, 95). Dinner only. The best way to find this hole-in-the-wall joint is to walk 2 blocks up Cavour from Via Fori Imperiali and take a left on the tiny street (Carrette) just past V. Tor di Conte. Delicious, wood-fired pizza is nearly the only thing on the menu.

L'ANTICA CORNETTERIA, Via Labicana, 78 (near S. Clemente). Pop in to this non-stop bakery for a sack of their extraordinary *cornetti* in a wide variety of flavors.

CAFÉ CAFÉ, Via dei Santi Quattro Coronari, 44 (at the Colosseum). Open from 11am, this is a tearoom with all-day light dining. Sunday brunch buffet, 11:30am-4pm.

CAFFÈ S. CLEMENTE, Via San Giovanni in Laterano, 124a. Quick snacks, coffee and drinks can be found right across from the eponymous basilica. There are a few seats inside and outside.

LA NAUMACHIA, Via Celimontana, 7. Rustic and reliable pizzeria with pleasing Italian dishes, like artichoke risotto and seasonal specialties. Inexpensive. Open daily from 11am.

LI RIONI, Via dei S. Quattro Coronati, 24. Go here for a fun vibe and excellent pizza. Hours vary, but usually closed Tuesdays and August 15-30. Dinner only, but, at time of press, there's talk of expanding to lunch service. Kids will love the outdoor seating in summer, and the cute interior, which looks like an old Roman street scene. It's packed after 9pm, so go early.

LUZZI, Via San Giovanni in Laterano, 88. Lunch and dinner. Closed Wednesdays. This busy trattoria has a variety of homemade pastas and roasted meats. At night, they add pizza to the menu. Moderate prices and good food are a rare combination within five minutes walk of the Colosseum.

PART TWO

MEDIEVAL & RENAISSANCE INFLUENCES

Having begun in and around Rome's Forums, we now leave the ancient city to explore the aesthetically-pleasing Medieval and Renaissance zones encompassing the Campo dei Fiori and Piazza Navona. Though Roman topography is the product of thousands of years, our definition here applies to the major Renaissance restructuring and urban beautification of this medieval warren of streets, now lined with the finest of Renaissance palaces. And though nearly everything in Rome, from St. Peter's to Piazza Navona, wears a Baroque face, the beautifying hand of the Renaissance gave it its "good bones."

Piazza Navona and the Pantheon both lie within this zone. And while Navona is unquestionably Baroque, it has a foot in many eras—it was an ancient circus, paved and developed in the latter part of the 15th century, and many of its buildings are from the Renaissance period. The Pantheon, though ancient, has a delightful Renaissance fountain in front and holds the tomb of the great Raphael within.

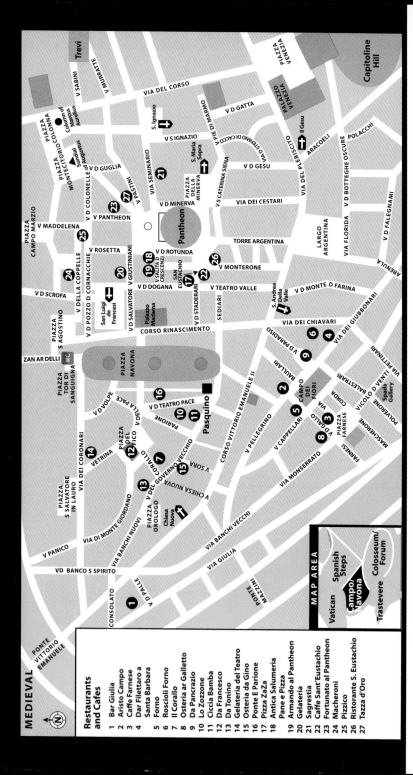

MEDIEVAL

Restaurants and Cafes

1 Bar Giulia
2 Aristo Campo
3 Caffe Farnese
4 Dar Filettaro a Santa Barbara
5 Forno
6 Roscioli Forno
7 Il Corallo
8 Osteria ar Galletto
9 Da Pancrazio
10 Lo Zozzone
11 Ciccia Bamba
12 Da Francesco
13 Da Tonino
14 Gelateria del Teatro
15 Osteria da Gino
16 Ponte E Parione
17 Pizza ZaZa
18 Antica Salumeria
19 Pane e Pizza
20 Gelateria
21 Sagrestia
22 Caffe Sant'Eustachio
23 Fortunato al Pantheon
24 Macheroni
25 Pizzico
26 Ristorante S. Eustachio
27 Tazza d'Oro

PONTE VITTORIO EMANUELE

CONSOLATO

V D BANCO S SPIRITO

V PANICO

PIAZZA S SALVATORE IN LAURO

VIA DEI CORONARI

PIAZZA TOR DI SANGUIGNA

ZAN AR DELLI

WC

PIAZZA NAVONA

PIAZZA S AGOSTINO

V D SCROFA

V D POZZO D CORNACCHIE

V DELLA COPPELLE

PIAZZA CAMPO MARZIO

PIAZZA MADDALENA

V PANTHEON

V ROSETTA

PIAZZA COLONNA

Column of Marcus Aurelius

Sundial of Augustus

PIAZZA MONTECITORIO

V D COLONNELLE

V PASTINI

VIA SEMINARIO

V D GUGLIA

V SABINI

V MURRATTE

Trevi

VIA DEL CORSO

S. Ignazio

V S IGNAZIO

V PIE DI MARMO

V D GATTA

S. Maria Sopra

PIAZZA DELLA MINERVA

V D MINERVA

V S CATERINA SIENA

V D GESU

Pantheon

TORRE ARGENTINA

VIA DEI CESTARI

V MONTERONE

V TEATRO VALLE

SEDIARI

S. Andrea Della Valle

VIA DEI CHIAVARI

LARGO ARGENTINA

VIA FLORIDA

V D MONTE DI FARINA

V D BOTTEGHE OSCURE

POLACCHI

ARACOELI

Il Gesu

V D PLEBISCITO

STEFANO DI CACCO

VIA DELLA GATTA

PALAZZO VENEZIA

PIAZZA VENEZIA

Capitoline Hill

ARENULA

VIA PETTINARI

Spada Gallery

PIAZZA FARNESE

FARNESI

MASCHERONE

V D VENTI

POLVERONE

V GALLO

V D BALESTRARI

CAMPO DEI FIORI

VIA MONSERRATO

VIA GIULIA

PONTE MAZZINI

VIA BANCHI VECCHI

Chiesa Nuova

PIAZZA OROLOGO

V DEL GOVERNO VECCHIO

V CHIESA NUOVA

V SORA

V D MONTE GIORDANO

VIA BANCHI NUOVI

V D PALLE

VIA BANCHI VECCHI

PIAZZA DEL FICO

VETRINA

V D PACE

V D VOLPE

LA PACE

PARIONE

V D TEATRO PACE

Pasquino

CORSO VITTORIO EMANUELE II

V PELLEGRINO

V CAPPELLARI

V D PARADISO

CORSO RINASCIMENTO

Palazzo Madama

San Luigi de Francesi

V D SALVATORE

V GIUSTINIANI

V D DOGANA

V D STADERARI

V SANTA CHIARA

V CRESCENZI

V D ROTUNDA

SAN EUSTACHIO

BAULLARI

VIA D GIUBBONARI

CORDA

V PENITENZA

MASCHERONE

PONTE VITTORIO EMANUELE

MAP AREA

Vatican

Spanish Steps

Campo Navona

Colosseum/ Forum

Trastevere

THE CAMPO DEI FIORI ZONE

CAMPO DEI FIORI *is two blocks south of Piazza Navona. The markets are open daily 7am-2pm, except Sundays.* This is the heart of the posh triangular area defined by the Tiber River and Corso Vittorio Emanuele II that first reached its peak in the Renaissance. Primarily a lively, outdoor fruit and vegetable market, the Campo's mouthwatering pizza bakery and stalls that sell cheap t-shirts and beaded jewelry make it a winner with kids. Half a block off the Campo is **Palazzo Farnese,** occupied by the French Embassy since 1635.

GALLERIA SPADA (1544), *Piazza Capo di Ferro,13. Open Tues.-Sat., 8:30am-7:30pm. Closed Mondays, Dec. 25 & Jan. 1. Information: Tel. 06-683-2409 or galleriaborghese. it. Tickets € 5, or online: ticketone.it (booking fee applies).* This small but mighty art collection and amazing trompe l'oeil garden are a few blocks from the Campo dei Fiori.

Timing and Tips

Too many families pack their days with museums and sights, effectively denying themselves the true native experience of "productive ambling." Discovering your own finds is one of the joys of travel, and this is the perfect place to let your kids do the discovering. Take an hour or so to wander this charming and vibrant zone, not including café downtime. And come hungry. Coffee, fresh-baked bread and ripe fruits are all part of the experience.

The **CAMPO DEI FIORI** zone was a medieval tangle of streets populated by a hodgepodge of craftsmen and a few inns, until its elegant transformation around 1450 when the papacy returned to Rome from Avignon. Finding the former palace (at San Giovanni in Laterano) too run down, the papal court moved near St. Peter's. That put this triangle of land, formerly part of the ancient *Campus Martius,* smack in between Rome's two greatest religious and political centers: the Vatican and the Capitoline Hill. Campo dei Fiori underwent a total transformation: Streets were widened to accommodate the major papal processions that now passed through, and inns, commerce and an elite clientele gravitated to the swanky new neighborhood.

Campo became the "it" place to live and work, the Via Veneto of its day. Popes, artists and society's elite, like **Pope Paul III Farnese** and artists **Caravaggio** and Raphael moved in, but so did notorious characters who gave the Campo its dramatic mystique. Vannozza Catanei, infamous mistress to Renaissance pope Alexander VI Borgia, owned an inn on the square. Her illegitimate daughter by that pope was the equally infamous Lucrezia Borgia, whom biographers continue to find worth writing about. Brilliant but troubled Caravaggio fought a duel here. And **Pope Urban VIII** once executed two monks and their accomplice for a botched assassination attempt on his life.

Today's Campo is no less colorful. Dozens of white-tented market stalls hawk everything from fresh fish on ice to sunglasses and beads. The chaos of barrels of exotic imported spices and baskets of produce is only marginally under control. Vendors do legally rent spaces, and many families have been renting the same stalls for generations.

Shopping here is much today what it was 600 years ago. Via Cappellari (street of hatmakers), Giubbonari (jerkins or jackets), Chiavi (locksmiths) and Pettinari (wool combers) were named after the trades that dominated them in medieval times. Today, funky, eclectic shops line the piazza and its neighboring streets, selling everything from handmade soaps to tailored clothing and skateboard gear. At night, the square is turned over to 20-somethings who congregate around its statue and while away the wee hours in Campo's many after-hours bars.

The zone is packed with great restaurants for every taste and budget. A good choice is **Da Pancrazio**, carved into the ruins of the ancient *Teatro di Pompeo* (61-55 BC) off the east side of the Campo. Pompey built his theater at the height of his political popularity and personal wealth. As part of its opening festivities, 500 lions and 18 elephants were reputedly slaughtered. Murder continued to distinguish the theater—it was here that Caesar met his untimely end.

NERO AND THE THEATER OF POMPEY

*W*hen Nero was on a campaign to associate himself with Apollo Phoebus, the Sun God, he made everything golden to reinforce the association. Coins were minted with his image surrounded by golden rays of light. He dressed like a charioteer to emulate Apollo and his sun-pulling chariot; he built the gold and jewel-encrusted palace, the Golden House; and he held a special "Golden Day" on which every surface in Pompey's theater was gilded. Sun bouncing off all that gold might have caused some serious blinding, but Nero had a solar awning specially made. When the crowds looked up at it, they beheld their emperor depicted as the Sun God blazing in the sky overhead.

Just off the Campo is **PALAZZO FARNESE,** the gigantic and extraordinary High Renaissance home begun by **Pope Paul III Farnese**

in 1514 when he was but a Cardinal (finished by his grandson, Cardinal Alessandro Farnese, in 1589). It is a great introduction to Rome's elegant world of Renaissance living. Bramante designed the lower portion, and **Michelangelo** designed the famous upper façade, central *loggia* (biggest) window and high cornice as well as the interior third story and attic. An equally-famous courtyard and breathtaking frescoes inside require a special permit from the French Embassy for entry.

A block further, **THE SPADA PALACE** is a gorgeous example of a 16th-century home complete with pretty, faded frescos on the outside and a statue-filled courtyard within. Its tiny Galleria has a mighty art collection that includes works by **Michelangelo**, Andrea del Sarto, Titian, Rubens, Reni, Annibale Carracci and Gentileschi, but Francesco Borromini's surprising trompe l'oeil in the garden is the reason you're popping by with kids. It's a slam-dunk.

THE WALKING TOUR

Upon arriving, head directly to the **Forno Campo de' Fiori**, arguably the best bakery in Rome. Wide-eyed children will have a tough time choosing which of the freshly made goodies and still-warm breads they want.

PEEK INTO THE OVEN ROOM

See the three-to-four-foot-long slabs of raw dough being prepared in the rustic oven room to the right of the bakery? Some of them will become *Pizza Bianca,* tasty pizza bread with no sauce, while others become delicious *Pizza Rosso,*

pizza with sauce. If you're lucky, they chop it up right
in front of you with great deft strokes. Grab a piece!

With delicious, warm bread in hand, explore the colorful and eclectic
Campo and its free-for-all atmosphere. Let kids pick out and purchase
their own *frutta di fresca* (fresh fruit), wash it in one of the drinking
fountains, and you're set for breakfast on the fly.

LOOK FOR THE FIGURE OF DEATH!

Giordano Bruno is the ominously dark, hooded statue in the
center of the square (1889). Public executions were commonly
held here during the 17th century, when Bruno was burned alive
during the inquisition. His crime was heresy: he supported the
ideas of his friend Galileo, whose telescope proved Earth was
not the center of the universe.

When you've had enough of the Campo, take Via Baullari or Vicolo
del Gallo to the adjoining **Piazza Farnese.** Now it's your turn: after the
crazy Campo, get a cup of wonderful coffee at **Caffè Farnese** and relax
at one of its outdoor tables on the peaceful piazza while kids romp safely
out of the heavy crowds.

FIND THE FARNESE FLEURS-DE-LIS

The palace crest is the first place you'll look, but what about
those gigantic fountain toppers on the huge Egyptian granite
bathtubs dominating the square? The tubs were scavenged

from the **Baths of Caracalla** and used as private boxes from which the Farnese viewed public events. In 1626, they were converted to fountains; the majestic Farnese irises were added still later.

DOING THE WINDOWS

Expounding on the palace's architectural details falls beyond our scope, but point out the windows. Notice how each story differs from the others. Those on the second story alternate from one style to another, as though they're beating a rhythm. Antonio Da Sangallo, who designed them to protrude from the façade, set new, dynamic standards for the Renaissance powerhouse with his three-dimensional trendsetters. Michelangelo expanded on that theme when he capped the building with his giant cornice, which extends six feet beyond the building.

Ask kids to lead you behind the palace by taking **Via dei Farnesi,** on its right, to Via Giulia. We are, in effect, going around the Farnesi Palace by going around the block.

FIND MICHELANGELO'S BRIDGE

The ivy-covered viaduct was intended to span beautiful Via Giulia and continue over the Tiber, connecting Palazzo Farnese with Villa Farnesina, a Raphael-frescoed retreat with extensive gardens in Trastevere.

THROW YOUR FOOD!

Agostino Chigi, wealthy owner of Villa Farnesina, was a banker who threw extravagant parties. Dinner was served on silver dishes, which guests threw into the Tiber after each course. Imagine marching out the door and hurling your green beans into the water, plate and all! Chigi was no idiot. His secret underwater net ensured that every bit of silver would be retrieved after his guests had departed.

Also at the corner of Via Farnesi and Via Giulia, you'll come upon **Santa Maria dell'Orazione e Morte,** called the "Skull Church," because skulls and winged hourglasses dominate the façade.

Its Latin inscription is a reminder of the fleeting nature of life, and it reads like one in the creepy **Capuchin Cemetery** on Via Veneto: "Today what we are, tomorrow you will be." The church was dedicated to a good death for all and, in 16th-century Rome, its priests fished bodies out of the Tiber behind it to give them a proper burial.

Palazzo Falconieri is right of the church (No. 1, Via Giulia). Artist Francesco Borromini, who's about to trick you at our next stop, redesigned it in the 17th century. The strange falcon heads with women's bodies were heraldic symbols of the Odescalchi family who once owned it.

You are standing on the wide, straight-as-an-arrow and very elegant Via Giulia, which runs north from the Ponte Sisto. It was created by Renaissance Pope Julius II della Rovere to connect the new Vatican papal digs with the Capitoline Hill, and celebrated its 500-year anniversary in 2008. The movie-set feel of its cobbled stones is enhanced by its Renaissance buildings, high-end antique stores, charming churches and yet another superior coffee shop, **Bar Giulia**, where each cappuccino is a tiny work of art, the froth expertly shaped into a creamy, aromatic heart. It holds court at the north end of the street in Raphael's home (at No. 86).

Continue on **Via Giulia** (left) behind the Palace, and go left again on **Via Mascherone**. (Before you do, glance right to see the *Mascherone* fountain. This big face is ancient and was placed here by a Farnese relative.) At the end of the street, take a right on little **Vicolo dei Venti** instead of a left into Piazza Farnese. Go one block to the **Spada Palace.**

The interior palace garden is your target, where Baroque master Borromini is about to play a trick-of-the-eye on you. Look for a grand statue at the end of a long, column-lined path called the *Galleria Prospettica*. The path is off limits, but guards happily walk it for you, and when they do, the amazing truth is revealed.

HOW LONG IS THE PATH?

Before the guard walks, estimate the distance of the garden's path and the height of the statue at its end.

Compare your estimates with what you learn to be the truth. How close were you?

Borromini, a rival of Bernini, fooled you using light, space and careful dimensions. Better keep an eye on this fellow. You'll come across several of his brilliant designs, like those falcon-headed women of Palazzo Falconieri on Via Giulia. A few others: **San Carlino alle Quattro Fontane**, charming St. Ivo, and S. Agnese in Agone on Piazza Navona, which is the focus of our next chapter.

WHAT'S AROUND?

COLLALTI BICI
Via del Pellegrino, 82
Open 9am-1pm and 3:30-7:30pm. Closed all day Sunday and Monday morning.
Tel. 06-688-01084
Rents bicycles.
This is strictly a teen activity; it is too difficult for younger kids to ride on cobbled streets. See *Useful Information* section for more scooter & bike rental options.

VIA GIUBBONARI

from Campo dei Fiori to Via Arenula.
A popular, pedestrian-only street mall with eclectic shops that runs about five blocks.

High-energy funky shops such as McQueen, Liu-Jo, Groove, and I Love Tokyo cater to teens while high-couture boutiques like Empressa, Prototype, Manila Grace, and DaDada couture please adults. Shelli (No. 97) is an affordable jewelry shop for young girls, while Ferri (No. 93A) is a bit more upscale. The A.S. Roma store sits at the end of the street (entrance on Via Arenula #82), and is a soccer fan's dream. It stocks a host of high-quality Italian team soccer jerseys.

PALAZZO DELLA CANCELLERIA

1/2 block north of Campo dei Fiori at Corso Vittorio.
Often open, currently hosting a long-running Leonardo da Vinci exhibit.

Pause to view the beautiful exterior. It was built primarily with the winnings of a single night's gambling. The lucky winner was Raffaele Riario Sansoni. You'll see his family symbol, the rose, embedded around the building as well as two della Rovere crests sporting oak trees (Corso side of the building); Sixtus IV della Rovere was Sansoni's great-uncle. Besides

its famous courtyard, the palace has an infamous salon frescoed by Georgio Vasari, who bragged to **Michelangelo** that it took him only 100 days to paint the large space. Michelangelo retorted, "It looks like it!"

PONTE SISTO

Take in one of the classic views of St. Peter's dome from this pedestrian-only bridge over the Tiber.

Sixtus IV commissioned this new bridge, the first one built since ancient times. As you cross to Trastevere, notice the inscriptions on both edges. The one on the right asks you to say a prayer for Sixtus. Still, this is a **Michelangelo** moment. He designed the distant dome of St. Peter's, worked on nearby Palazzo Farnese and its ivy-covered bridge, and has some work in the Spada Gallery to boot. Just across the bridge, you can pick up pizza-to-go from Pizza Pazzo (crazy pizza) in Piazza Trilussa. See ***Extras in Rome*** for more on Trastevere.

PIAZZA NAVONA
TO THE PANTHEON

PIAZZA NAVONA, *Always fun; always open.* Its unique shape reveals its ancient past as the Stadium of Domitian (96 AD), large enough to hold 30,000 spectators. The beautiful piazza is a vision of warm, sun-lit tones by day and a hotspot at night.

SAN LUIGI DEI FRANCESI (1518-89), *Via del Salvatore at Piazza S. L. dei Francesi. Open daily 8am-12:30pm and 3:30-7pm.* Free. It contains three Caravaggio masterpieces.

THE PANTHEON, also called *Santa Maria ad Martyres* (Circa 125 BC). *Open daily, 9am-7:30pm; Sun., 9am-6pm; holidays, 9am-1pm. Closed Jan. 1, May 1, and Dec. 25. Tel. 06-6830-0230. Masses held Sat., 5pm and Sun., 10:30am. Free. Audio guides are available for a suggested donation of € 3.* Of special note: the famous Mass of Roses, on Pentecost Sunday (seven weeks after Easter), when millions of rose petals fall from the opening.

Timing and Tips

Plan for 1-2 hours of relaxed rambling, best done late afternoon to accommodate church closings between noon and 3pm. Before or after your tour, dine in this restaurant-rich zone. Many choose to visit the festively lit Pantheon and its lively piazza at night, but if you have time for just one visit, see the spectacular interior by day.

Kids light up over the excitement, fountains and wide-open space of **PIAZZA NAVONA**. Stone lions, horses and other creatures from the sea to the sky add to its circus-like atmosphere. As the day wears on, artists, street performers, students, Romans and tourists flow in and out of the enormous space, as do a plethora of vendors hawking small toys and laser lights.

What makes Piazza Navona a must-see, however, is its central fountain, the work of the brilliant **Gian Lorenzo Bernini,** primarily responsible for the Baroque face of modern Rome. This is our intro-

duction to his extensive Roman works. Baroque art is highly dramatic, but the life of this artist had a drama all its own, largely due to an intense rivalry with fellow artist Borromini.

Bernini, an affable society darling, won the best commissions, while Borromini, a troubled and obsessed genius, tragically committed suicide in his prime. In Piazza Navona, you can see both rivals at work— Borromini's façade of **Sant'Agnese in Agone** faces Bernini's *Four Rivers* fountain. The two artists worked on many of the same projects: Propaganda Fide Palace at Piazza di Spagna, St. Peter's and the Barberini Palace, for example.

Borromini was, without question, the senior architect of the two, having apprenticed under Carlo Maderno, then head architect for

St. Peter's. The two artists got on well at first, but the friendship cooled when Borromini was hired merely to assist Bernini on the design of St. Peter's massive *baldacchino* (papal canopy). To the bitter end, Borromini claimed the final design was his own.

Bernini suffered a humiliation when his bell tower additions to St. Peter's proved unstable and were taken down at his own expense. Borromini criticized them openly, further fueling the feud.

Piazza Navona owes much to Renaissance planning and design; it was then that it was first paved and adorned with noble family palaces (another result of the papal move to Vatican digs). The Pamphilj family, whose son became Pope **Innocent X,** turned it into the Baroque beauty we see today. They lived in a palace on the southern end and contributed that splendid palace (rebuilt by Innocent), the church of S. Agnese in Agone and **Bernini's** *Four Rivers* Fountain.

When Innocent X took the papal throne after **Urban VIII,** he inherited a church nearly bankrupt from Urban's flagrant spending. His dislike for the Barberini seemed to shade his view of their favored artist, too. Innocent refused to let Bernini compete for Navona's central fountain commission. A friend and admirer, Prince Ludovisi, put Bernini's silver model in the pope's path and, upon seeing it, Innocent could do nothing but hire him.

To his credit, Innocent put aside personal dislikes to create Rome's most recognizable piazza. But he was never much liked, harsh man that he was, and when he died, his body was left unattended for three days, until a few workers finally prepared the corpse and held vigil. Relatives eventually provided for a funeral.

Family vote on a favorite sight in Rome: the breathtaking **PANTHEON,** hands down. It almost hovers with an energy and life

force of its own. See for yourself when you turn a corner off a narrow, cobbled street and come upon the massive, ancient edifice.

Long ago, another building stood here. Agrippa built it (27 BC) to commemorate the victory of Actium, where he and Octavian (later called **Augustus**) defeated Antony and Cleopatra. After a devastating fire destroyed it, emperor and architect **Hadrian** replaced that damaged structure with the Pantheon. Puzzlingly, the Latin inscription on its pediment reads, "Marcus Agrippa built this." No one can say why Hadrian would defer credit, but most think he wanted to pay homage to—and thus politically connect himself with—the great Agrippa. Perhaps he was just being coy. What is certain is that Hadrian made this temple to all the gods unique, as singular as his back-to-back temple to Venus and Roma in the Forum.

The Pantheon's dome is a testament to ancient Rome's genius with concrete and masonry. Some 5,000 tons of concrete were poured over a temporary wooden frame with concrete being mixed increasingly lighter as it went higher; from a basalt base to light pumice at the top. A solid concrete dome would be too heavy, so craftsmen lightened the load every possible way—the recesses of the coffered ceiling reduced the load, as did the giant *oculus*, or hole, in its ceiling. Walls 20 feet thick at the bottom support it.

The Pantheon remained a pagan temple until 608 AD, when Byzantine Emperor Phocas donated it to the Church. Phocas, you may recall, has a column dedicated to him in the Forum in honor of this very gift (the last monument erected there). Becoming a Christian church saved the Pantheon from destruction; most temples were destroyed or stripped for materials as they fell into disrepair. **Pope Urban VIII** did lift a couple of tons of bronze from the portico for his armory, but the Pantheon remains Rome's only intact building from classical times.

THE WALKING TOUR

Approach Piazza Navona from the south. But before entering the square, turn left and go one block (Via Pasquino) to sneak a peek at **Pasquino,** Rome's most famous "talking statue." Like Marforio atop Capitoline Hill, this statue wore handwritten signs that criticized political or religious dictates—and it still does! Pasquino was the first to squawk, and thus was coined the term *pasquinades* for public lampoons. **Michelangelo** thought this was one of the most beautiful statues he'd ever seen. Piazza di Pasquino is the start of Via Governo Vecchio (see **What's Around?**), a charming street packed with excellent family restaurants and eclectic shops connecting Navona with Castel Sant'Angelo.

During the 19th century, the piazza was flooded every weekend in August for naval games and mock sea battles, like the staged *naumachia* sea battles of antiquity.

Doubling back to Navona, make your way to its prize, the central **Fountain of the Four Rivers**, *Fontana dei Quattro Fiumi*, that **Bernini** designed in 1651.

The prized ancient obelisk with the names of the Flavian emperors Titus, Vespasian and Domitian written on it in hieroglyphics pales in artistic comparison to the spectacle Bernini carved to hold it. He went above and beyond designing a traditional, heavy, support base; the opening in the center makes it seem too light to support such a massive weight, and many critics thought it would topple. They say Bernini showed up with a string, and tied one end to the obelisk and the

other to a nearby building. "There," he said, "that ought to hold it." The master personally sculpted the rock, the palm tree and most of the wildlife himself.

KIDS! CAN YOU FIND THE NILE?

The fabulous fountain is populated with anthropomorphic rivers: the Danube, Nile, Río della Plata (in the Americas) and Ganges. The Nile's head is shrouded, symbolic of its source being then unknown.

MORE BERNINI

*Bernini also redesigned della Porta's **Fountain of the Moor** at the south end, unifying the look of the Piazza. Many years later, Bernini reputedly drove past the **Four Rivers** and looked the other way, crying, "How ashamed I am to have done so poorly!" (Hibbard)*

WHY PLATA'S HORROR-MOVIE POSE?

Longstanding rumor has it that Bernini's *Plata* (America) shields his eyes from the "horrible" design of Borromini's **S. Agnese.** In fact, most sources agree that the obelisk symbolizes Divine Light and Plata is shielding his eyes from the celestial blaze. Besides, S. Agnese is an astounding work of architecture,  and it was completed *after* Bernini's fountain. But with such a dramatic rivalry between the two artists, the rumor remains the more popular explanation.

The word *Navona* probably comes from the Greek term *agones,* meaning foot races. Foot races were held here when it was a stadium. In fact, only athletic contests took place in stadiums; horse races took place in a circus, like Circus Maximus.

HOW MANY DOVES ROOST IN NAVONA?

The dove was a part of the **Pamphilj** family crest. Look on the papal escutcheons being straightened by the Danube (Europe) and the Nile (Africa) and on the iron fence of S. Agnese. How about the church itself? One is about to get away!
Look for it atop the obelisk.

Find the little-known entrance gate outside the north end of Navona, in Piazza Tor Sanguigna, to go beneath Piazza Navona, where you can view a tiny excavation of Domitian's stadium. It's only open on weekends, but you can get a feel for its walls and artifacts through the open viewing window any time.

After exploring Navona and its impressive toy store **Al Sogno,** at the north end (see *What's Around?*), make your way to the Pantheon by taking the Corsia Agonale, adjacent to the central fountain, to busy Corso Rinascimento. Across the Corso, you'll see the mighty Baroque Palazzo Madama, formerly a Medici palace and now home to the Italian Senate. Leo X, born Giovanni de' Medici in Florence, was the first Medici to wear the papal tiara. He supported great artists like Raphael and Bramante. Skirt the palace and its colorful guards along its left side, down Via del Salvatore.

At the end of the block, the street becomes the pedestrian-only Via Giustiniani. Before continuing down that street, stop briefly at the French-national church **San Luigi dei Francesi** (1518-89), on the left, for a look at three of **Caravaggio's** most famous masterpieces. This cycle of St. Matthew was among his first ecclesiastical commissions in Rome.

Via Giustiniani offers a good cut pizza place and above-average gelato. For truly excellent gelato, Gelateria del Teatro is a few short blocks away, but not the direction we are currently headed (see *Let's Eat* for info). With kids happily devouring ice cream, continue down Giustiniani to the **Pantheon.** Approaching the grand piazza from this narrow, cobbled road has great impact.

In fact, the whole deal with the Pantheon is visual impact. Enjoying it doesn't need to get any more sophisticated. Stunning as it looks on the outside, the genius of its architecture lies within: the height and diameter are the same size (43.3m), so that a sphere, like a giant beach ball, could fit perfectly inside it.

Adding to the wow factor is the gigantic circular opening, or oculus, that creates a striking shaft of light. As the sun shifts throughout the day, the natural spotlight moves. It highlighted strategically placed statues of historic figures and planetary gods (Venus, Mars, Jupiter, Neptune, Pluto, Saturn, Uranus) that once stood in the niches.

The Pantheon is an excellent place to be in case of rain. Watching rain falling through the oculus will lift everyone's mood. And there's plenty of roof left to keep you dry!

Bernini added turrets to the Pantheon, but they were taken down by 1883. They were commonly referred to as the "ass ears of Bernini."

It's crowded in the Pantheon—and not just with the living! Your first clue is the temple's Christian name, Saint Mary of the Martyrs. To make something holy, you had to have a relic, so the Church dumped a bunch of martyrs' bones under the floor. Undocumented lore says 20-30 wagonloads were transferred from Christian catacombs. You'll also find the remains of Savoy kings Victor Emanuel II and Umberto I; Italy's first queen, Margherita; and a handful of humble artists, including Raphael and Annibale Carracci, both in rather plain-looking tombs.

CAN YOU FIND URBAN'S I.O.U?

Look outside, near the top of the massive doors for a plaque acknowledging that **Pope Urban VIII** stripped tons of bronze from the Pantheon. Most of it was used to make dozens of cannon for the papal fortress, Castel Sant'Angelo. However, the portion **Bernini** used for St. Peter's grand *Baldacchino* (altar canopy) is what really got him in trouble, resulting in the most famous pasquinade of all: *What the Barbarians didn't do* (during the sack of Rome), *the Barberinis did!*

KIDS!

In Urban's defense, reuse of old materials was nothing new, and he saved the Church a massive amount on import costs. And, at least he left a sign acknowledging his lift!

The Renaissance fountain in the piazza supports an obelisk of Ramses the Great, a remnant from the nearby Temple of Isis (now gone). In fact, many relics from that ancient temple are scattered about the streets of Rome.

KIDS! COUNT THE COLUMNS AND FIND URBAN'S BEE

The portico has 16 gigantic, granite Corinthian columns with white marble bases and capitals. Kids tend to go around each one, touching them as they tally. Three on the left are replacements with symbols of the restorers on their capitals.

At this point, you've seen this zone's highlights: Piazza Navona and the Pantheon. If you have an extra half-hour, take the kids on a treasure hunt behind the Pantheon for an elephant, a giant foot and an ancient stray cat. But first, a coffee break.

Teens may wish to wait on the steps of the Pantheon piazza, enjoying a little downtime and independence, while you take in an aromatic cup of coffee from one of the two most famous coffee shops in Rome: Taza D'Oro, on Via d. Pastini, or my favorite, Sant'Eustachio il Caffe, where we are heading, now.

Take Salita di Crescenzi (to the right of the Pantheon's portico, as you face it), and immediately veer left on Via S. Eustachio and follow it, turning right into Piazza S. Eustachio. You'll find pretty Cafe San Eustachio at No. 82. It's easy to spot its signature bright yellow. And remember, they add sugar for you, so say, "senza Zucchero (*zu-ker-o*), if you don't prefer it.

KIDS! FIND THE CROSS IN ANTLERS

A cross on top of a church is expected, but in a deer's antlers? This church is dedicated to S. Eustace, who lived during Hadrian's reign. He is the patron saint of the chase, because he saw a vision of Christ in the antlers of a deer. He was martyred for refusing to worship Jupiter.

When everyone's ready, take Via delle Polombella, behind the Pantheon, to **Piazza della Minerva.**

KIDS! ELEPHANT HUNT!

Can you find **Bernini's** baby elephant (1667)? Like the one at the Pantheon, its diminutive obelisk originally belonged to the ancient Temple of Isis, which was near here but is now gone. The inscription reads, "A strong mind is needed to support solid knowledge." Very Jesuit.

The elephant statue adorns the rare Roman-Gothic (but clearly finished during the Renaissance) church of **Santa Maria Sopra Minerva,** distinguished by Filippino Lippi's 1489 frescoes of Medici popes as boys over the altar of the Carafa Chapel (right transept). The boys became Popes **Leo X** and Clement VII, both buried behind the altar. Kids can look out for Medici heraldic symbols, too.

Michelangelo's Greek-looking *Christ Bearing the Cross* is left of the main altar. In the north transept, **Bernini** created Sister Maria Raggi's unique memorial (1643). The small but colorful piece looks like wind-blown fabric anchored to one of the pillars with a cross-shaped stickpin.

HOW HIGH DID THE TIBER RISE?

Outside, on the right façade of the church, look for a flood marker from December 24, 1598. Before the Tiber's banks were fortified, the river periodically engulfed the streets. The private **rooms of St. Ignatius** (see *What's Around?*) were salvaged from a building that suffered extensive damage on that very day.

Continue your walking treasure hunt:

From Piazza Minerva, take Via Caterina da Siena, right of the church, which turns into Via Piè di Marmo (literally, "foot of marble street") and follow it one block. There, at the corner of S. Stefano dei Cacco, you will practically trip over an **enormous marble foot**, remnant of a colossal statue.

Continue another block down Piè di Marmo (great chocolate shop at No. 21/22) to Via della Gatta (Street of the Cat), and turn right, going about half a block into a piazza.

KIDS!

WHERE'S THE CAT?

Legend says the cat's gaze falls upon buried Egyptian treasure. Look up on a building ledge in Piazza Grazioli to find this **Egyptian cat**, yet another remnant from the Temple of Isis.

You're now positioned to go view one of two spectacular trompe l'oeils: the stupefying ceiling and false dome of **St. Ignatius** church and the vestibule in the private rooms of St. Ignatius (only open late afternoon) next to **Il Gesù,** both painted by Fra Andrea Pozzo (see *What's Around?*). Both are tremendous.

FRESCO IN FASHION

Ceiling frescoes were the rage in 17th-century Rome. Standouts at the height of the trend:

1597-1601: Annibale Carracci's *Loves of the Gods*, Palazzo Farnese

1613-1614: Reni's *Aurora*, Casino Rospigliosi

1633-1639: Pietro Cortona's *Triumph of the Barberini*, Palazzo Barberini

1674-1679: Baciccio's *Adoration of the name of Jesus,* Il Gesù

1691-1694: Andrea Pozzo's *Glorification of St. Ignatius,* St. Ignazio, and his corridor of S. Ignatius' rooms, in the college next door to Il Gesù

WHAT'S AROUND?

NAVONA

AL SOGNO

Piazza Navona, 53
Tel. 06-686-4198
Web site: alsogno.com
Here's an upscale toy store known for its selection of collectable model figurines, like gladiators and WWII legends, chess pieces, stuffed animals and gorgeous dolls. Expensive!

BERTÈ

Piazza Navona, 108
Tel. 06-687-5011
This older toy store on Piazza Navona carries nice baby items and toys, but it's not as unique as Al Sogno.

INTERNET POINT

Via Corso Vittorio Emanuele II, 129
Check your e-mail and surf the Web from this very large Internet place at the corner of Corso Rinascimento, near the pretty church of Sant'Andrea della Valle.

VIA DEL CORONARI

A lovely Renaissance street running between the north end of Piazza Navona and Castel Sant'Angelo.
Window-shop your way past marble bas-reliefs, mosaics, antiques and other wonders. Along with loads of quick and casual restaurants, from home-made pastas to bakeries, you'll find one of Rome's finest gelato shops, and strolling traffic-free is a joy. Hadrian's kid-pleasing castle is easily found off the west end of the street.

> Made, No. 25, offers lovely cupcakes, scones, bagel sandwiches, and carrot cakes.

> Gelateria del Teatro, No. 66, boasts a charming setting and superior gelati made with fresh ingredients, ranging from pure chocolate to seasonal delights such as pumpkin chocolate chip or pear & honey. Kids love to watch the process from the huge viewing window.

VIA DEL GOVERNO VECCHIO

Starts at Piazza Pasquino and continues northward towards Castel Sant'Angelo.
With great restaurants, an intriguing bookstore with a wonderful assortment of Italian posters, and shops that range from couture to eclectic resale, there's something for everyone. Like Via del Coronari (above), this street is also pedestrian-only. Dotted among the many shops, you'll find plenty of restaurants. Among the kid-friendly, Tonino, at the north end, dishes up authentic, Italian fare, while the Abbey Pub fits the bill for burgers. A few shops for teens and tots:

> Altro Quando, No. 80, is a sliver of a store filled with cool movie posters and books.

> Legno e Fantasia, No. 102, stocks wooden and classic toys, from romper horses to doll houses.

PANTHEON

BARTOLUCCI
Via dei Pastini, 98. Tel. 06-691-90894. Web site: bartolucci.com.
Pinocchio lives in this charming artisan shop selling loads of pinewood toys, clocks, and clever objects, all handcrafted by the Bartolucci family.

CITTÀ DEL SOLE
Via della Scrofa, 65. Tel. 06-688-03805. Web site: cittadelsole.it.
This earthy toy store north of the Pantheon leans toward educational toys, wooden puzzles and quality children's books.

CONFETTERIA MORIONDO & GARIGLIO
Via Pié di Marmo, 21/22
Closed Sundays Open 9am-1pm and 3:30-7:30pm
Tel. 06-699-0856
As a former chocolatier to royalty, the boxes of handmade chocolates, truffles, caramels and other confections from this old-guard establishment reek of class. Hushed tones come naturally when you step inside the lush store, covered in rich wood and dark-red walls. What's been good enough for the royal House of Savoy since 1886 is certainly good enough for your mob.

IL GESÙ (1568) and THE ROOMS OF ST. IGNATIUS
West of Palazzo Venezia on Via del Plebiscito (Piazza del Gesù).
€ 10. Ages 17 and under, € 5. Ages 10 years and under, free.
Open Mon.-Sat., 4-6pm; Sun., 10am-noon
In the college to the right of Il Gesù are the beautifully preserved private rooms of St. Ignatius.
The Jesuit founder spent the last 12 years of his life here, until July 1556. Andrea Pozzo designed the vestibule's amazing trompe l'oeil (ca. 1680), which has a carnival mirror effect. Stand on the marble rose in the center and everything makes sense; but the figures twist out of proportion when you step away. Remaining rooms display artifacts from St. Ignatius' life. Kids can see how they measure up to a saint, because a bronze cast of his head is placed exactly at his height. Jesuits live, work and pray here—Silence is required.

Next door, in **Il Gesù,** the gigantic jewel-and-marble-encrusted altar to St. Ignatius deserves a look. It seems the floor will cave in under the gilded bronze and lapis lazuli monolith. Rising from all that glitz is the statue of St. Ignatius, in what has always seemed to me to be a

Broadway pose. Baroque art is theatrical, but this takes the cake. At 5:30pm every day, music and lights draw you to a descending painting (left chapel), which reveals the dramatic silver statue. **Bernini**, master of the Baroque, so loved this church that he is said to have attended its evening vespers every night for years (Hibbard). Kids may like the tiny, year-round nativity, or *presepio*, in the first chapel on the right. Push the button to peek into the window while being serenaded with *Silent Night*.

    Farnese irises inside the church tell us the Farnese family footed the bill for this first Jesuit structure. **Paul III** had approved the new order of monks during the Counter-Reformation of the 16th century.

    Two shields grace the outside of the church: one carries the pope's coat of arms, the other, **SPQR**. It means that the church is under the protection of the Roman people because the Capitoline Hill is within its parish boundaries. There are only two other churches in Rome with such a privilege: S. Maria D'Aracoeli and S. Marco in Piazza Venezia.

SANT'IGNAZIO DI LOYOLA (1626-85)
Piazza S. Ignazio
Open 7:30am-12:30pm and 3:30-7:15pm

The trompe l'oeil ceiling fresco by Fra Andrea Pozzo is spectacular with its huge bodies that seem to have their gigantic feet dangling overhead. You won't be sure where the real architecture stops and the painting begins. Grade-school kids versed in geography may spot all the continents written on the ceiling's shields—marking destinations reached by the traveling Jesuits. Stand on the yellow disk set into the floor for the fullest 3-D effect. Don't leave without viewing the equally astounding trompe l'oeil dome.

Tip: As in most churches, look for a coin box and drop in the proper change to illuminate the art and ceilings.

LET'S EAT!

CAMPO DEI FIORI

ARISTO CAMPO, Piazza Campo dei Fiori, 50. Sandwiches to go. The pork sandwich is a Roman classic.

BAR GIULIA, Via Giulia, 84. Closed Sundays. This teeny, sparkling coffee shop on the north end of Via Giulia serves cappuccino with heart-shaped froth. The coffee is art, the staff is charming and the location, in the shadow of the Florentine church, is quite lovely.

CAFFÈ FARNESE, Piazza Farnese, 106, at Via dei Baullari. Open from 7am. This pretty bar on the piazza offers excellent coffees deftly made by a pair of able baristas. Join the locals sitting at outdoor tables reading their morning papers or stand inside for a quick cappuccino and a *cornetto* (like a croissant).

FILETTI DI BACCALÀ, or Dar Filettaro a Santa Barbara, Via Giubbonari at Largo Librari, 88. Opens nightly around 6pm. Closed Sundays. For a secret backdoor experience, head straight back to the kitchen and ask the cook for a fried cod filet to go: "*Una filetta porta via, per favore.*" You pay the chef, she drops the fish and soon hands you a piping-hot crispy treat wrapped in waxed paper. The taste is amazing.

IL FORNAIO, Via dei Baullari, 4, between Corso Vittorio Emanuele II and Campo dei Fiori. More deli than bakery, this efficient countershop stocks lunchmeats, salads, sandwiches and baked goods perfect for picnics.

FORNO CAMPO DÉ FIORI, No. 22 on the piazza, next to La Carbonara. Mon.-Fri., 7am-2pm and 5-8pm; Sat., 7am-2pm. Closed Sundays. This is Rome's best bakery, and it's extremely crowded at opening times. Nothing compares to their fresh Pizza Bianca or Pizza Rosso, piping hot from the massive ovens. They doubled their space by moving the cookies and sandwiches to a new shop across the street.

ROSCIOLI FORNO, Via dei Chiavari, 34, just off Via Giubbonari. The Roscioli family has delivered exceptional breads, cut pizza, bakery treats and sandwiches for generations. Open 7am-7pm, Monday to Saturday. A small hot buffet is set up in its back room around lunch. Follow your nose!

Forno Campo dei Fiori

OSTERIA AR GALLETTO, Vicolo del Gallo, 1, Piazza Farnese, 102. Lunch and dinner. Closed Sundays. Alfresco dining on the Piazza lets kids play in the square while you wait for your meal and enjoy splendid food in an equally splendid setting. Moderate.

RISTORANTE DA PANCRAZIO, Piazza del Biscione, 92/94 (Via Grotta Pinta, 20). Lunch and dinner. Closed Wednesdays. Eat above the ancient Theater of Pompey, where Brutus and Cassius murdered Caesar. The basement rooms, reserved for private parties, are carved around the ruins and display many relics. The staff is happy to let you take a look, providing the space is free. Ask permission. Moderate.

POINT OF NO RETURN

*J*ulius Caesar grew up in the great Republican age of Rome, after the expulsion of the last tyrannical king—an era considered Rome's halcyon days. At the fall of the Republic, power struggles gave way to three legendary generals: Crassus, Pompey and Caesar, who formed the first triumvirate, or group of three people controlling the city. Tensions grew along with Caesar's power. Finally, as Caesar and his army returned from victory in Gaul, they came to the Rubicon River, the point where no army was allowed to cross into Rome. The river became famous when Caesar crossed it to march on Rome saying, "The die is cast!" To this day, the term, "Crossing the Rubicon," means going past the point of no return.

Caesar became dictator for life—too powerful, too much like a king— when the tyranny of the kings was still fresh in people's minds. On the Ides of March, March 15, 44 BC, his senators stabbed him to death in the Theatre of Pompey.

PIAZZA NAVONA

CICCIA BOMBA, Via del Governo Vecchio, 76. Lunch and dinner. Closed Wednesdays. This solid pizzeria, with a nice selection of pastas, grooves from its tiny spot on a bustling street. Very casual and inexpensive.

DA FRANCESCO, Piazza del Fico, 29. Wednesday-Monday. Lunch and dinner. Dinner starts at 7pm at this popular pizzeria in a lovely, ivy-clad square—earlier than most places. This is especially helpful for kids who have trouble adapting to Italy's later dinner hour. And note that pizza is served only in the evenings. Let's talk real Roman pizza: thin crusts and fresh ingredients. And Francesco has a well-rounded menu to accompany its pizza. No reservations accepted, and crowds form out front, so go early.

DA TONINO, Via del Governo Vecchio, 18. Lunch and dinner. Closed Sundays. Locals love this secret spot with great food in an unpretentious, family-friendly setting with an extremely low-key staff. No frills and no credit cards.

FATTO IN CASA, Via del Governo Vecchio, 125. Open all day. Loads of options, like pastas and burgers, please most kids. As the name suggests, some of the pasta is made in house. Check the chalkboard for daily specials. The average fare is complimented by a big bright, light space, an outdoor terrace, and free Wi-fi.

GELATERIA DEL TEATRO, Via Coronari, 65-66. This charming gelateria in an impossibly picturesque location tops most "Best Gelato" lists for a reason. The gelato is fresh, organic, creamy, and creative, using pure chocolate, garden herbs, and ripe fruits. Keep it simple or go with one of their complex flavor combinations, such as sage and raspberry or ricotta, almond, and fig. Your taste buds will thank you, and your kids will love watching the chefs prepare their creations behind a big glass window.

Geateria del Teatro

IL CORALLO, Via del Corallo, 11. Open lunch through dinner. Most restaurants offer pizza only for dinner, so if you're looking for excellent, thin-crust, Roman pizza for lunch, this is your spot. Nice indoor and outdoor space a few steps from Piazza Navona.

LA MONTECARLO, Vicolo Savelli, 13, just off the large Corso Vittorio Emanuele II, only a few blocks from Piazza Navona. Lunch and dinner. Closed Mondays. This hopping pizza place fills up early and stays that way, and it's no secret why: delicious pizza, huge portions, and a gregarious waitstaff. The ultracasual style is perfect for families. The pastas and salads are large enough to share, and they are reasonably priced at 8-10 Euros. The pizza is superior; the pastas are mediocre but kid pleasing—as is having the order arrive on a huge silver platter, à la medieval times. Don't worry if there's a line; they can seat a lot of people, and they serve them almost as fast as they order.

LO ZOZZONE, Via del Teatro Pace, 32. Weekdays, 9am-9pm; weekends, from 10am. It can't be beat for sandwiches made to order. Huge slices of fresh Pizza Bianca are halved and filled with up to three deli ingredients. The medium, which goes for under € 3, is huge.

MADE CREATIVE BAKERY, Via dei Coronari, 25. Open Mon.-Sat. 11am-7pm, Sunday, 11am-6pm. Familiar American treats are served in this spotless storefront, from bagels to carrot cake, brownies, and cake pops.

PASTICCERIA CINQUE LUNE, Corso Rinascimento, 89. The alluring scents of fresh baked goods will help you find this small bakery between Piazza Navona and the Pantheon.

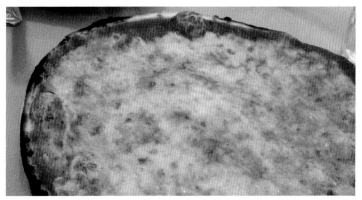

Il Corallo

PANTHEON

ANGELO FEROCI, Via della Maddalena, 15. A butcher shop? Yes. Artistic window displays highlight the prettiest selection of prepared meats you'll ever see. The spotless interior with its marble counter and efficient staff offers dishes like lasagna, meatballs and stuffed zucchini that make it possible to easily serve a tasty feast in a vacation rental apartment.

ANTICA SALUMERIA PANE E PIZZA, Piazza della Rotunda, 4. Traditional deli counter at the Pantheon makes tasty sandwiches (but skip the pizza) that you can eat on the steps of the piazza, taking in the ambiance while you snack.

ARMANDO AL PANTHEON, Salita dè Crescenzi, 31. Lunch and dinner. Closed Saturday nights and Sundays. Around the corner from the Pantheon and away from the crowds, tiny Armando's serves authentic Roman fare. Kid favorites: ravioli, spaghetti and simple but elegant meat dishes. Moderate.

CAFFÈ SANT'EUSTACHIO, Piazza Sant'Eustachio, 82. Open from 8:30am. A sought-after coffee shop for two good reasons—it's lovely inside and out, and they roast their own beans. In summer, try the fabulous iced *granita di caffè*. And note that coffee here is served already sugared; ask for "*senza zucchero*" (without sugar) if you prefer it that way.

FORTUNATO AL PANTHEON, Via Pantheon, 55. Lunch and dinner. Closed Sundays. Old school Roman cooking brings a following of die-hard locals that grows larger each year. Moderate.

GELATO DI SAN CRISPINO, Piazza della Maddalena, 3. Open daily. Closed on Tuesdays in autumn and winter. Zero preservatives are the hallmark of this famous franchise—that, and some pretty delicious ice cream! Sophisticated flavors like chestnut and rum or walnut and fig complement classic crowd-pleasers like cinnamon, lemon, chocolate, and vanilla.

GIOLITTI, Via Uffici dei Vicario, 40. Open daily. The gelato is no longer the best-tasting, but the reputation of this pretty, sparkling 1930s-style soda fountain keeps 'em coming in droves.

LA SAGRESTIA, Via del Seminario, 89. Closed Wednesdays. Family-run casual trattoria with Italian favorites and wood-fired pizza set in the shadow of the Pantheon. Moderate.

MACCHERONI, Piazza delle Coppelle, 44. Lunch and dinner. Closed Sundays. Young crowds make for a lively, kid-friendly restaurant that pleases every age. You may go back more than once. Moderate.

PIZZICO, Piazza Maddelena, 8. Lunch and dinner. In a popular square north of the Pantheon, this casual yet attractive place specializes in the thicker-crust pizza of Naples. Moderate.

RISTORANTE S. EUSTACHIO, Piazza dei Caprettari, 63 (Piazza Sant'Eustachio). Lunch and dinner. Closed Sundays. A block west of the Pantheon, this restaurant is attractive indoors and out, and it offers a pleasing menu of pasta, meats and fish to go with its atmosphere. Share the special *fritto vegetariano* appetizer of shredded, fried zucchini over a Jewish-style artichoke (*carciofi alla giudia*) topped with cheese. Moderate.

ZAZÀ, Piazza Sant'Eustachio, 49. Cut pizza (*pizza al taglio)* made with organic ingredients is all they serve from this tiny shop with outdoor seating. It's the best pizza-to-go in the area, and you'll find it just across from the famous Cafe Sant'Eustachio. Inexpensive and very good.

TAZZA D'ORO, Via degli Orfani, 84, just off the Pantheon. This coffee shop roasts their own beans and, among the coffees, they are famous for their *Granita di Cafè*, shaved iced coffee topped with whipped cream.

La Sagrestia's pasta fagioli

PART THREE

BAROQUE & MODERN ROME

We began by exploring Ancient Rome, then moved northwest to the old Campus Martius, a triangular-shaped plain nestled in the bend of the Tiber River that retains Medieval and Renaissance streets and palaces. Now, we move east of the Corso to the Trevi, the Spanish Steps, the Via Veneto and Villa Borghese, contemporary (by Roman standards) areas steeped primarily in the Baroque.

"You do not have to love Roman ruins to love Rome, but you have to love the Baroque; otherwise, you will think Rome is florid and vulgar and recoil from its extravagance."

Barbara Grizzuti Harrison, *Italian Days*

MODERN

Restaurants and Cafes

1 Alfredo Ristorante
2 Fatamorgana Gelato
3 Il Margutta RistorArte
4 Ciampini
5 Baccano
6 Eataly Hamburgeria
7 Casino Valadier
8 Marguta Osteria
9 Otello Alla Concordia
10 Giolitti
11 Re Degli Amici
12 Al Moro
13 Il Gelato di San Crispino
14 Boscaiolo Pizzeria
15 Café de Paris - Doney
16 Colline Emiliane
17 Da Tullio Ristorante
18 Forno Cerulli
19 Hard Rock Café

MAP AREA

Vatican
Spanish Steps
Campo/Navona
Colosseum/Forum
Trastevere

Borghese Gallery

Bioparco Zoo

VIA UCCELLIERA

VILLA BORGHESE

GALOPPATOIO

VIALE DEL MURO TORTO

VIA PORTA PINCIANA

VILLA MEDICI

VIALE TRINITA DEI MONTI

VIALE DEL OROLOGIO

Pincio

VIALE DELL'OBELISCO

VIA VALADIER

VIALE VILLA MEDICI

Santa Maria del Popolo

PIAZZA DEL POPOLO

VIA DI RIPETTA

Ara Pacis

PONTE CAVOUR

Augustus' Mausoleum

PIAZZA AUGUSTO IMPERATORE

VIA TOMACELLI

VIA DELL'ARANCIO

VIA FONTANELLA BORGHESE

VIA DELLA SCROFA

VIA DI CAMPO MARZIO

VIA UFFICI D. VICARIO

VIA D. VICARIO

To Pantheon

VIA DEI PASTINI

VIA GUGLIA

VIA DI PIETRA

Column of Marcus Aurelius

PIAZZA COLONNA

Sundial of Augustus

PIAZZA S SILVESTRO

VIA DEL CORSO

V LAURINA

VIA DEL BABUINO

VIA MARGUTTA

VIA VITTORIA

VIA D CROCE

VIA D CONDOTTI

VIA FRATTINA

VIA DELLA VITE

Spanish Steps

VIA SISTINA

V GREGORIANA

VIA DUE MACELLI

V F CRISPI

VIA ARTISTI

VIA LUDOVISI

VIA LIGURIA

VIA VITTORIO VENETO

Santa Maria della Concezione

Triton's Fountain

VIA DEGLI AVIGNONESI

VD STAMPERIA

VIA PANETTERIA

VIA LAVATORE

PROPAGANDA VD NAZZARENO

VIA DEL TRITONE

VIA DELLE MURATTE

Trevi

VC SCANDERBEG

VINCENZO

VIA DELLA DATARIA

VIA DEL QUIRINALE

Quirinale Hill President's Palace

Barberini National Gallery of Classical Art

VIA BARBERINI

VIA QUATTRO FONTINO

V S NICOLA DE TOLENTINO

PIAZZA NAVONA

THE TREVI FOUNTAIN

THE TREVI FOUNTAIN by Nicola Salvi *(1732-1762) is just off the Corso at Via Muratte and is perhaps the most centrally located monument in Rome: west is the Pantheon, north are the Spanish Steps, east is Triton's Fountain and south are the Forums.*

COLUMN OF MARCUS AURELIUS (2nd century AD). *Piazza Colonna at Via del Corso, north of the Trevi.* This soaring monument holds court in a large piazza connected to another (Piazza Montecitorio), where you'll find the equally impressive "Sundial of Augustus." If you prefer to shop, the Galleria Sordi complex is just across the Corso.

Timing and Tips

It takes no time to see the dramatic Trevi, so tack it on when convenient. An early-morning visit will provide some breathing room at this otherwise tourist-choked site. Better yet, make it the start of an evening walk like the one outlined below.

The crashing, splashing **TREVI** is a splendid example of high Baroque art, and it serves as our gateway to modern Rome (again, by Roman standards). The initial thrill and sensory overload upon encountering the Trevi is marvelous. This fountain is the splendid finale of the Roman aqueduct, the *Acqua Vergine* (Virgin Water), built by Agrippa in 19 BC (aqueduct, not fountain) that supplies most fountains in the historic center, and it is a real crowd pleaser. Tell kids that, like them, the gushing water has been busy all over town.

Discovering the Trevi's large spectacle at the end of a tiny, narrow street is spectacular. High drama is, of course, the calling card of Baroque art, and designer Nicola Salvi put as much dramatic staging into the Trevi as he could. He crafted sea gods, rough rocks, swaying trees and dynamic rearing horses with theatrical precision. Even the little balconied scenes look like theater stages once did.

In nearby Piazza Colonna, you'll find **THE COLUMN OF MARCUS AURELIUS.** Like Trajan's storytelling, scroll-like Column at the Imperial Forums, this one covers Marcus Aurelius' victorious German campaigns. Aurelius was a solider, emperor, author and philosopher. His no-nonsense book, *Meditations,* can be found in nearly every Roman bookstore.

Use the Trevi as a great start (or finish, by reversing the order) to a *passeggiata*, Italy's traditional evening stroll. As the sun sets, the fountain is bathed in a beautiful light and, once dark, it is lit to spectacular results. Teenagers love being out and about at night, and this walk is a good way to sightsee after the sun goes down. You'll visit the Trevi, the Column of Marcus Aurelius, the Pantheon and Piazza Navona.

THE WALKING TOUR

Begin at the Trevi Fountain.

DOES THE VIEWING AREA LOOK FAMILIAR?
See how it curves like theater seating around a stage. Sit down and enjoy the show. Think about **Bernini** and his *Four Rivers* fountain of Piazza Navona. Would he have praise or contempt for this over-the-top fountain?

The Trevi is uniquely carved into the south end of Palazzo Poli, the building it caps. Look for rough, incomplete hunks of building that seem to magically morph into fountain.

Take a close look at the two bas-reliefs at the top. In the upper right, a goddess or girl (virgin) shows Marcus Agrippa where to dig for water. If you've been to the Pantheon, recall the line, "Marcus Agrippa built this," on its pediment—**Hadrian's** tip of the hat to Agrippa who first built a temple there. Help kids make the Agrippa connection by pointing him out here and to his name on the **Pantheon** when there.

The left relief shows Agrippa explaining his aqueduct plans to **Augustus** for approval. Agrippa was Augustus' right-hand man and successfully fought for him in the Battle of Actium against Antony and Cleopatra.

Some €800,000 is thrown into the Trevi annually. They are collected daily: Euros, European Union coins, go to the Caritas organization of the Catholic Church; foreign coins are donated to the Red Cross.

FIND THE ACE OF CUPS.
The Trevi also serves as a drinking fountain: look for its offshoot called the *Ace of Cups*. That's one spectacular drink of water! (Hint: Look on the right side.)

A bothersome barber on the piazza criticized and harassed Salvi as he worked, day in and day out. So, one night, the clever artist built a large basin (the *Ace of Cups*) on the right balustrade, completely blocking the barber from his view.

Turn your back to the fountain and toss a coin in—over your left shoulder if you want to come back to Rome. Then, stroll down pleasant **Via della Muratte**, a pedestrian-only street that leads you to the Pantheon (on the left as you face the fountain). Shops, colorful street vendors and restaurants line the way, making the walk action-packed and entertaining.

When you come to the big street of **Via del Corso**, cross it and continue to the Pantheon on **Via d. Pietra**.

Or:
Go right at the Corso and jog half a block to see the **Column of Marcus Aurelius** and its adjoining square with an obelisk called the **Sundial of Augustus** (Piazza Montecitorio). Both are fun, wide-open places.

WHO'S ON TOP?

Just as a statue of Saint Peter replaced one of Trajan atop his column, so here saint usurped emperor: Marcus Aurelius was replaced with Saint Paul in 1589.

Remember the flak **Urban VIII** caught for stripping bronze off the Pantheon? Before him, Pope Sixtus V melted down a bunch of cannons and the giant bronze doors of Castel Sant'Angelo to make the saintly statues that top Rome's two relief-decorated columns.

CAN YOU FIND THE WINDOWS?

During the Middle Ages, people paid a small fee to climb the column's interior staircase (no longer accessible) and enjoy the view. See the little windows that lit the cramped interior?

Wander over to adjoining **Piazza Montecitorio** to find a famous obelisk brought by Augustus from Heliopolis and made into a giant sundial. The Montecitorio Palace (north side of the piazza), planned and built by **Bernini** in 1650, now serves the Italian Parliament.

From the Sundial, duck down **Via Uffici d. Vicario** to try a gelato from popular **Giolitti** (at No. 40). Then, return and head south on **Via d. Guglia,** veering right onto **Via Pastini** and into the Pantheon square. After a pause at the Pantheon, follow pedestrian-only **Via Giustiniani**, to finish our evening in festive Piazza Navona, where it seems everyone in Rome gathers in the evening.

WHAT'S AROUND?

With a lot within walking distance, let kids choose from a short list: the sunset panorama from the Quirinal Hill is nice, early morning hours may best be spent at the Forums, or teens may wish to shop the Corso. Its north end has a high concentration of funky teen-friendly shops, but there's something for everyone along the long, outdoor mall.

CITTÀ DELL'ACQUA (City of Water)

Vicolo del Puttarello, 25. Find it easily: with your back to the Trevi, find the church on your left and take the street on its right side (V. S. Vicenzo). Immediately, take the pedestrian walk-through on the left (Vicolo dei Modelli). Just follow it around, staying to the right on Vicolo del Puttarello. The whole walk is about half a block!
Wed.-Fri. 11am-5:30pm, Sat. and Sun. 11am-7pm, closed Dec. 25, and Jan. 1. Tel. 339-778-6192. Tickets, € 3. Ages 17 and under, free.

Sneak over to these imperial-age excavations like you're on a secret mission. You'll be amazed and virtually alone in ancient Rome! A small theater store is the secret portal to an underground world with a rare condo building from the age of Nero (64 AD). You may recall that after most of Rome burned, Nero planned a great new city, the Nova Urbs. Until now, it was only known of through literary works.

GALLERIA SORDI

Via del Corso at Piazza Colonna
10am-10pm daily

This gorgeous and historic building, with mosaic floors and refined marble and glass, holds equally elegant stores. Of note are the many fine Italian leather goods shops, like Piquandro, Nannini, and The Bridge (which has created iconic bags, briefcases, and luggage since 1969). Stylish shops like Pinko, Trussardi, and Zara share the mall with kid-pleasing Gusella/Imaginarium, which sells beautiful children's clothing and toys. Feltrinelli Italian bookstore has an English language section, and for the basics, find La Rinascente, Rome's classic department store.

MARINA MENASCI

Via del Lavatore, 87
Tel. 06-678-1981 (near the Trevi)
Exclusively wood-carved toys that invoke the spirit of Pinocchio.

PIAZZA QUIRINALE

President's Palace tours: Sundays only, 8:30am-noon. Closed the month of August and major holidays.
Tel. 06-46991
Tickets € 5
Web site: quirinale.it
Changing of the Guard*: weekdays, 3:15pm; holidays, 4pm*
From the Trevi, go south on Via S. Vincenzo, turn left on Via della Dataria, and climb the steps at the end of the street.

Quick, enjoyable navigating takes you through a few serpentine backstreets and up to the Palazzo Quirinale (1573). Originally a papal summer palace, the Quirinal, as most call it, became residence of the king upon Italy's Unification (1870) and is currently home to the Italian President. Tours are entirely worth any effort it takes to get inside.

Enormous statues of Castor and Pollux, their trusty horses, and yet another ancient Egyptian obelisk dominate the Quirinal Piazza. And check out the towering guard standing in the palace entrance. Required to be over six feet tall, these elite guards are intimidating visions with grand horsehair-topped helmets.

Only fair views are available from this crest of one of Rome's original seven hills, but the vast space of the giant piazza, which seems to magically pop out of Rome's cramped streets, is wonderful. **Bernini** designed the large papal window over the main door as well as the *manica lunga,* the "long sleeve" of a building addition, running down Via del Quirinale.

The regal pomp of **The Changing of the Guard** is a highlight for many kids. Though not on the scale of London's Buckingham Palace, the president's magnificent Cavalry Guards are splendid in military breastplates and shining golden helmets. They ride on horseback around the palace before entering the piazza.

ROMA POINT

Piazza Colonna, 360
Mon.-Sat., 10am-7:30pm
AS Roma store sells fan merchandise for the beloved soccer team. A must for any soccer fan. Upstairs, you can purchase tickets to in-town games.

SPANISH STEPS LOOP

PIAZZA DI SPAGNA. Famous for its cascade of steps, this piazza and its surroundings were virtually uninhabited until the 17th century. The so-called Spanish Steps climb in three sets up to the earlier 16th-century church of Trinità dei Monti.

THE PINCIO GARDENS and terrace, located above the **Piazza del Popolo**, are a small portion of **Villa Borghese**. Delightful garden paths lead to a fantastic view, pedal-karts, an obelisk, a water clock, and even a puppet theater (see **Villa Borghese**). Reach them from Piazza Trinità dei Monti by the uphill road left of the church or, alternatively, by stairs from Piazza del Popolo. *Free.*

PIAZZA DEL POPOLO caps the north end of Via del Corso with its vast square. **Santa Maria del Popolo,** built in 1099, can be found at the piazza's northeast end (No. 12). Hours: *Mon.-Sat., 7am-noon and 4-7pm; Sun. 8am-1:30pm and 4:30-7:30pm.*

Timing and Tips

Allow 2-3 hours (including playtime) to climb from the bottom of the Spanish Steps up to the church and even higher to the Pincio before looping down to Piazza del Popolo. This tour is an outdoor adventure with plenty of opportunity for kids to expend energy.

The pulsing heart of tourist Rome is **PIAZZA DI SPAGNA**, begun in the 1580s by Sixtus V, who broke with tradition when he decided to expand rather than beautify the overcrowded city center. By bringing water to unused tracts of land where development costs were cheap, he effectively created a whole new zone, one that proved especially attractive to foreigners. Wide, straight streets connected the new zone to major meccas like Santa Maria Maggiore and Piazza del Popolo. First, artists pounced on the cheaper accommodations, then hotels sprang up and then the tourists came, as they continue to do, in hoards.

Piazza di Spagna was originally called Piazza dei Francia because French kings, not Spaniards, financed the construction of these lovely Steps in 1723. The French wanted to connect the piazza with the French church of Trinità dei Monti, built over 200 years earlier in 1493. But when the Spanish Embassy moved in (No. 56), the new name stuck.

The view from atop the Steps is classic, and no trip to Rome is complete without taking it in. The people-watching is entertaining given the crowds and the fact that the surrounding streets comprise a high-end mall. But otherwise, there's little else actually to *do*—unless you're a young adult. Year-round, the piazza is a meeting place for young tourists and Romans with their indispensable *telefonini* (cell phones). They make the piazza a convivial, energetic place.

Strolling **THE PINCIO** was one of the classic walks British gentry took on their Grand Tour in the 1800s. The expansive and lush gardens are a kid's dream. Pedal go-karts are available for rent just at the top of the hill; you can also rent skates, bikes and even golf carts to enjoy the greenery. But simply taking a walk through the delightful gardens to the Piazzale Napoleone I terrace with its

commanding view is a joy and a welcome respite from the heat and pavement of the city. Take to the gardens for your own Grand Tour.

PIAZZA DEL POPOLO is the quintessential Italian piazza, a place of social congregation that originally provided its community's only water source and escape from tiny apartments. Though Piazza Navona tops most tour lists, the grand, absolutely cavernous Piazza del Popolo should not be missed. Its prized view down the entire length of the Corso allows you to see all the way to the enormous Victor Emanuel II monument.

The vast oval shape of the piazza was laid out in 1538, and we have **Pope Paul III Farnese** to thank for commissioning its redesign.

Striking twin churches, Santa Maria dei Miracoli and Santa Maria in Montesanto, boast beautiful Baroque façades enhanced by **Bernini.** Other highlights include a gorgeous central fountain added during Valadier's redesign in the 1800s; a massive 13th-century BC obelisk from Heliopolis, the second oldest in Rome, originally positioned at Circus Maximus; and **Santa Maria del Popolo**, a church full of **Caravaggios.**

THE WALKING TOUR

Stand at the bottom of the Spanish Steps and look up. In spring and summer, the way is outfitted with an extravagant array of pink azaleas lining the balustrades, top to bottom, and spilling into lavish masses along the landings. Reason enough to go and be awed. The lovely, mellow-colored mass of travertine steps cascades down the slope in three distinct waves, breaking over three separate landings, meant to echo the Trinity theme of the church above: three landings, three staircases, and three manifestations of Christian God.

> At the southern-most end of the piazza, you can find the enormous **College of Propaganda Fide** sitting between Via di Propaganda and Via Due Macelli. Bernini rebuilt its Piazza di Spagna exterior while Borromini designed its Via di Propaganda side. Borromini was known for his concave/convex designs, as you can see displayed on the windows there.

Take a look at the ingenious *Fontana della Barcaccia,* the fountain at the base of the stairs. It is the oldest feature of the piazza, built in 1629. While accounting books show that Pietro Bernini got paid for it, art historians believe it was done in collaboration with his talented son, Gian Lorenzo, who was then already a brilliant allegorical designer. The boat design may pay homage to ancient, staged naval battles that were conducted here by flooding the area, but many believe it's an allegorical representation of the Church: always under attack, never sinking. Depictions of the Church as a vessel to salvation were common, as you'll see when we come to St. Peter's portico. Still others believe the significance is held in the type of boat: *Barcaccie* were famous for hauling wine casks from the nearby Ripetta port. Italians always go with the best story, so pick your favorite and enjoy.

WHY IS THE BOAT SINKING?

Bernini's partially below-ground *barcaccia*—at a perfect height for a child—accommodates the low water pressure of the Acqua Vergine at this point. From here, the pressure rises until it comes to a spectacular end at the **Trevi Fountain**.

Urban VIII commissioned the boat fountain, so look for Barberini bees on the stem and stern between water cannons; the family suns spout water fore and aft. Find the suns again atop the giant *baldacchino* in St. Peter's.

WHERE'S YOUR WALDO?

Have a family member blend in with the massive crowds on the Steps and take a photo. Blow it up and play *Where's Waldo* at home, framing the photo for a great memento.

Even with massive crowds, there's plenty of room for kids to play. Now, hike up the stairs to the church piazza above.

HOW MANY STEPS ARE THERE?

Have each member of your party count as he or she climbs.
Compare your answers at the top.
Did all of you count 137?

Stop at the top to watch the artists who come to draw or paint one of
the most beloved views of Rome. Check out the Egyptian obelisk (ca.
200 AD), too. Its hieroglyphs are copied from the one in Piazza del
Popolo, which you'll see
further along our tour.

Before continuing, you
may wish to make a
quick detour down Via
Gregoriana to view the
quirky **House of the
Monsters** (see *What's
Around?*), where all
the windows and doors
are set into gigantic,
monstrous mouths.
Then, return to climb
steep Viale d. Trinità dei
Monti, left of the church,
up to the **Pincio.**

On the way up, you'll pass the elegant **Villa Medici** on the right, where
Galileo served his house arrest in the 1630s during the Inquisition (look
for a column just beyond the villa with a plaque acknowledging it). In
1803, Napoleon acquired the villa, and it is now home to the French
Academy in Rome. Its splendid formal gardens are occasionally open for
limited hours. Notice the cannonball in the center of its fountain, across
from the main doors. Queen Cristina of Sweden was given the honor
of shooting a cannon from Castel Sant'Angelo; allegedly, her bad aim
sent it hurtling toward Villa Medici instead of harmlessly up into the air.
Eventually, the ball was set into the fountain.

WHERE DID THE CANNONBALL HIT?

See if you can find a dent it could have made in those huge
bronze doors.

Also near here is famous **Ciampini**, whose charming glass conservatory may prompt you to stop for drinks. Lunch here is not appealing to children, but its little café (the uphill entrance) provides a lovely drink break. At the top of the hill is gorgeous, neoclassic **Casina Valadier café**, recently reopened after years of restoration. It was Valadier's home while he designed the Piazza and gardens; now you can get coffee, drinks or lunch there (with a kids' menu, too). A third refreshment choice is the simple gazebo snack bar in the Pincio Gardens.

Immediately after Villa Medici, veer right up the steeper path that leads directly to the Casina and the Pincio gardens.

Once on the Pincio, rent pedal-powered go-karts (no age limit), and kids will be more than happy to zip alongside while you stroll the gardens. Put them on the lookout for another obelisk. Grab a coffee and a bench to enjoy the Italian sun while happy kids cruise around in plain view.

When everyone has had enough, take the steps on either side of the **Napoleone I Belvedere Terrace** to **Piazza del Popolo** below.

SPHINX OR LION?

Egyptian-style fountains flank the ancient obelisk. These lions look very different from Bernini's big cat in the *Four Rivers* fountain at Piazza Navona. Their sphinx-like design compliments the Egyptian obelisk, but they are 19th-century Roman—neither Egyptian nor old.

Striking twin Baroque churches, Santa Maria dei Miracoli and Santa Maria in Montesanto (both façades modified by **Bernini**), adorn the piazza's south end while older **Santa Maria del Popolo** holds court on the north. Skip the interiors of the former. Don't miss the major art in the latter.

Two mega-famous **Caravaggio** paintings warrant your time in **Santa Maria del Popolo:** *The Crucifixion of St. Peter* and *The Conversion of St. Paul,* both in the first chapel left of the choir. Don't forget to illuminate them by dropping a coin in the box. Renovated once by **Bernini,** this church also contains famous frescoes by Pinturicchio and statues by both Raphael and Bernini. The façade inscriptions and oak tree crest tell us it was Sixtus IV della Rovere who had the church built in 1472 over what was formerly a small chapel.

GHOST IN THE TREES

A chapel was erected here to cover the tombs of Nero's nefarious Domitia family (Nero was buried here) because the site was believed to be haunted. A walnut tree was also cut down because superstitious Romans thought Domitia demons occupied it in the form of crows.

KIDS!

HOW MANY SKELETONS INSIDE?

Check out the disconcerting skeleton behind bars by the front doors of Santa Maria del Popolo, and count how many others you can find. Check the floor of the Chigi chapel on the left for a skeleton carrying a family crest. Its Latin inscription says, "[From] death to the heavens." There are lots of skulls in this church. Rome has a taste for the macabre: skeletons pop up all over the place, from the Skull Church façade on Via Giulia to the bizarre displays of the Capuchin cemetery.

Do the skulls make this church feel different from, say, a church like S. Agnese in Piazza Navona, which has a dove as its central theme?

Before leaving the square, check out the ancient city gate, **Porta del Popolo,** redesigned by **Bernini** for the Queen of Sweden's entrance in 1655 (the same queen that shot a cannonball at Villa Medici).

Depending on when you started, have lunch at one of the many restaurants in this zone or explore some of the English-language bookshops, elegant children's clothing boutiques and teen-friendly shops listed in *What's Around?*

WHAT'S AROUND?

ANGLO AMERICAN BOOK CO.
Via della Vite, 102
Tel. 06-679-5222
Books of all kinds printed in English can be found here. The selection for adults as well as children is always ample. Its location near the Spanish Steps makes it one of the most convenient.

ARA PACIS *(Altar of Peace, 13 BC)*
Lungotevere in Augusta, west of the Spanish Steps. Open Tues.-Sun. 9am-7pm; Dec. 24 & 31, 9am-2pm. Closed Mondays, Jan. 1, May 1, and Dec. 25. Tickets € 8.50. Ages 5 and under, free. Audio guides € 4. Web site: arapacis.it. Online booking: omniticket.it. Strollers permitted.
The newly reopened Altar of Peace is the latest success of Roman restoration, a striking contrast to the still-decrepit mausoleum of **Augustus** (28 BC) next door. The Altar is a block of marble with friezes that was made to commemorate the Empire's long-lasting peace that Augustus won with his victories in Spain and Gaul. It looks terrific, protected in a shiny high-tech structure by U.S. architect Richard Meier.

Over the centuries, pieces of its famous white marble friezes were scattered among museums around the world until they were reunited in the 1930s. Pick out the famous depiction of Aeneas (right of main entrance) and the portraits of Augustus and his royal entourage.

Nearby is the slated-for-restoration tomb of Rome's first and greatest emperor. Augustus built the mausoleum, gigantic but by no means Hadrianic, for himself and the Imperial family members. Eight emperors were interred before space ran out, leaving Trajan in the market for new eternal digs (under his eponymous column). Hadrian followed; his splendid tomb is now known as Castel Sant'Angelo.

BERNINI'S HOME
Via Della Mercede, 11
A plaque with Bernini's profile marks his modest palace. No entry. Of all ironies, the church of **San Andrea della Fratte** by Borromini stands across the street. Will these two rivals ever leave each others' shadows?

VIA DEL BABUINO
Runs north from the Spanish Steps to Piazza del Popolo.
This street is home to high-end antique shops and *Babuino,* who is one of Rome's talking statues, called "Baboon" because it's so unattractive. Never met a kid who didn't agree. Some children's shops:

Pinco Pallino, Via del Babuino, 115. Tel. 06-691-90549. The sophisticated creations of Imelde & Stefano Cavallieri are the stuff of heirlooms and paintings.

Pure Gold, Via del Babuino, 150. Tel. 06-323-5464. Closed Sundays. The finest party dresses from top fashion designers—for girls only. Expensive.

BONPOINT
Piazza San Lorenzo in Lucina, 25
Tel. 06-687-1548
Traditional children's clothing for well-heeled kids (from infants to 10 year olds). Bonpoint excels at stocking crisp suits, wool coats and knitted sweaters.

CALICO LION
Via della Vite, 80
Tel. 06-678-4626
Elegant clothing for kids 8 years old and up in one of the nicest stores in the area.

VIA CONDOTTI
From the Spanish Steps to Via del Corso
Rome's most exclusive shops are on and around this posh street.
Caffè Greco, *No. 86,* has been a meeting place for travelers, intellectuals and artists such as Goethe, Byron and Keats for centuries.

VIA DEL CORSO
From Piazza del Popolo to Piazza Venezia
Shops on this street are more affordable than those on Condotti. The north end has a large concentration of teen-friendly shops where you'll find jock-pleasing shoe and jersey stores like Adidas (No. 475), Nike Roma (No. 478) and Puma (No. 403).

Diesel, *No. 186-188,* is the flagship store of this mecca of jeans and cool clothes.

Miss Sixty, *No. 179.* Internationally known Roman-label clothing for funky teens and young adults (or young at heart). The same designer's **Energie** and **Killah** stores share space.

VIA FRATTINA
From the Corso to Piazza di Spagna
A few choice children's stores dot this posh street. Well-healed kids will find colorful knits at Gallo *(No. 123)*, high fashions at Armani Jr. *(No. 34a)*, and, the beloved:

> Pure Sermonetta, *Via Frattina, No. 111.*
> The answer for high-fashion kids looking for brands like Diesel, Dolce & Gabana Jr., Fendi, and Burberry.

HOUSE OF MONSTERS
Via Gregoriana, 28
Hunt for the house with giant monsters devouring the windows and front door. It's a few paces from the top of the Spanish Steps. The little palace was designed by Baroque painter, Federico Zuccari in 1592, and is now a fine-arts library.

LADIA
Via Vittoria, 13
Simply stunning baby clothes and special occasion children's garments are lovely, but pricey. They are closed Sundays and Monday morning.

LAVORI ARTIGINALI FEMMINILI
Via Capo le Case, 6
Tel. 06-679-2992
Haute baby clothes for special occasions.

THE VIA VENETO ZONE

TRITON'S FOUNTAIN, *Fontana di Tritone, Piazza Barberini.* Bernini's powerful sea god, a travertine masterpiece on two scallop shells supported by four dolphins, has commanded the square since 1642.

VIA VITTORIO VENETO, or Via Veneto, is a major modern (1886) artery of Rome, lined with luxurious hotels, upscale clothiers and lots of cafés and restaurants that cater to foreigners. It runs north from Piazza Barberini. Lovely but undeniably touristy, its south end holds Eataly's tasty l'hamburgheria, the Hard Rock Café, the bizarre Bone Church and Triton's Fountain. Classic Cafè de Paris and Cafè Doney, hold court on the north end, directly across the street from one another.

SANTA MARIA DELLA CONCEZIONE, *Via Vittorio Veneto, 27. Crypt open daily, 9am-7pm. Closed Thursdays. Tel. 06-888-03695. Tickets, €6. Ages 17 and under, €4. Audio guide, €4.* This church, commonly known as "the Bone Church," is so called because its adjoining Capuchin Cemetery includes several rooms decorated with human bones.

Timing and Tips

If you're not an art devotee, you're in for about a half-hour tour. Start at **Triton's Fountain** and then walk a short way up legendary Via Veneto to see the **Bone Church**. Although most children are fine in the cemetery, some may be frightened by the skeletons and others might dislike the musty smell.

Steps from the "Bone" church, you'll find the superior l'Hamburgheria by Eataly, slinging Italian style burgers (hot dogs, fries), using native Italian meats and cheeses, while Hard Rock Cafè, a few steps further, offers American style (even Italian kids enjoy its glass outdoor terrace). Hamburgers can delight the homesick child—and happy kids are better travelers.

Art appreciators with the time and inclination may visit **Barberini Palace**, now one of Rome's greatest museums. It's a powerhouse filled with 12th-18th century art (see **_What's Around?_**).

Swanky **VIA VENETO** was the backdrop to great films of the 50's and 60's, like Fellini's _La Dolce Vita_. It is still home to grand hotels such as the Majestic and the Regina Baglioni; sparkling cafés like Café de Paris, Doney and Harry's Bar; as well as the refined U.S. Embassy (Palazzo Margherita).

Fittingly enough, Via Veneto rises from glistening Piazza Barberini where Bernini's glorious sea-god **TRITON** blows his conch shell to proclaim the Barberini family's glory. The land around the fountain, once entirely in the family's holdings, was dominated by the palace of Urban VIII. Built and beautified by the likes of Maderno, Borromini and the prolific Bernini, the fine palace is one reason this part of town represents some of the best of the Baroque.

A few steps away, the Capuchin order of Franciscans buried their dead in the indoor cemetery of **SANTA MARIA DELLA CONCEZIONE**. When the limited amount of sacred soil ran out (around 4,000 friars interred), the Capuchins began digging up the oldest graves to make room for the new. Bones piled up, and someone got the idea to decorate with them—walls to ceilings. The artistic results are at once creepy and fascinating.

THE WALKING TOUR

Begin at **Triton's Fountain.** Piazza Barberini, one of Rome's central traffic squares, can be rather daunting to cross, but don't see this fountain from across the street or, worse, from inside a car or tour bus. Only up close can you fully appreciate its size and magnificence. Watch the sparkling jet shoot sky-high; listen to the terrific splash it makes when it hits the shell; hear the rumble become a roar as thousands of droplets cascade off.

GUESS WHO PAID FOR TRITON?
Look for escutcheons with the papal tiara, crossed keys and a heraldic trio of bees. Yup, those Barberinis!

Until the 18th century, unidentified corpses were displayed in this square so that they could be claimed.

Make your way up the right side of Via Veneto, stopping briefly to admire **Bernini's *Fountain of the Bees** (Fontana delle Api, 1644).* The low, open shell provided water to horses and other animals. The original fountain, carved from Luna marble, stood at the low end of the square, allowing it to naturally fill with run-off from Triton. Humans drank first, animals second.

BEE CAREFUL

*The Bee Fountain honored **Urban VIII**'s 22nd year in office, but he died eight days before his anniversary, making the original inscription look arrogant. To quell negative gossip, Urban's nephew changed it to read, "21 years."*

This travertine copy was created when the Luna version, taken down during a 19th-century street reorganization, could not be reassembled. It uses only one portion of Bernini's original—the middle section with the center bee and the folds of shell connected to it.

CAN YOU FIND THE REAL BEE?
Only one of the original bees drinks at the waterspouts.
(Hint: Its color gives it away.)

Continue up the street to Santa Maria della Concezione. The church was built for Cardinal Antonio Barberini, Urban's older brother and a Capuchin monk. Recall that this is Barberini-ville: The family once owned all the land around the piazza. Antonio's tombstone lies unmarked before the main altar of the church. To find it, look for a Latin inscription, *"hic jacet pulvis, cinis et nihil"* (here lies nothing but dust and ashes). And check out the spooky painting, *Saint Michael the Archangel Defeating the Devil* by Guido Reni (1635), before heading to the Capuchin Cemetery to marvel at its ossified artifacts.

DEVIL MAY CARE

*R*eni *was apparently a rebel with some real moxie. They say he hated* ***Innocent X*** *enough to use his likeness for the devil's face in his St. Michael painting.*

HOW IS A MONK LIKE A CUP OF COFFEE?

Cappuccio means hood. *Capuchin* friars got their names because they wear, as St. Francis of Assisi wore, hooded brown robes. The coffee drink *cappuccino* is so-called because it wears a hood of light brown froth resembling a Capuchin hood.

KIDS!

In the Capuchin Cemetery, to the right of the church, don't forget to look up at the ceilings. Hovering over skeletons in monk robes, amid moldings of clavicles and shoulder blades, is a young Barberini princess, sickle in one hand, scale in the other. It was a high honor for laypersons (albeit nobles) like the tiny princess to be buried here.

Look for a sign that reads, "That which you are, we were; that which we are, you will be." (You'll find a similar inscription on the Skull Church of **Via Giulia**, behind the Farnese Palace.) On the way out, consider buying at least some postcards depicting the strange rooms since no photos are allowed. Kids will relish showing them to friends at home. Some stories are just better with pictures.

From here, consider touring the Barberini National Gallery of Classical Art (see ***What's Around?***), enjoying Villa Borghese's park at the top of the Via Veneto, or taking in the Galleria Borghese. The latter two are the subjects of our next chapter, and they are far enough from Piazza Barberini for you to save time and energy by taking transportation.

Another option: walk up Via Sistina to the top of the Spanish Steps, covered in the previous chapter.

WHAT'S AROUND?

BARBERINI NATIONAL GALLERY OF CLASSICAL ART

Galleria Nazionale d'Arte Antica, Via delle Quattro Fontane, 13.
Open Tues.-Sun., 8:30am-7pm. Closed Mondays, Jan. 1, & Dec. 25.
Tel. 06-328-10
Web site: galleriaborghese.it/barberini/it.
Tickets € 7. Audio guides, € 3. Book online: tosc.it; booking fee applies.

Since 1947, when the Italian state bought **Urban VIII's** family palace, Barberini's Baroque tour-de-force on the Quirinal Hill has been home to the National Gallery. Enjoy one astounding masterpiece after the next while kids figure out where the pope slept, ate and held marvelous parties. A multitude of family symbols decorate the walls, ceilings, columns and windows.

This astounding collection of treasures includes paintings by **Caravaggio**, Fra Angelico, Filippino Lippi, Perugino, Bronzino, **Bernini**, Guercino, Poussin, Annibale Carracci and Raphael. (Don't miss his well-known portrait, *La Fornarina,* "The Baker's Daughter." She was Raphael's girlfriend; look for his name tied around her arm). Later, you can eat at Romolo, a restaurant in La Fornarina's one-time garden. For more on the Gallery, see ***Extras in Rome***.

VIA DELLE QUATTRO FONTANE (*Street of the Four Fountains*), a few blocks away from Piazza Barberini, boasts a fountain on each of its intersection's four corners where it crosses with Via del Quirinale. A visit to this intersection and the following two nearby churches is best considered with teens.

From each of the four river gods lounging on their corner fountains, you can spot three distant obelisks that mark the crests of the Quirinal, Esquiline and Pincian Hills: at Piazza Quirinale, Santa Maria Maggiore (south), and Trinità dei Monti (north). Be aware, the street is heavily congested. Two tiny churches, San Carlino (also on this corner) and Sant'Andrea (a half block away), offer a comparison study of two brilliant architects from the same era: the rivals Borromini and Bernini. Their immediate proximity to one another and one odd surprise leave no time for boredom.

SAN CARLINO ALLE QUATTRO FONTANE (1665-76)

Via del Quirinale, 23, at Via Quattro Fontane. Open Mon.-Fri. 10am-1pm and 3pm-6pm; Sat., 10am-1pm; Sun., noon-1pm.

Here a parent can confidently answer the age-old question, "What can I do with math?" Borromini's sophisticated, crazy church and charming cloister were revolutionary in his time, and they continue to be some of the most beautiful mathematically expressed pieces of architecture. Exclusively an architect (never a painter or sculptor), Borromini was devoted to mathematical principles. For this, his first commission in Rome, he ingeniously transformed an awkward corner building into a flowing masterpiece where the walls seem to undulate, inside and out. Notice that Borromini shunned marbles and rich embellishments, preferring to let the beauty of the architecture do the impressing. He always used common Roman brick and painted the interiors a simple white.

SANT'ANDREA AL QUIRINALE (1658-78)

Via del Quirinale, 29
Open daily, 8am-noon and 4-7pm. Closed Tuesdays.

Innocent X's nephew, Prince Camillo Pamphilj, hired **Bernini** to design this beautiful church half a block from San Carlino. Bernini's son, Domenico, wrote that his father was more pleased with its execution than with any of his other works.

Inside, windows above the cornices and within the upper lantern make the church seem lighter as it goes heavenward. Breaking from the tradition of depicting a church's name-saint in a flat painting, Bernini uniquely rendered St. Andrew in 3-D, floating on a cloud above the altar. There is a painting, too, and it works with the sculpture. St. Andrew is shown being crucified in the painting and then, above the painting, you see him ascending to heaven led by the dove of the Holy Spirit.

CAN YOU FIND SLEEPY STANISLAUS?

Go through the doors right of the altar (the sign says "Rooms of Saint Stanislaus"). Pass the souvenirs and Jesuit offices and ascend the staircase. See that man sleeping several rooms away? Sneak up on the poor guy...and see who is more surprised. Stanislaus, a Polish saint, died here in the 1500s. Kids will do a double take as they figure out he's only a sculpture. Quell ensuing chatter to be respectful of the Jesuit offices.

Outside, find the Pamphilj coat of arms; spotting their dove is quick work for kids who have seen it in places like S. Agnese in Agone and atop the obelisk, both in Piazza Navona.

GALLERIA BORGHESE

VILLA BORGHESE is an expansive park on the north side of the city center, fanning out from the Pincio Gardens. Hundreds of acres of gardens, paths, shade trees, fountains, statuary and delightful ponds provide lovely opportunities to unwind. Among the attractions on the grounds of this 17th-century villa are the Galleria Borghese, a charming puppet theater (*San Carlino*), a playhouse and playground (*Casina di Raffaello*), and the zoo (*Bioparco Giardino Zoologico di Roma*). Further, the park is host to rides of all kinds, from pony and train rides to roller blades and golf carts! *What's Around?* has the details. Villa Borghese was the first of Rome's large public parks to offer Wi-Fi hotspots.

GALLERIA BORGHESE, *Piazza Scipione Borghese, 5. Open Tues.-Sun., 8:30am-7:30pm, entrance limited to 2-hour time slots beginning at 9am (11am, 1pm, etc.). Mandatory reservations: Tel. 06-328-10 or book on-line at galleriaborghese.it. Tickets € 11. Audio guides € 5. Daily tours in English, 9:10am and 11:10am, additional € 6 each. Tickets online: tosc.it (booking fee applies).*

Timing and Tips

Expect to spend 2 hours exploring the museum and a bit of the surrounding grounds. To avoid disappointment, you must reserve Galleria tickets in advance and purchase them at least 30 minutes before your reserved 2-hour time slot. Waiting may not be too terrible a prospect given the pleasant, citrus-tree-filled Borghese gardens where kids may run free before being reigned in for the museum tour.

Time your gallery visit for when children are fresh and more likely to be orderly. Your ace-in-the-hole, should you need one, is a visit afterwards to the zoo or one of the many other attractions on park grounds. Alternatively, the park's bike, surrey, and go-kart rentals (all pedal-powered) are sure to keep boredom at bay while you make a search party for the park's monuments, tiny temples and lovely little lake.

If you've got tots or tuckered-out young kids, take a ride on the little Bioparco Express train that circumnavigates the zoo. It runs Saturdays and Sundays, € 1 a ride. Public bathrooms are located near the Borghese lake, in the *Casina di Raffaello* playhouse and at the north end of the Pincio gardens.

VILLA BORGHESE is the largest mass of green space found inside the ancient center of the city, or *centro*. The villa, including the Casino Borghese, which houses **THE GALLERIA BORGHESE**, was the product of Pope Paul V's nephew, Cardinal Scipione Borghese, who began work on the property in 1605.

The Cardinal's magnificent private collection of sculpture and paintings is on display here in the building he had built for the purpose. The astute 17th-century collector accumulated some of the world's greatest art, ancient and modern.

In 1902, the Italian State purchased the Casino and its contents to make them available to the public, and the slow process of locating and restoring the Cardinal's original collection began. One by one, lost pieces were found and restored to the collection.

Expect to be wowed by powerhouse artists like **Bernini,** Raphael, Titian (his *Sacred and Profane Love* in room XX is spectacular), Canova, Rubens and **Caravaggio**. More than for any other artist, the gallery is a tribute to Bernini, with many of his greatest mythological sculptures. Even his first sculpture is here (Jupiter and a Faun with Amalthea, the she-goat).

Rather than describe all of the masterpieces in the museum, the tour below focuses on major works in a way that appeals to children and spotlights artists on our short list of Romans to know.

THE WALKING TOUR

All rooms are numbered and, though you certainly don't have to move through the museum in that order, it is how we'll proceed. Generally speaking, grand sculpture is on the ground floor and the bulk of paintings are upstairs.

Starting in the opulent Entrance Hall, look up to find **the sculpture of a horse and rider** near the ceiling that looks as though it's flying through the wall. The rider is Marcus Curtius flinging himself into the **Forum**'s disastrous chasm that became known as the *Lacus Curtius*. Pietro Bernini, father to Gian Lorenzo, created the rider and attached it to a horse recycled from antiquity.

LEGENDARY LEAP

*L*ivy *tells us the Romans believed the chasm would close if they threw in their most prized possessions. Nothing worked until soldier Marcus Curtius, knowing the army was Rome's most prized possession, charged into the chasm horse and all.*

Eagles and dragons from the Borghese coat of arms are abundant throughout the museum since it was the Cardinal's villa. Here in the entrance hall, two cherubs hold up the family heraldic symbols in white and gold stucco (on the short ends). Kids can find plenty more eagles at the Vatican since Pope Paul V was a Borghese.

Proceed to **Room I.** The reclining *Paolina Bonaparte as Venus,* masterfully sculpted by Antonio Canova in 1805, greets you. When

Napoleon's sister Paulina married Camillo Borghese, the Borghese family was forced to sell a large portion of their priceless collection to the greedy emperor.

Notice how soft the marble mattress looks, creasing and bending under the weight of her body. Paulina's skin looks smooth because Canova used to rub the marble with pink wax so that the skin of his creations glowed.

WHY IS PAULINA HOLDING AN APPLE?

Napoleon's sister is depicted holding an apple to identify her with Venus, who won a golden apple in a beauty contest. Seems none of the Bonapartes were short on ego.

ONE BAD APPLE...

*T*he appropriately-named goddess Discord offered a golden apple for the fairest goddess. Paris, a prince of Troy and a mere mortal, was selected to be an unbiased judge of the beauty contest. The goddesses tried to bribe him with eternal life and endless wealth. But Venus won his favor by offering him the most beautiful woman on earth, Helen (of Troy), already married to a Greek king. Her abduction sparked the Trojan War. Today, when someone is very beautiful we say she has "a face to launch a thousand ships," as Helen's did.

Look up on the ceiling for a painting depicting the *Golden Apple* contest. In most rooms here, the sculptures and paintings are related in theme. And don't forget to look for Borghese family symbols: eagles and dragons. This room even has an eagle-riding cherub.

Now move to **Room II**.

The last sculpture Bernini created for Borghese was the masterful ***David***. The artist's ability to capture the dramatic is in full flower; notice the recoiling body and tensed muscles, just about to launch the legendary slingshot on Goliath.

Point out an elusive Borghese symbol: the lyre at David's feet is decorated with an eagle's head.

FIND THE SLINGSHOT

Bernini is said to have looked into a mirror while putting his hand over fire to create David's resolute facial expression. If that's true, this is also a self-portrait. In fact, Bernini will show you what he looked like in two self-portraits, and he'll show you how Cardinal Borghese looked in two busts, all upstairs in **Room XIV**.

ARE YOU UP TO A HERCULEAN TASK?

How many renderings of Hercules can you find in this room dedicated to the strong man? The sarcophagus depicts ten of Hercules' labors, but there's also a bust of Herc, a rendering of baby Herc and even an old man Herc.

Proceed to **Room III** and get ready for…trouble. Bernini's next extraordinary works expose two crimes. Troublemaker gods Pluto and Apollo are both trying to capture girls they are smitten with. One is successful; the other is not.

CATCH APOLLO RED-HANDED

Bernini's action-packed pieces offer up not only the peak dramatic moment but also powerful emotion, as *Apollo and Daphne* demonstrates. Apollo's about to catch the object of his desire, but just as he touches her, Daphne turns into a tree to escape. Daphne's body takes root as branches grow from her hair and fingers.

MYTH OF APOLLO AND DAPHNE

The nymph Daphne refused to marry; she only wanted to hunt and hang out with her friends. Amorous Apollo had other ideas, and he gave chase. Terrified, Daphne called out to her father, the river god, begging for help to keep her from Apollo's grasp. He did so by turning her into a laurel tree.

Sad Apollo spent his days sitting under his beloved tree, wearing her leaves as a crown. Roman emperors wore the laurel leaf crown after Apollo, god of inspiration.

FIND APOLLO'S CLONES

Play Apollo hide and seek.

Look up! He's at it again, chasing Daphne on the ceiling.

Can you find more? (Hint: Apollo was also god of music.

In **Room IV** (Gallery of the Emperors), you'll find that now it's **Pluto**, King of the Underworld, who is up to no good.

CAN YOU FIND PLUTO'S TRIDENT?

Like his brother Neptune, King of the Seas, Pluto carries a trident. Where is it? Why did he drop it? Unlike Apollo, Pluto gets his girl. We discover him having just caught poor Persephone, about to bring her down to the underworld to reign as his queen.

This room, devoted to Ovid's story of Proserpina (Persephone), features Bernini's sculpture ***Proserpina and Pluto.*** Zero in on the realistic depressions Pluto's fingers make in Proserpina's skin with his firm grasp. The marble seems more like clay or dough; a fine example of Bernini's masterly skill as a marble cutter. This grouping has a third character—check out Cerberus, the three-headed hound who guards the gates of the Underworld. See how his eye follows you wherever you move in the room. Head's up on the three-headed hound: he's also keeping watch on the museum's portico.

Room VI features the masterful ***Aeneas*** sculptural grouping. It's a product of three minds: **Bernini, Augustus** and poet Virgil. It embodies the important ancient Roman ideal of *pietas*: loyalty to God, country and family, in that order. Aeneas bears his responsibility to the gods, his country and his family quite literally. With his little son by his side, he carries his father, Anchises (who is holding the family's household gods), out of the fallen city of Troy to begin a new, great race in Italy—the Romans.

Augustus hired Virgil to write a story like the Greek *Odyssey,* of a Roman hero who embodied the virtues of *pietas*. Virgil delivered *The Aeneid,* the action epic of Aeneas, whose lineage rooted Romans to the pedigreed Greeks and their gods; the Greek mortal Anchises was Aeneas' father and goddess Venus was his mother.

WHOSE SKIN DO YOU FIT IN?

Observe the texture on all three people in the Aeneas grouping. See how virtuoso Bernini made each character's skin different? Compare the boy's doughy flesh with the firm, muscular tone of Aeneas and the saggy, paper-thin skin of the aging father.

Room VI is also called the Room of the Gladiator because it is decorated with scenes of fighting. Look up at the ceiling to see the gods taking sides over the Battle of Troy. Those in favor of war against Troy are on the left—Minerva in her helmet and Neptune with his trident; those against the war—Mars, Venus and Cupid among them—amass on the right. That's Jupiter, the Roman version of Zeus, in the middle.

CAN YOU FIND 8 HEROES, 1 GOD AND... A WARTHOG?

KIDS!

1. **A host of gladiators** (six *are in a line with shields in partial relief and more are under the frescoes of piles of shields*)
2. **A guy fighting a lion**
3. **Aeneas with his father**
4. **A warthog**
5. **Lovely Leda and a swan** (Zeus in disguise)

Room VII features Egyptian hieroglyphics and graphics on the floors and walls. Note the Sphinx over the doors.

Room VIII displays most of the museum's **Caravaggio** paintings. The give-away is the dancing satyr in the center of the room. Look for its tail.

Bacchus (Il Bacchino malato) is among Caravaggio's earliest works and a self-portrait. More compelling, perhaps, is this master's interpretation of *David*. Compare this painting to Bernini's sculpture in **Room II.** Recall that Bernini chose to express that moment of action when David launches the stone. Caravaggio chose to show the gory results. His *David* holds the dripping, severed head of Goliath. Bernini loved action; Caravaggio loved dark drama.

WHERE IS THE SLINGSHOT THIS TIME?

Want to know what Caravaggio looked like? He gave his face to the bloated head of Goliath. Compare it with his earlier self-portrait as Bacchus, and you'll get a sense of how life was going for this troubled artist who had to flee Rome on a murder charge. Other Caravaggio standouts: the powerful *Saint Jerome,* the controversial *Madonna of the Palafrenieri* (removed from St. Peter's for reasons of decorum), the famous *St. John the Baptist.*

Continue upstairs to the picture gallery, and find in **Room XIV** two **self-portraits of G. L. Bernini** and his nearly identical busts of **Scipione Borghese.**

DOUBLE TAKE

Cardinal Borghese commissioned a bust from his favorite protégé, Bernini. Although an unfortunate crack developed on the forehead, Bernini completed the bust anyway. According to biographer Charles Scribner, Bernini unveiled the work, crack and all, to his eager patron who was disappointed but understanding. Then, Bernini presented a second, perfect bust of his benefactor, which he'd been working on in secret, thereby surprising the delighted Cardinal.

CAN YOU CRACK THE CASE OF IDENTICAL BUSTS?

Which bust was the first, and which was the second one? Can you see the crack in the forehead? How else are they different? Bernini purposely made them nearly identical, yet slightly different. He wanted each work to be unique and not a copy.

When you've all had enough, take a brief refreshment break in the museum's small bar before tackling the park or the zoo. It's pricey, but restaurants and cafés are scarce around here. If you've promised a trip to the **zoo** (see *What's Around?*), take Viale Uccelliera, on your right as you exit the Galleria. A brief and pleasant walk brings you to the zoo entrance at Piazza del Giardino Zoologico.

WHAT'S AROUND?

BIOPARCO GIARDINO ZOOLOGICO DI ROMA *(The Zoo),*
Piazzale del Giardino Zoologico, 1, in Villa Borghese.
Open daily, Mar. 29-Oct. 26, 9:30am-6pm; Oct. 27-Mar. 29, 9:30am-5pm.
Tel. 06-360-8211
Tickets, € 15 adults. Ages 11 and under, € 12. Babies, free.
Web site: bioparco.it.

Refurbishments of the 1911 zoo have transformed the entrance and many of the animal habitats into a lovely setting, though a few of the habitats are still a bit archaic. Young children don't seem to notice, however. The zoo is working on upgrading all its exhibits and has a really pleasing new children's play area.

CASINA DI RAFFAELLO *(playhouse and playground)*
Viale della Casina di Raffaello
Open Tues.-Fri., 10am-3:30pm, Sat., Sun. and holidays, 10am-6pm.
Closed Mondays, Jan. 1, May 1, and Dec. 25 and 30.
Web site: casinadiraffaello.it
Note: Some activities require a small fee and reservation.
Best for ages 12 and under.
This is a lovely building in the park, located at the Piazza di Siena. Just look for a line of strollers. Inside the playhouse you'll find rooms stocked with wonderful costumes for playing dress up—bring a camera! More crafts and a bathroom are inside, while a top-notch playground with lots of activities is just outside. On weekends, you'll be able to find the pony rides from here (on Viale J.W. Goethe).

SAN CARLINO PUPPET THEATER *(Teatro dei Burattini San Carlino)*
Viale dei Bambini on the Pincio Hill, at the Water Clock (Viale dell'Orologio)
Weekends only, closed in August.
Tel. 06-699-22117
Tickets range from € 10-12.50. Reservations required.
Web site: sancarlino.it.
If you're looking to catch an authentic Italian puppet show, this is the place. Each show lasts one hour; check the Web site for shows and times.

Borghese Gardens

LET'S EAT!

SPANISH STEPS

Myriad restaurants leave no shortage of places to eat here. On average, food is mediocre; you pay for location. Some reliable choices:

ALFREDO RISTORANTE L'ORIGINALE, Piazza Augusto Imperatore, 30. Closed lunch Mondays. This is the real deal, the originators of Fettuccine Alfredo. Check out the photos of celebrities who have visited. Moderate.

CASINA VALADIER, Piazza Bucarest terrace atop the Pincio Hill. 18th-century architect Valadier's gorgeous home makes for a swanky coffee break in a leafy park with views of Piazza del Popolo and St. Peter's dome in the distance. And there's a kid's lunch menu. Moderate.

CAFFE CIAMPINI, Viale Trinità dei Monti, 1, at Villa Medici. Open 8am-1am (even open Christmas day). Limited credit cards accepted. Take a break amid Art Nouveau charm, rooftop views and flowering plants. Café drinks at the bar are inexpensive, but a sit-down lunch will cost you plenty.

CIAMPINI, Piazza S. Lorenzo in Lucina, 29. Closed Sundays. Legendary gelateria and café started by Angelo Ciampini, holds court on this picturesque square. Salads and light meals accompany the coffee and gelato.

FATAMORGANA GELATO, Via Laurina, 10, steps from Piazza del Popolo. One of Rome's finest gelaterie now has a chain of storefronts dotting the city. Like all of the best gelato, no thickeners, preservatives, or food coloring are added. With a focus on health, many flavors are gluten-free, low-calorie, lactose-free and even sugar-free.

IL MARGUTTA RISTORARTE, Via Margutta, 118. Absolutely delicious vegetarian brunch is served daily, with loads of palate-pleasing choices for everyone. Dishes such as quiche, polenta, mashed potatoes, beans, and a host of hot and cold fare are high on taste. The colorful, artistic interior is spacious and can accommodate many. Good thing, because they are popular with the locals!

OSTERIA MARGUTTA, Via Margutta, 82. Take lunch or dinner in this romantic restaurant on the "street of the artists" (where Gregory Peck lived in *Roman Holiday*). Upscale homemade pastas like linguini with prawns are wonderful. Moderate. Closed Sundays.

OTELLO ALLA CONCORDIA, Via della Croce, 81. Closed Sundays. A shady interior courtyard lets you eat outside but away from Spanish Steps crowds. Terrific food at moderate prices.

RE DEGLI AMICI, Via della Croce, 33B. Lunch and dinner. Traditional fare is served up at this popular spot a stone's throw from the Steps. Outside tables go quickly, but kids like the indoor space with its familiar scenes of Rome. Moderate.

TREVI

AL MORO, Vicolo Bollette, 13. One of few nice restaurants in this touristy zone, Moro was a favorite of movie director, Fellini. Moderate to expensive.

BACCANO BISTROT, Via delle Muratte, 23. Paris in Rome? Yes. This fresh take on an old classic serves classic bistrot burgers and fare all day long, from 10am to 2am. It's a good, safe bet in this otherwise, heavy tourist zone.

IL GELATO DI SAN CRISPINO, Via della Panetteria, 42. Another top shop, S. Crispino specializes in smooth gelato in seasonal flavors like ginger, raspberry or cinnamon. From the Trevi, walk east down Via Lavatore and take a left on Panetteria. Before you turn, look right to see the back door of the President's Palace.

THE VIA VENETO ZONE

IL BOSCAIOLO, Via degli Artisti, 37. Open lunch and dinner, Tues. to Fri., dinner only Sat. and Sun. Closed Mondays. Kids are happy in this humble pizzeria with good local fare supporting its wood-burning oven (*forno*) baked pizzas, just off the pricier Via Veneto. Inexpensive.

CAFÉ DE PARIS, Via Vittorio Veneto, 90. Open 8am daily. Coffee and snacks are presented in sparkling dessert and sandwich (*panini*) cases: the most elegant ham and cheese you're likely to find.

COLLINE EMILIANE, Via degli Avignonesi, 22. Closed Sunday nights and Mondays. A block from Triton's fountain, this modest but elegant restaurant serves mouth-watering hearty dishes from the Emilia Romagna region. Dinner books up fast, so reservations are essential for this not-to-be-missed, homemade cooking. Moderate.

DA TULLIO RISTORANTE, Via S. Nicola da Tolentino, 26. Closed Sundays. Top Roman steakhouse, clubby and crowded, where the steaks are roasted in a wood-burning oven along with other meat and fish dishes. From Triton's Fountain, take the street left of the Bernini Bristol Hotel. Moderate.

FORNO CERULLI, Via di S. Nicola da Tolentino 53, has been baking up pizza and baked goods since 1937. Today's menu also includes pastas, salads, and sandwiches made with their fresh breads.

HARD ROCK CAFÉ, Via Vittorio Veneto, 62a. Familiar, American-style burgers and mood-elevating rock music are a treat for kids, especially homesick ones. Moderate.

L'HAMBURGHERIA DI EATALY, Via Veneto, 11. New in 2013, this hamburger place may have an American theme, but the hamburgers, hotdogs, and fries are all created from locally-grown products. Eataly is a proponent of the Slow Food movement. Kids don't care. Just get them the goods.

PART FOUR

PAPAL ROME

We've seen the heart of Ancient Rome, explored the Renaissance influences around Campo dei Fiori and walked the richly-Baroque zone east of the Corso. Now, we move across the Tiber to the *Borgo* and the hub of Christian Rome: St. Peter's Basilica, the Vatican museums and Castel Sant'Angelo.

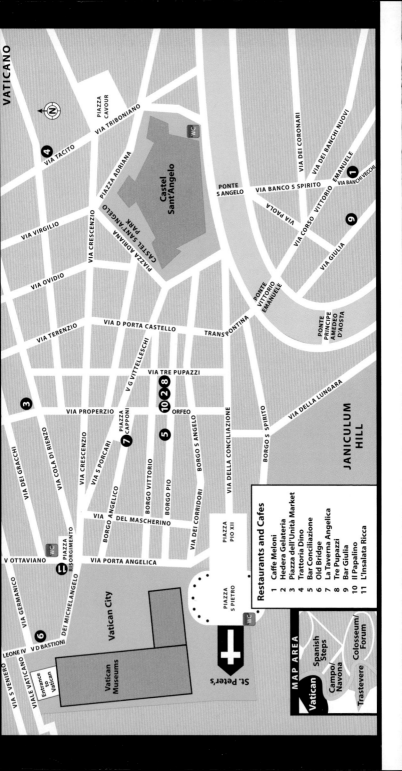

Restaurants and Cafes

1 Caffe Meloni
2 Hedera Gelateria
3 Piazza dell'Unità Market
4 Trattoria Dino
5 Bar Conciliazione
6 Old Bridge
7 La Taverna Angelica
8 Tre Pupazzi
9 Bar Giulia
10 Il Papalino
11 L'Insalata Ricca

MAP AREA

Vatican Spanish
Steps
Campo/
Navona
Colosseum/
Forum
Trastevere

ST. PETER'S & THE BORGO

Climbing ST. PETER'S DOME is at the top of every kid's list. *Open 8am-dusk. Tickets € 7 with elevator, € 5 without.* While it is possible to climb from the ground floor all the way to the lantern above the cupola, you may prefer taking the elevator to the *loggia* roof (halfway) and climbing to the top from there.

ST. PETER'S BASILICA (16th century). *Open daily 7am-7pm, until 6:30pm in winter. Closed Wednesday mornings during papal audiences held in the square. Web site: Vatican.va. There is no entry fee for the Basilica and its grottoes, but for a small fee you may rent audio guides from the bag check to the right of the Basilica.* You may not enter St. Peter's with bared knees or shoulders.

CASTEL SANT'ANGELO, *Lungotevere Castello, 50. Open 9am-7:30pm. Closed Mondays, Jan 1, & Dec. 25. Tel. 06-32810. Tickets € 10.50, audio guides € 4. Web site: castelsantangelo.com. Online tickets: tosc.it (booking fee applies).* This is the papal fortress dominating the east end of Via Conciliazione. A covered passageway connects it to St. Peter's at the west end.

Timing and Tips

Gorgeous St. Peter's can easily demand 2-3 hours from an adult, an unreasonable chunk of time for even the most diehard of tourists, let alone parents with children. Instead, we'll avoid dreaded Vatican burnout by taking the family up to the dome and through the Basilica at an enjoyable pace. You can climb the dome in an hour, see the church in an hour, and traverse the grottoes in about 30 minutes (grottoes are by no means essential). Families traveling with young children, handicapped persons, or with anyone who suffers from claustrophobia should make use of the dome's elevator rather than attempting to climb it from the ground up.

Combining a tour of St. Peter's with the Vatican Museums and Sistine Chapel is not recommended. It's simply way too much in one day for youngsters.

After an early break for lunch in one of the many restaurants, bakeries and cafés along the charming Borgo Pio, head for Castel Sant'Angelo. Better yet, visit the Castel during lunch hour, because tourist-choked tours there are no fun. Alternatively, save the fortress for those hours before dinner when most tourists are headed back to their hotels.

Not in his wildest dreams could **Nero** have imagined that the site of his diabolical circus—where St. Peter was martyred and where many Christians were burned as human torches for night games—would become the epicenter of Christianity. The bodies of these martyrs were conveniently buried in an adjacent cemetery, part of which is directly under **ST. PETER'S BASILICA**. St. Peter's grave became a shrine until Constantine, the emperor who converted to Christianity, built a church over it in the 4th century. After being replaced by today's amazing edifice, Constantine's original church is now known as "Old St. Peter's."

St. Peter's must surely hold the record for longest remaining work in progress. "Old St. Peter's" was already 1,000 years old by the time Pope Julius II destroyed it to begin the gigantic new basilica over its ruins in 1506. New St. Peter's was finally completed in 1626, though work inside would continue many more years.

Bernini was chief architect of St. Peter's during nearly 50 years of the basilica's evolution, having worked for at least five popes. His work here is extensive, although he is most well-known for the Colonnade outside and the giant *Baldacchino* (say *"bal-da-keen-o"*) inside, built with bronze stripped from the Pantheon. The dollhouse-like tabernacle in the SS. Sacramento Chapel, though not often mentioned among his greatest works, is certainly among the treasures here.

Seeing St. Peter's through Bernini's perspective is a good key to understanding the trove of artistic treasures. His recurring theme is of stepping from darkness into the light (awareness of God). We are going to be constantly drawn to the divine light, which you will see at the far end of the church in the form of a golden ray. As you stand in the church's piazza, you will see how Bernini's columns seem to march toward the church. Your eyes will follow them, stopping briefly at the center obelisk, but continuing up those massive steps that lead right through the front doors.

Once inside, the eye continues to be pulled through the church; first toward Bernini's great bronze *Baldacchino* (altar canopy), then further still to a celestial glow at the far end of the church. This is the *Cathedra Petri*, an amber-colored window that produces a golden aura as sunlight streams through. It's meant to symbolize the radiant light of the Holy Spirit.

Bernini was only one of an all-star lineup of brilliant artists lending their talents to the Vatican. **Michelangelo**, for instance, was responsible for the basilica's Greek cross plan (later altered by Maderno). You can best appreciate the master's architectural work on the western exterior, but you can only gain access to it by taking the garden tour (off-limits if you don't), which takes you past a nice portion, but kids *hate* the garden tour. Michelangelo also created the famous *Pietà* sculpture of Mary with Christ's crucified body across her lap, in the first chapel. He even designed the colorful uniforms of the Swiss Guards who stand at the Vatican City gates. Michelangelo took over construction of the church when he was 72 years old; it is commonly believed that **Pope Paul III Farnese** never paid him for his work.

What kids will most appreciate Michelangelo for, however, is **ST. PETER'S DOME.** Climbing it is an unforgettable experience. From ground level to lantern, it's a challenging 537 steps! But, you can cheat by taking the elevator half the way. A refreshing terrace, the thrill of victory, and fantastic views reward those who make it to the top—no building in Rome's center is higher.

Whether you choose to climb the dome or not, do take the elevator to the loggia roof where you will be able to walk around the dome's inner drum, check out its gigantic mosaic letters up close, and look down at the art-struck people below. And you can take a break at the rooftop snack bar or browse the nun-run gift shop before heading down.

For kids, **CASTEL SANT'ANGELO**, the tomb-turned-fortress, is probably the coolest museum in Rome. **Hadrian**, that emperor with

a penchant for the humongous, built this monument in 135 AD as a final resting place for himself, his wife, his adopted son and several more emperors. If you are intrigued by Hadrian's massive sense of scale, you may want to check out the ruins of Hadrian's sprawling suburban villa, where you see even more clearly how the scale of this tomb fits the emperor's grandiose style (see ***Extras outside Rome***).

The tomb went on to play many parts in Rome's checkered past: as a fort, a prison that once held famous artist Benvenuto Cellini, and as a papal palace that also served as fortress for the pope during attacks on the Vatican. Pope Clemente VII put it to this last purpose during the 1527 sack of Rome.

Today, it's a wonderful labyrinth of some 58 rooms. Children can bound up its ramp and ramparts, roam around gorgeous papal apartments and discover old weapons, flags and cannonballs. Soldier lookouts, narrow corridors and sudden terraces appeal to kids while beautiful frescoes, coffered libraries and elegant artifacts satisfy adults. There's even a small-but-mighty museum of military weapons that spans the ages; many of its pikes, armor and uniforms were excavated here. Don't stop until you find yourself on the upper-most roof terrace enjoying glorious views in the company of the bronze angel you've seen from the street.

THE WALKING TOUR

Get an early start: first thing in the morning, make your way to the giant obelisk in Piazza San Pietro.

In the center of the piazza is a pink granite Egyptian obelisk dating from 1835 BC. Caligula brought it to Rome and placed in the Vatican circus then occupying this site. Two powerful fountains flank it.

FIND THE MAGIC CIRCLES

Different disks set into the pavement mean different things.

White circles with dark granite centers say "*centro del colonnato.*" Find one between each fountain and the obelisk, stand on it and look at the colonnade. You'll experience the illusion that there is only one row of columns in the colonnade instead of four.

All-white disks are etched with blowing winds. These represent the points of a compass. They encircle the obelisk.

A somber red porphyry disk on the right side of the Piazza near the security checkpoint. This marks the place where Pope John Paul II was shot on May 13, 1981.

KIDS!

Alexander VII Chigi commissioned **Bernini** to create the **Colonnade** and redesign the square in 1656. Its 284 travertine Doric columns are topped by 140 colossal statues of saints and martyrs—an impressive lineup intended to awe. Bernini explained that his design formed the arms of Mother Church, embracing pilgrims as they come forward.

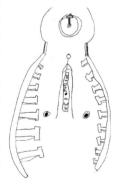

The 10 year old who drew this picture was asked to draw St. Peter's—but where's the church? You can see how strongly the columns, obelisk and the optical-illusion disks impress a young tourist.

All visitors funnel through the security checkpoint on the right, regardless of whether you want to go inside the church or climb the dome. We're going to start with the dome, so after the checkpoint, follow the crowds up to the basilica, then veer right rather than entering it.

But first, do pause on the **portico.** Of the five sets of gigantic bronze doors, the set farthest to the right is the *porta santa,* or sacred door, opened only by the pope during proclaimed Holy Years (usually every 25 years). The pope opens the door with a special silver hammer and chisel. Then, pilgrims are allowed to walk through it as they pray.

The **central bronze doors** were created by Florentine artist Antonio Filarete for Old St. Peter's (the Constantinian basilica) and are in the same style of Ghiberti's Baptistry doors in Florence. They took a dozen years to craft, from 1433-1445. The bottom panels depict St. Peter being crucified upside down and Nero seated on his throne.

CAN YOU FIND WHO MADE THE DOORS?
Filarete seems to have had a sense of humor. Look on the bottom interior of the door to find a carving of the artist (he's the one on the right) and his caravan of workers. It's a signature of sorts.

The doors farthest to the left are modern, designed in 1947 by Giacomo Manzu, who won a coveted competition to create them. They are called the *Doors of Death* because the creepy subject matter depicts the final hours of Christ and the Virgin.

FIND YOUR MUMMY
Early Christians prepared bodies for burial by wrapping them in bandages, mummy-style, as one of the panels near the bottom of the Doors of Death shows.

Two equestrian statues flank the portico like bookends. On the far right as you face the church is Bernini's smashing **Constantine** at the moment of conversion. The lackluster one on the left is of **Charlemagne,** who was crowned emperor here on Christmas Day in 800 AD.

Now look above the central doors. Barely visible in the recess is what remains of Giotto's famous 1298 mosaic, the ***Navicella,*** another of the precious few items retained from Old St. Peter's. In it, Christ walks on water. Note the boat in the background, often a symbol for the Church. You will see boat symbolism throughout your Roman journeys. Recall, for instance, Bernini's boat fountain in the Piazza di Spagna as an allegory for the Church, always under attack but never quite sinking. When you stand on the terrace of the dome's lantern, you'll be reminded again; it feels like you're standing on a ship's deck. The flooring undulates to the tread of many tourists as you survey Christendom from the magnificent crow's nest.

To climb **the dome**, do not enter the church. Go instead to the courtyard on the right, past Bernini's equestrian statue of Constantine, to find the dome entrance and elevator/ticket booth. When you've finished your tour of the dome, you'll be deposited inside the church for the next leg of our journey.

Purchase tickets with elevator access (recommended) to the *Loggia.* Great photo ops await you: phenomenal views of the piazza below, close-ups of the giant statues that line the rooftop, and views of the dome itself. Ring around the interior of the mosaic-lined dome and check out those giant black letters on a golden background—they're nearly 7 feet tall! What's more, two roof buildings, formerly for workers, house a snack bar and an eclectic gift shop.

The able and willing can climb the dome's 323 steps to the lantern terrace from here. Notice how the stairs become smaller and shorter, turning to iron, and then to tiny marble ones. Windows provide welcome light and air. Remember to look for them when you're back in the piazza to see how high you've gone. The slanted ceiling becomes more and more severe, following the shape of the dome, making you feel a bit like Alice in Wonderland, growing much too big for the space. Even the handrails morph from substantial brass to a final rustic rope-pull hanging from the ceiling. Shake off the urge to quit because you won't have to come down this way; there's a nice, wide path down the central staircase. The feeling of finally bursting forth onto the terrace is a triumph you'll treasure.

Once on the rooftop lookout, spy into the pope's gardens behind the church.

CAN YOU FIND THESE VATICAN VISTAS?
1. The pope's crest made out of topiary and flowers
2. The Vatican's train station, radio station and heliport
3. A **Borghese** eagle perched over a fountain
4. A copy of the Grotto of Lourdes, a gift from French Catholics

See if you can spot the fortified **Pope's Wall**. The covered passageway connected the church with Castel Sant'Angelo so the pope could make a run for the fortress when Rome fell under attack. Imagine running its length, arrows and cannon shot flying about.

Upon descending the dome, you'll be inside the church. Begin your tour of **St. Peter's** by the central front doors. Yes, it's daunting. There are probably more masterpieces per square foot here than anywhere else in Italy, save the Vatican museums, of course! But fear not —we'll hit all the high-lights from door to apse, working up the right side.

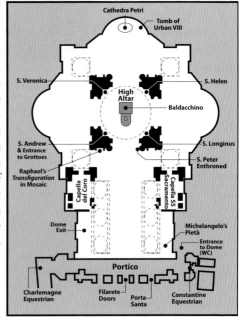

CAN YOU FIND THE EMPEROR'S CIRCLE?

Look at the floor just inside the central doors. See the giant inlaid porphyry circle? It's from Old St. Peter's. Holy Roman Emperors would kneel on it in order to be crowned, Charlemagne being the first to bow on Christmas Day, 800 AD. You saw him on his horse on the portico.

Here in the nave, note the pillars. **Bernini** designed much of the decoration for **Innocent X Pamphilj**. You'll see plenty of Pamphilj doves here and, of course, you'll find plenty of **Barberini** bees. Only a heavenly exterminator could eliminate Urban's swarm.

WOULD THE WORLD'S BIGGEST CATHEDRALS FIT IN HERE?

As you proceed, be on the lookout for stars running down the floor of the central nave. They are footprints of a sort, marking where giants like St. Paul's in London and the Cathedral of Seville would reach if they were put inside St. Peter's. Each bears a cathedral's name and indicates its length.

Michelangelo's *Pietà* masterpiece, which he carved at the age of 24, occupies the first chapel on the right aisle. The only known sculpture to bear his signature, it was enclosed in glass in 1972 after suffering some damage due to a vandal attack.

FIND MICHELANGELO'S SIGNATURE

Standing near the *Pietà* one afternoon, Michelangelo overheard a group speculating on who might have carved this beauty. They mentioned several respected artists, but never considered him. Miffed, the young and unproven artist snuck back that night and carved his name on the statue as proof positive. (Look on the ribbon falling off the Virgin's left shoulder.)

Continue up the right aisle to the **Chapel of SS. Sacramento,** a chapel reserved for prayer, so silence is mandatory. Duck in to catch Bernini's stunning tabernacle, or *ciborium*, his last commission for St. Peter's. Like an ornate dollhouse, the *ciborium* is a miniature version of Bramante's life-sized *tempietto* at San Pietro in Montorio on the Janiculum Hill. The details are exquisite: a dome with mini-papal keys, tiny Corinthian pilasters, columns of lapis lazuli and bronze, a gilded statue of Christ to top the whole thing off. As usual, Borromini is not far behind his rival;

he made the pretty iron entry gate to the chapel. Flanking the right altar are spiraled marble columns original to Old St. Peter's—said to be the inspiration behind Bernini's twisting *Baldacchino* columns. A few more of them can be found around the church. And don't miss the **Barberini** bees hovering over both of the chapel's side doors.

Now, make a beeline for Bernini's gigantic *Baldacchino* in the center of the church, directly under Michelangelo's dome. Look up. You will see the magnificent, mosaic-covered cupola whose seven-foot-tall letters seem dwarfed from this perspective. At ground level, four niches surround you, each of which contains a giant (three times life-size) statue of a saint.

> The word *baldachin*, originally from Baghdad, means a silk cloth. Silk canopies marked sacred spots and distinguished important people. Many Middle Age and Renaissance paintings place monarchs and religious figures under baldachins. This bronze canopy covers the papal altar and, directly below it, St. Peter's grave.

Part architecture, part sculpture, the *Baldacchino* has been called both brilliant and monstrous! Mark Twain likened it to a four-poster bed. It is certainly gigantic, but the cavernous church, two football fields long, makes the canopy's proportions deceiving. Who would guess that the height of the *Baldacchino* is a whopping eight stories (29 meters), the same height as the **Palazzo Farnese**? It took Bernini nine years to complete.

ARE THE COLUMNS IDENTICAL?

How are the twisting columns of the *Baldacchino* different from each other? Some run clockwise; others, counter-clockwise. (If you noticed this feature unprompted, start applying to schools of architecture!)

BORN TO BUILD

*O*ne day, as many great artists worked on St. Peter's, Pietro Bernini, young Gian Lorenzo in his arms, surveyed the site with master painter Annibale Carracci. Carracci mused that the great church would need an even greater master to create something worthy for the central crossing. He pointed to infant Gian Lorenzo and said, "Maybe he will do it."

The *Baldacchino* marks the center of the church, but more importantly, it calls attention to the core of the Christian faith. St. Peter was, of course, the Church's first pope; that Christ handed him the keys to heaven supported each succeeding pope's authority. Note how the columns are entwined with laurel, a symbol of martyrdom to remind you of Christ's sacrifice.

The baldachin was completed a week after **Galileo** was jailed in 1633.

SEARCH THE BALDACCHINO

1. **A cross on a globe** (Look up for this representation of Christ's victory.)
2. **Four angels** (They seem to be holding the columns up with garlands.)
3. **Barberini bees** (They buzz about the columns, and four enormous bronze ones hover by the globe.)
4. **Barberini suns** (The same ones decorating the boat fountain at the Spanish Steps top each column.)
5. **8 Barberini papal escutcheons** (Look at the column bases.)

Four saints surround the *Baldacchino*, one in each niche of the dome's supporting piers: S. Helen, S. Longinus, S. Andrew and S. Veronica. They attest to Christ's sacrifice on the cross. Constantine's mother, St. Helen, brought back a piece of the cross to Rome; Roman Centurion St. Longinus converted when he poked Jesus (on the cross) with his lance; Peter's brother, St. Andrew, was crucified on an X-shaped cross; and St. Veronica retained a sacred image of Christ's face on her veil after she used it to wipe his brow as he carried his own cross. Frescoes on the niches above each statue depict the events that made them saints, and relics from each are stored in the niche above Veronica, with the exception of poor Andrew's head, which was given to the Greek Orthodox Church. They are displayed once a year on the fifth Sunday of Lent. Altogether, we are meant to see tangible, highly glorified proof of Christ's passion and the authority vested in the pope on earth.

Look closely at Longinus, the Roman Centurion. He is velvety and more impressive than the other figures. Artists who carved the other statues made them to look smooth at close viewing. But, because they are displayed up and away from the viewer, the smooth features are lost, and the sculptures lose definition. **Bernini** knew this would happen, so he devised a rake tool that made grooves in the marble, helping the statue catch and reflect light. You can see the grooves up close, but stand further away and the effect is clearly better than the others.

WHY IS ST. PETER'S TOE SO SHINY?

Tradition dictates that each passerby touch or kiss the first pope's foot for good graces. You'll find **St. Peter**, sitting under his own special canopy, around the corner from St. Longinus.

Cut directly across the church to find the famous mosaic version of Raphael's *Transfiguration* behind the pier of St. Andrew. The *Transfiguration* was Raphael's last painting, though he didn't have time to complete it, and it was placed over his deathbed. The original painting is inside the Vatican museums.

Now you're ready for the apse, whose altar is dedicated to St. Peter's Chair, or *Cathedra Petri*.

Bernini began the fabulous alabaster window above the gilded throne of St. Peter in 1657 and completed it in 1666. You have arrived here as he intended, moving from the dark recesses of the Basilica into the light of the Holy Spirit as cast by heavenly rays of warm, yellow-orange light from the amber-colored oval window. The sculpture group below the window—two angels holding the keys to heaven and a papal tiara, and a golden chair floating at the center—projects the idea that the popes hold the keys to the heavenly kingdom. The chair supposedly belonged to St. Peter, but it dates from the 9th century.

Two papal tombs flank the Cathedra Petri window. To the right is **Urban VIII Barberini**, and to the left is **Paul III Farnese**. It should come as no surprise that these VIPs hold court on this highly prestigious turf.

Urban VIII commissioned Bernini to design his glorious tomb. Note its intriguing, even cheeky, winged angel of death riding the sarcophagus like a sleigh. Death is writing Urban's name on his scroll, checking him off his list of new souls. *Divine Love*, the statue holding an infant on the left side of the tomb, was originally nude, but modest Pope Innocent XI had it covered.

WHAT HAPPENED TO URBAN'S CREST?

You would think that those Barberini bees would be here on this tomb of all places. But Bernini liked to expand the norms. Here, he has set the heraldic bees free. They make a trail from the sarcophagus to Urban.

At this point you've seen the highlights of St. Peter's and can make for the doors. If you're looking for more, however—about a half hour more—take the stairs by St. Andrew to the grottoes below, called the **Tombe dei Papi**. They occupy the space between the basilica above them and the foundation of the older basilica below them. Some 20 popes (including John Paul II), a couple of queens and an emperor are buried here, making it currently rather crowded. Save the grottoes for last, as they will lead you outside the church.

The grottoes are not to be confused with the **Scavi** tour, which is an underground exploration of the ancient cemetery beneath even this space. When people rave about "the tour under St. Peter's," it is most assuredly the awesome Scavi (Italian for "excavations") they are referring to. The Scavi tour, described in **What's Around?**, requires advance reservations.

CAN YOU FIND THE BONES OF ST. PETER?

Hint: You're getting close when you find a tomb flanked by angels and lions. The remains are behind glass and not really visible. Still, it's the highlight of the otherwise somber grottoes.

When you emerge from the grottoes, you will be outside the church in the right courtyard where you began your tour of the dome.

At this point, satisfy everyone's need for a break—and sustenance, especially after all that climbing—en route to Castel Sant'Angelo. The large Via della Conciliazione, that killjoy of a road made by Mussolini, will lead you there directly but, instead, take this opportunity to enjoy a bit of the *Borgo,* the medieval papal zone.

From Piazza San Pietro, slip through Bernini's colonnade about midway on the left (back to the church), and you'll find yourselves looking at the fortified papal wall that connects St. Peter's with Castel Sant'Angelo. Go one block past it and turn on Borgo Pio, a medieval, mostly pedestrian-only street packed with restaurants, cafés, bakeries and pizza places (see *What's Around?*). The idea is to stop for an early lunch or sizable snack, then hit Castel Sant'Angelo while everyone else breaks for lunch. If it's a bit too early for lunch, try the diner-like Bar Conciliazione at the east end with its family-sized booths and air-conditioning.

When you're refreshed, continue to **Castel Sant'Angelo** and enter from the front, by the bridge.

HEAVENLY HEALING

*A*ccording to legend, St. Gregory the Great prayed continually for Rome's relief from the ravages of a plague. Finally, as he crossed the bridge built by **Hadrian**, he looked up and saw an angel sheathing his sword atop the tomb. The plague ended, and Gregory was convinced that his vision was of St. Michael defeating the dreaded disease. Ever since, the tomb has been called the Castle of the Angel.

Immediately before the ticket (*biglietti*) office, look for large models depicting the castle during different stages of its long career. Papal crest enthusiasts, accustomed to seeing their targets from a distance, are in for a real treat because hunks of old crests are displayed here at nose level. A Medici, a **Barberini** and a **Farnese** are among those shields available for up-close inspection. Their heraldic family symbols (balls, bees, irises) can be found throughout the papal apartments.

Recall how **Urban VIII Barberini** stripped the bronze off the Pantheon; some of it, as you now know, was used for St. Peter's *Baldacchino*, but the bulk went into fortifying this castle with a phalanx of cannon. Urban also had one of the interior staircases built.

CAN YOU FIND A SURPRISE ATTACK?

As you climb the interior ramp, look up. Those hatches you see were once used to dispense hot oil on advancing enemies.

The castle unfolds in many directions at the end of the ramp, making navigating by a set plan pretty tough. Here are some highlights to look for as you work your way up and through the fortress:

On the first floor at the end of the ramp, you'll encounter a long staircase. Halfway up, there's a bridge right in the center of the building, below which the urns containing the Imperial ashes were kept.

The stairs up to the second floor place you in a courtyard with the angel statue that originally topped the building. At the far end of this courtyard, **Leo X Medici** contributed several additions, including a **chapel** whose façade was the work of **Michelangelo.** Leo liked to host theatrical performances here.

On the second floor, the **Sala dell'Apollo** with its delicate frescoes is one of the most popular and easy-to-find rooms. But look for the teensy tiny **bathroom of Clement VII,** too. It's up a set of narrow stairs off the courtyard, where you'll also find a spitting fountain, a stack of cannonballs and an old well.

On the third floor, check out the enormous wall paintings in the **Room of Paul III Farnese.** One side shows **Hadrian**, the castle's pagan owner; the other shows the angel, representing its Christian stewards. Find the circular **treasure room of Paul III** in the very center, and take the steps at the right up to the topmost terrace with the angel.

WHOSE CREST IS UNDER THE BRONZE ANGEL?

It's a mystery, all right. With the identifying elements long scratched away, you'll just have to guess.

Once outside, try to locate the *passetto,* that escape route built in 1277 so that popes under siege at the basilica could reach Hadrian's handy fortress of a tomb. Unstable structural conditions keep it closed, but a portion of the 600-meter long passage is open on very limited occasions. Jump at the chance for a peek if it's offered.

As you descend, you may wish to stop at the third-floor terrace bar for refreshments served with a terrific view of Michelangelo's dome. Ask your climbers to try to figure out which of the now-speck-sized windows in the dome they may have passed along the way. Other easily identifiable monuments: the Vittoriano and the Pantheon.

To exit and return to the city center, cross the **Bridge of Angels** (*Ponte S. Angelo*) directly in front of Castel Sant'Angelo. When **Hadrian** built the bridge, then called the *Pons Aelius,* in 134 AD, it was the widest of its kind in the ancient world. It has been rebuilt since then, but the three central arches under the middle are part of the original structure**.**

Bernini added the gorgeous, flowing baroque angels that crown the span, turning what had been a place of public executions into a bridge of reflection and beauty. Two of these were carved by Bernini personally, but were so prized that only copies were installed; his originals are in San Andrea delle Fratte, across from Bernini's home between the Trevi and the Spanish Steps, in a church designed by Borromini.

KIDS! WHAT IS EACH ANGEL HOLDING?

Those who know their Bible can try to identify the objects, each a symbol of the passion of Christ. Pilgrims en route to St. Peter's were meant to see these angels and reflect on Christ's trial and crucifixion..

WHAT'S AROUND?

BORGO PIO is a picturesque, mostly pedestrian-only street a block north of the papal corridor (and Via della Conciliazione) that runs between Castel Sant'Angelo and St. Peter's Basilica.

Cheap souvenirs and religious articles abound at the west end (near St. Peter's), where on nearby Via Mascherino you'll also find stores that sell knit hats and scarves sporting soccer team logos, printed silk scarves and towels, and bins of €2 souvenirs perfect for

kids with pint-sized budgets. The better cafes, bakeries, and restaurants are located on the east end (near Castel Sant'Angelo). Quick stops:

- **Antico Forno,** *No. 7/8,* sells bread, pizza and sweets.
- **Hedera Gelato,** *No. 179,* at the charming Papal fountain.
- **Bar Latteria**, *No. 48,* is a simple and warm coffee bar.
- **Pane e Pizza,** *No. 159,* sells fresh-from-the oven goodies.

CASTEL SANT'ANGELO PARK consists of the shady grounds that surround the fortress.

This almost-secret park makes an especially pleasant place to recharge after the Vatican. Largely un-crowded, it offers grassy lawns, slides and playground equipment for younger children and a lot of open areas for pickup games of soccer. Consider bringing picnic fixings from nearby Borgo Pio and kick back.

VIA DEI CORONARI. Beautiful antique shops and plenty of food options line this lovely street that runs between Castel Sant'Angelo and Piazza Navona.

When walking between the two, sneak in some shopping. Kids may not notice!

Once the primary access route for St. Peter's, the street was named for the rosary makers who sold their beads to pilgrims en route to the church.

Now it's lined with eclectic antique shops that sell everything from marble statuary to antique telescopes. Among the kid-pleasing restaurants, don't miss a spectacular gelato from Gelateria del Teatro *(No. 66)*.

PAPAL AUDIENCES *are held every Wednesday in St. Peter's Square at 10:30am. They are free, though a ticket is required.* In the event of inclement weather, they move into the Papal Audience Hall, left of the church. In summer, audiences may be held at Castel Gandolfo, the pope's summer palace outside Rome. For tickets in advance, w*rite to: Prefettura della Casa Pontificia, Città del Vaticano, 00120 Roma; Tel. 06-698-83017; or Fax 06-698-85863. Alternatively, you may order tickets from Santa Susanna, the American church in Rome. Web site: santasusanna.org.*

In Rome, the easy way to get tickets is from the Swiss Guard at the Bronze Doors *(Portone di Bronzo)* located at the colonnade right of the church just beyond the security check. Swiss guards speak English and a host of other languages with proficiency. Anyone may show up after 3pm the night *before* an audience to request as many tickets as desired. There are usually a fair number available, though no guarantees. If you are unable to procure tickets, go anyway and watch the action from beyond the square's limits. No tickets are required for the pope's blessing at noon on Sundays.

THE SCAVI TOUR explores the ancient necropolis excavations under St. Peter's. *From 9am-5pm. Closed Sundays. Tel. 06-698-85318, fax 06-698-73017. Tickets € 13 adults. Advance booking is essential. E-mail: scavi@fsp.va (recommended mode) or Fax: (39) 06-698-73017. Info online: Vatican.va. Children under 15 are not permitted to enter. Proper attire required.*

This 60-minute tour takes you underneath St. Peter's to tour the "City of the Dead," a 2,000-year-old necropolis that includes the grave of St. Peter and an excavated portion of completely intact, tomb-lined streets. The tour is truly spectacular and requires booking well in advance.

To make arrangements or to meet your guide, having already purchased tickets, go to the Scavi office through the **Arch of the Bells** (left of the Basilica). The Swiss Guards at the Arch will direct you.

SISTINE CHAPEL
& VATICAN MUSEUMS

THE VATICAN MUSEUMS, *Viale Vaticano, 13. It pays to check the ever-changing schedule ahead of time, but as a rule hours are weekdays, 9am-6pm. Closed Sundays and all major public and religious holidays, except 9am-2pm the last Sunday of each month, for which admission is waived (and the crowds increase commensurately). Last entry is always 1.5 hours before closing. Tel. 06-698-83332. Tickets € 16 adults, € 8 ages 6-18, ages 5 and under, free. Be prepared to pay by cash at the Vatican ticketbooths. Additional € 7 per audio guide rental. Two-hour guided tours are available for € 31 adults, € 25 kids. To schedule a tour, fax reservation requests to 39-06-6987-3250, or e-mail: visiteguidatesingoli.musei@scv.va. Web site: mv.vatican.va. SKIP THE LINE: You may book a specific entry time at biglietteriamusei.vatican.va for an additional € 4 per person.*

Timing and Tips

The best way to avoid notoriously long entry lines is to visit the museums in the afternoon on weekdays or during the papal audience, held every Wednesday morning. With many pilgrims gathered in St. Peter's piazza for the audience, you'll have significantly less of the massive crowds to deal with. I call this play "papal interference." Or, for a fee, buy "skip the line" tickets directly from the Vatican.

Once inside the Vatican museums, you will be tempted, given the high admission prices and the sheer breadth, to spend more than two hours. Don't. This tour narrows the gargantuan task of touring the papal treasures to its two prime jewels: the **Sistine Chapel** and the **Raphael Rooms** (*stanze*) in the Vatican palace. If you put on blinders getting to these popular rooms, your entire tour, entrance to exit, will be around one hour to an hour and a half. And that's at a very child-friendly pace.

Note: Exiting the Sistine Chapel through its door marked "Groups" is a shortcut, leaving you on the right side of St. Peter's Basilica rather than walking back to the exit/entrance, though it is reserved for official groups. Further, audio tours must be returned to the rental desk

Those who want to see more after visiting the Sistine should stop at the nice cafeteria for a break and then head to the museum side of the Vatican collections. The famous *Apollo Belvedere* and accompanying sculptures in the courtyard of the **Museo Pio Clementino** and the kid-pleasing **Egyptian Museum** are right next to each other and worth the easy effort.

If you've got two mornings to spend at the Vatican, so much the better to avoid overload. See the Palace (the Sistine and Raphael rooms) one day and the museums on the other. A final tip: bring binoculars—the Sistine ceiling is a long way up!

Bathrooms are located on the far-left side of the entrance hall (downstairs), near the cafeteria, near the post office at the exit, near the Raphael Rooms, and near the coffee bar by the Sistine Chapel. Most women's bathrooms have baby-changing facilities.

THE SISTINE CHAPEL and the collections of the **VATICAN MUSEUMS** contain some of the most famous and prized art in the world. It takes a staff of over 300 people to maintain and preserve the massive amount of works commissioned and collected by pontiffs over the years. Though the Sistine Chapel was begun by Sixtus IV della

Rovere (1471-1484), we really have his nephew, Julius II della Rovere (1503-1513) to thank for starting the Vatican collection with a few choice sculptures placed in the Octagonal Courtyard. Julius II also had the foresight to hire **Michelangelo** to fresco the Sistine ceiling, Bramante to head up construction on the new St. Peter's Basilica and Raphael to paint his private living quarters. (No fan of the former Borgia pope, Julius refused to live in Alexander VI's equally gorgeous apartments.)

Of course, many other popes had a hand at the stewardship of this masterpiece-packed palace. Pope Nicholas V (1447-1455) commissioned Fra Angelico to fresco his Capella Niccolina; Leo X, a Medici pope, completed the Raphael Rooms; and two popes from the 18th century are responsible for opening the museums to the public: Clement XIV (1769-1774) and Pius VI (1775-1799). The Pio Clementino Museum is named after them.

THE WALKING TOUR

From the entrance atrium, everyone is directed up the *Scala Simonetti* escalator. When you arrive at the second-floor atrium, you'll find yourselves looking at an info desk where you can rent audio guides. Around the left, with signs that direct you to the Sistine, is a great long hall. The first part is dedicated to candelabra, sculpture and art; the second, to maps (*Galleria delle Carte Geografiche*).

This hallway will take you to our two main targets, the **Raphael Rooms** and the **Sistine Chapel**, both clearly marked. The Vatican often changes routes and accessibility, so be prepared to go with the flow and keep your eye out for signs.

MAKE THE ULTIMATE CREST TALLY

They're all here: dragons, stars, balls, writing tablets, trees, eagles, fleurs-de-lis, mountains, arms, lions and bees, to name a few. Make a graph or chart by drawing or writing down each symbol you find. Add a tally mark for each one you spot.

Crests and family symbols were powerful advertising tools, kind of a brand name—like today's Nike swoosh—plastered everywhere. When we see corporate symbols at ball games, in magazines and on athletes, we get the impression of a powerful-yet-benevolent company. Papal symbols on public works sent the same message. Count up each symbol, and decide which pope had the most PR power.

You can match the symbols you've found to their respective popes with the help of a book or poster, usually available in the museum bookstores.

Fly past the following few rooms, until you get to the **Stanze di Raffaello,** arguably Raphael's greatest works. He was just 26 years old when he conceived of the designs; painting them was a 22-year-long endeavor, finished by his students (from 1498-1520). The **Stanza della Segnature** is most revered. The current Vatican route threads visitors through all four rooms in the following order.

The first and largest room is the **Sala d. Constantino.** As the name implies, all the frescoes have to do with Emperor Constantine, who made Christianity the official religion of Rome, thereby ending the persecutions in the 4th century. It has an especially action-packed rendition of the Battle of the Milvian Bridge, before which Constantine had a vision of the Cross that prompted his conversion. He saw a cross in the sky and was told that he would win the battle under that sign. Another wall here shows him donating Rome to the Church (an act called the Donation of Constantine, one that gave the pope control over the Papal States). The ceiling is a blatant show of Christianity triumphing over the pagan city. Though Raphael designed the room, acolytes of the artist did the actual painting.

Cut over to the adjoining room for a peek into the often-missed **Capella Niccolina,** the private chapel of Nicholas V. The tiny room is one of the oldest parts of the palace, and it features beautiful, delicate frescoes by master Fra Angelico (ca. 1440).

Move to the third room, the **Stanza della Segnature.** The most famous fresco in this room is *School of Athens,* whose central figures are Plato and Aristotle. Each figure points to his area of philosophy—Plato, heavenward; Aristotle, earthbound. They are surrounded by power-thinkers like Pythagoras, Socrates and Euclid.

WHERE'S MICHELANGELO?

KIDS!

After Raphael snuck into the Sistine Chapel to see what **Michelangelo** was up to, he was so struck by what he had seen that he painted Michelangelo into his school of great thinkers. Michelangelo was a brooding fellow, always lost in his work. Which of these thinkers could he be? (Hint: He's not in a Greek toga, nor is he barefoot.)

Michelangelo is accurately portrayed in Renaissance clothing, leaning against a block of marble. Raphael also put himself in the painting. He's staring at you from the extreme right, wearing a black beret. Maybe that's why we always associate great artists with berets.

Look above the opening left of the *School of Athens* for more portraits (in groups ascending and descending a hill). You'll see blind Homer bracketed by poets Dante and Virgil among them. All three crafted celebrated epic poems that continue to be studied today—Homer composed the *Odyssey* and the *Iliad* in the 8th century BC, Virgil wrote the *Aeneid* around 30 BC, and Dante wrote the *Divine Comedy* around 1300 AD. On the wall opposite the *School of Athens*, find Dante again in the crowd on the right (with laurel leaves on his head).

The final Raphael Room, the **Stanza dell'Incendio,** is dedicated to popes named Leo (since the 800s). Most of the depictions, however, relate in some way to **Leo X Medici**.

WHERE'S AENEAS?

Bernini's sculpture of Aeneas at the Borghese Gallery shows Virgil's hero fleeing from burning Troy and carrying his father and his household gods to a new land. Strangely enough, Aeneas shows up in this room, too, which is named after a fire. See if you can find him in the illustration of *Fire in the Borgo*, meant to recall a conflagration in the 800s that was extinguished when the pope made the sign of the cross from the *loggia* of St. Peter's.

The chapel of **Urban VIII** immediately follows, after which you have the option of going downstairs to the Borgia apartments (the ones Julius II shunned) or directly to the Sistine Chapel (left). We, too, are going to take a pass on Alexander VI's living quarters.

The Sistine Chapel (1473-81) is a visual feast, one whose centerpiece is unquestionably Michelangelo's, but whose other fare is no less dazzling, served up by the likes of Pinturicchio, Botticelli, Perugino and Ghirlandaio. Find Perugino's wall fresco of ***Christ Delivering the Keys of the Kingdom to Saint Peter*** (1481-1483) and share this appreciation of it with kids:

WHERE DO THE LINES MEET?

Notice how the lines of the fresco end just beyond the central door of the church. This is an example of a new science in painting at the time called "point of convergence," a way to show perspective and depth.

IS THAT ST. PETER'S?

The church in the painting looks different from St. Peter's because Perugino was using another idea new to his time: a *central plan church*, built more like a round temple than a nave-and-transept crossed church.

KIDS!

PAGAN ARCHES IN A CHRISTIAN PAINTING?

The arches are modeled on the Arch of Constantine, which you probably saw in the Forum. By integrating them into Christian art, Perugino managed to suggest that Christianity was in continuity with paganism, a natural evolution of early beliefs. Thus, ancient Rome and modern Rome are in harmony. Look on the wall directly opposite this to see the arch again in Botticelli's *Punishment of Korah*.

DON'T FORGET THE KEYS!

The main subject is Christ giving the keys to St. Peter. Christ is passing on the divine right to mind the store (earth and its inhabitants) when he turns over the keys to Peter, the first pope. All those keys in crests, walls, fountains, paintings and buildings represent this significant moment.

Now behold **Michelangelo's** stupendous ceiling. It took him nearly five years (1508-12) to complete the fresco—some 5,800 square feet of it— *alone*, according to art historians. In fact, Michelangelo is said to have jibed Raphael for relying on a large group of assistants to get his work done.

The whole thing began when Julius II, on the prodding of Bramante, hired Michelangelo to fresco only the sides and lunettes of the chapel ceiling. It was a curious choice: Michelangelo was a sculptor, and Julius had many of Italy's greatest fresco painters already on the payroll. Michelangelo might well have taken a pass; but not only did he accept the job, he also insisted on painting the entire ceiling, calling the pope's plan a "poor thing."

ARTISTIC ENVY

Sources say Bramante, the pope's master architect, was jealous of Michelangelo and afraid his talents would pale in comparison. Also, Bramante wanted to promote his young friend Raphael, who had recently arrived in Rome from Urbino, Bramante's hometown. The architect persuaded Pope Julius that Michelangelo should work on the ceiling, certain that the great artist would flee the monumental task or stay and fail; either way, Michelangelo would be out of the way. Bramante underestimated his rival in both respects.

Nine ceiling panels depict the Bible's Genesis story, beginning with *God's Separation of Light and Dark.*

FIND THE FLOOD

The depiction of the flood is the first panel Michelangelo painted. He wasn't sure he could paint well enough so, rather than start at the panel right in front of the entrance, he picked this inconspicuous spot. He repainted a portion of it, so the oldest figures on the ceiling are the group huddling under a tent on the rock at the left. Impossible to imagine his insecurity when looking at the stupendous outcome!

Look at the third panel, just below *The Flood*. The two nude figures wrestling with a garland may look familiar. Recall that Michelangelo oversaw transporting the sensational, ancient *Laocoön* sculpture from the farm field where it was discovered to the Vatican holdings (which we'll see further along). The poses of these two figures are clearly inspired by the struggling figures of that pagan grouping.

Beginning with *The Creation of Adam,* notice that all the subsequent panels have much larger figures and very few characters. That's because Michelangelo took down the scaffolding at the halfway mark, saw his work from the ground and decided that the images were too small.

FIND THE MOON

In the last three panels nearest the altar wall, God is separating darkness from light; creating the sun, moon and planets; and separating sky from water. Notice Michelangelo's new foreshortening technique: the figures seem to be flying in space, unlike the flat depictions of his earlier panels. But who's that giving you "the moon"?

Now compare the first panel by the entrance with the last panel by the altar. The first is cluttered with lots of scenery and small figures; the last is striking for its simplicity: no scenery and one huge figure—God. You can see how much the artist grew and evolved during the process.

ARTISTIC ADMIRATION

R aphael was so affected by Michelangelo's frescoes that he reworked his own painting of Isaiah in S. Agostino. Vasari believes Michelangelo's influence on Raphael is most obvious in the painting of sibyls and prophets in Santa Maria della Pace; he hailed them as Raphael's greatest achievement. See for yourself. Both churches are near Piazza Navona.

Twenty years after finishing the torturous ceiling, Michelangelo was made to return to the scene of his backbreaking work when **Pope Paul III Farnese** tapped him for the job of painting the altar fresco, *The Last Judgment*. By then a consummate multitasker, the aged master painted the altar while also reorganizing the Campidoglio Piazza (from 1534-41). Even as an old man, however, Michelangelo infused his work with a passion and daring that caused controversy for years. The naked figures and the powerful, beardless Christ earned the appreciation of art lovers like **Farnese** while it earned only disdain from some later pontiffs, who wanted the fresco white-washed!

The fresco is enormous, so zero in on these items.

FIND ST. BARTHOLOMEW

This saint was skinned alive. See if you can find him in *The Last Judgment*. (Hint: He's the one holding his own skin.) Many experts think the face in the folds of his skin is Michelangelo's self-portrait.

Can you find St. Peter and his keys?

How about a soul who is being pulled up by rosary beads?

If your group is spent, exit the door on the right marked "Groups Only" (with backs to the altar), which will leave you at St. Peter's—and allow you to skip its entry line! Otherwise, take the door on the left and make your way down the impossibly long **Gallery of the Library** to the **Egyptian Museum** and the **Pio-Clementino Museum**.

Look in the library for the rotating display of Vatican correspondence. You may find a copy of the document written by Abraham Lincoln, or the letter from Galileo asking his friend, **Cardinal Barberini**, to allow him to serve his sentence under house arrest rather than in prison (see **Villa Medici**).

Currently, it is possible to take a right at the end of the library gallery and an immediate left up a short flight of stairs to the **Egyptian Museum,** which will be on the right. Though, for a quick refueling, you may want to pause first at the Vatican cafeteria just below this area.

The **EGYPTIAN MUSEUM** really appeals to kids. One of mine wanted his room painted just like its midnight blue walls with stars on the ceiling. The exotic, half-human, half-animal Egyptian gods and the ultra-cool sphinx never fail to grab a child's imagination. These statues, some of which date to 1300 BC, are among the oldest in the world. There are loads of artifacts such as rings, bowls, jewelry, papyrus and—best of all—real mummies.

When exiting the Egyptian Museum, do NOT go right to the Chiaramonti or the Braccio Nuovo. Go left, to the **Pio-Clementino** and head directly to these two important areas:

In the **courtyard** find the *Apollo Belvedere,* a 2nd-century Roman copy of a 4th-century BC Greek original of Apollo with his arrows slung on his back. It was found in the 15th century. You will also see the haunting *Laocoön* group, unearthed near **Nero's** Golden House in 1506; recall that **Michelangelo's** was inspired by it. The *Laocoön* (say "*lay-ock-oo-whan*") is a 1st-century marble by Agesander of Rhodes, probably based on a 2nd-century BC Greek original. Both the Apollo and the Laocoön are two of the most famous antiquities from the classical world, and both were installed here by Pope Julius II della Rovere. Many works of classical art had perished over time; some had not been seen for centuries, even in Ancient Roman times. They were known of only from the detailed accounts left by Pliny.

Finding these ancient Greek sculptures was a big deal for those Renaissance artists first exposed to them. Giorgio Vasari, art historian and student of Michelangelo, explained how this exposure accelerated the evolution of Renaissance style, as a leap from stiff, dry renderings to softer, more lifelike art. Michelangelo's style change, in particular, can be seen in his *Moses* statue in S. Pietro in Vincoli.

BEWARE OF GREEKS BEARING GIFTS

*V*irgil's Aeneid *tells how the Trojan priest Laocoön warned Troy against accepting the Greeks' gift, a giant horse with soldiers stashed inside. But the gods punish Laocoön for his interference, sending serpents to crush and drag him and his sons into the underworld. Troy accepts the horse, and the Greeks sneak out of it at night to vanquish Troy from within the city ramparts. This battle was the catalyst for Greek hero Aeneas to flee fallen Troy and seek his destiny in Italy, which is how the Romans connected themselves to the respected early Greek civilization and to the gods. Rome's founder, Romulus, and his twin, Remus, were descendants of Aeneas.*

Upon exiting the Vatican Museums, I'd call it a day—at least so far as museum touring goes.

WHAT'S AROUND?

VIA COLA DI RIENZO, *runs west from the Vatican to the Tiber.*
This is a where most Romans go for everything from clothing to
vegetables. It lacks the panache (and high prices) of areas like the
Spanish Steps, but if you wonder where the average Giuseppe goes for
his threads, this is it. For sustenance along the way, **Franchi,** No. 200,
is Rome's best deli while its neighbhor, **Castroni**, No. 196, is known for
hard-to-find international foodstuffs. This is where American ex-pats go
for such exotic foods as Aunt Jemima pancake mix.

PIAZZA RISORGIMENTO, *sits where the Vatican wall meets Via Cola
di Rienzo.* The medieval tangle of streets between this piazza, the Vatican
and Castel S. Angelo makes up the colorful zone known as the **Borgo.**
The large square accommodates many bus lines and a collection of
white-tented market stalls selling books, low-end jewelry, scarves,
t-shirts and other novelty items at fair prices.

LET'S EAT!

Eating well around the Vatican can be a challenge. Going on a full
stomach helps, and cold drink (*bibete*) carts are stationed in front of the
piazzas for desperate travelers. Your best bet for good food and a nice
selection is to head to **Borgo Pio**, one of the streets that connect the
Vatican with Castel Sant'Angelo.

CAFFÈ MELONI, Via Corso Vittorio Emanuele II, 298/300. A classic,
working Roman café at the north end of the Corso Vittorio, Meloni
runs at a hum. Efficient barristas serve up some of the city's best coffees.

Breakfast is an olfactory experience with the bewitching smells of fresh brewed coffee and piping hot *cornetti*.

TRATTORIA DINO, Via Tacito, 80. The locals flock to this place for a nice lunch or dinner, near Piazza Cavour. Moderate.

BAR CONCILIAZIONE, Via Borgo Pio, 162. This diner-like bar offers family-friendly casual dining around the Vatican. Though a little overpriced, it's perfect for a quick lunch of sandwiches, salads, pastas and desserts. There's also a coffee bar for drinks only.

IL PAPALINO, Via Borgo Pio, 172. Lunch and dinner. The wide menu, wood-fired pizza and terrific homemade pastas make this restaurant one of the best of the Borgo. Moderate.

HEDERA, Via Borgo Pio, 179, is a fresh, modern shop serving gelato, granite, and sorbet from its charming location next to an old papal fountain.

L'INSALATA RICCA, Piazza Risorgimento 4-5. Creative salads share the menu with a large selection of antipasti, pasta, light fare, and pizza at this inexpensive chain trattoria.

TAVERNA ANGELICA, Piazza Amerigo Capponi, 6. Mediterranean fare well-prepared in a reasonable restaurant. Open for lunch on Sundays; otherwise, dinner only. Moderate.

OLD BRIDGE, Via Bastioni dei Michelangelo, 5. A teeny but popular gelato shop near the Borgo Pio and the Vatican, at the south end of Via Leone IV.

PIAZZA DELL'UNITÀ, Via Cola di Rienzo. Housed in a fantastic 1928 neoclassical-style building a block long, this vast covered market will amaze you with its contents—part bazaar, part market. It's a great place to find everything from fruit and cheese to knife sharpeners and locksmiths. The sharp observer will notice SPQR engraved above the massive entrance arch.

TRE PUPAZZI, Via Borgo Pio, 183. Closed Sundays. Traditional Italian fare is served at this restaurant that's proved reliable over the years. It's especially charming in the evening when you can choose to dine al fresco. Moderate.

PART FIVE

DAY TRIPS AND MORE

These aren't must-sees on a first—and perhaps only—visit to the Eternal City, but they are the best outings with children if you have time enough for additional sightseeing.

EXTRAS IN ROME

BARBERINI NATIONAL GALLERY OF CLASSICAL ART (*Galleria Nazionale d'Arte Antica*), *Via delle Quattro Fontane, 13. Open Tues.-Sun., 8:30am-7pm. Closed Mondays, Jan. 1, & Dec. 25. Tel. 06-328-10. Web site: galleriaborghese.it. Tickets € 7. Tickets online: ticketeria. it (booking fee applies).* With kids, it's best to skip the offered tour of the 18th-century private apartments of Cornelia Costanza Barberini.

The Italian state bought **Urban VIII's** family palace in 1947, and the National Gallery has been exquisitely situated within ever since. Barberini's Baroque tour-de-force was the largest palace ever built for a pontiff. The Quirinal Palace, once the papal summer residence, is but a few blocks away. With an astounding collection of **Caravaggio,** Fra Angelico, Filippo Lippi, Perugino, Bronzino, **Bernini,** Guercino, Poussin, Annibale Carracci and Raphael (his well-known portrait *La Fornarina*, "The Baker's Daughter," with Raphael's name tied around her arm, is here), the gallery will require an hour or more for art lovers. Since a restoration is currently underway, many works of art have been moved or put into storage, but the most significant ones are displayed on a scheduled rotation.

Maderno, **Bernini,** Bronzino and Borromini designed the elegant palace and façade, a testament to the artistic eye of Urban VIII. Luxurious and grand, every level has remarkable details in the floors, ceilings and stairways. Kids can seek out countless marble, stone, glass and iron **Barberini** bees and suns that are embedded in window façades, iron grates (above the first gallery entrance), columns and frescoes.

Pietro da Cortona's awesome ceiling fresco, *Triumph of the Divine Providence*, celebrates the papacy of Urban VIII, applauding the wisdom of Divine Providence, which brought ancient Rome through the age of the emperors to the glorious age of the Barberini (papacy). Another highlight is an all-white portrait of Beatrice Cenci by **Guido Reni.** The simplicity of a beautiful girl in a white turban is a pleasant contrast to the over-the-top pomp of the ceiling frescoes.

THE CENCI

*T*wenty-two-year-old Beatrice Cenci, along with her brother and *stepmother, was executed in 1599 for having plotted the murder of her abusive father. To her death (a beheading in front of Castel Sant'Angelo), she refused to confess. Percy Bysshe Shelley was so taken by this painting that he wrote a play about the scandalous family entitled* The Cenci.

Borromini's third-floor oval windows and his breathtaking helical staircase are architectural gems and another chance at comparison with Bernini, who designed the rectangular staircase opposite it. Look for Bernini paintings, too: find the one of Urban VIII and another of *David*, with an enormous Goliath head.

Caravaggio has several paintings here, but kids will appreciate the gory, cartoon-like *Judith and Holofernes* (Giuditta e Oloferne). It depicts the Bible story of Judith killing her assailant. Note the expression on her maid's face. Those murderously-red, bulging eyes show she's up to the task of a slaying.

BATHS OF CARACALLA, *Viale delle Terme di Caracalla, 52. Open daily, 9am until 1 hour before sunset. Closed Jan. 1, May 1, and Dec. 25.* Tel. 06-399-67700. Tick- ets €7. Audio guide, €5. Online tickets: coop- culture.it. South of the Colosseum, the Baths are best arrived at by cab. Go early or just before closing to avoid blazing heat in high summer.

The massive ruins of Rome's most luxurious public baths are a great place for kids to romp and explore. Begun by Septimius Severus in 206

AD and opened by his son Caracalla a decade later, the Baths accommodated an estimated 1,600 people.

Imperial Rome had hundreds and hundreds of baths, from simple to grandiose in style. The rich and the poor worked out in the same gymnasiums; took hot, warm and cold baths; and met friends and influenced people. Caracalla's state-of-the-art facility had changing rooms, banquet halls, even libraries. There's far more open space here than in the Forum, and kids will delight in discovering bits of old tile flooring and such. The two gigantic tubs-turned-fountains in Piazza Farnese came from here. It's also where writers like Keats and Shelley used to hang out, composing amid the romantic, overgrown ruins.

BIKING THE APPIA ANTICA, *Parco Regionale dell'Appia Antica, Visitors Center, Via Appia Antica, 42, with bike hire at No. 58. Open 9:30am-5:30pm (4:30 in winter). Tel. 06-513-5316. €3 per hour or €15 per day. Web site: parcoappiaantica.it. Recommended only for teenagers on Sundays when the street is closed to traffic except for buses and taxis. Ask for a lock and make sure you get a park brochure.*

Rent bikes at the Visitors Center and struggle up this ancient military street as far as you can. (Even the very fit may need to walk the bikes at times.) The mostly downhill return, however, is a blast. Do remember to stay in control and check speed.

Bike the peaceful Roman countryside, pausing to inspect monuments like old Roman road markers and tombs (all are open Sundays). The park brochure explains the area, its monuments and the adjoining Caffarella Valley Park, which has been undergoing restoration to make its oak-and-elm strewn valley a desirable destination. Keep in mind that the Caffarella paths take you off the Appia Antica. A café (Bar Appia Antica, No. 175) and a few restaurants provide sustenance.

THE CANNON ON THE JANICULUM HILL, *(Gianicolo), Piazza Garibaldi.*

The park-like setting of Rome's highest hill offers a relaxing and beautiful respite from which you can see the majestic Garibaldi Statue and enjoy a wide-angle vista of Rome. What makes it of special interest to kids is the booming howitzer.

The lovely and important Janiculum is a long, thin hill south of the Vatican and west of the Tiber where Martial and Caesar once kept villas with expansive gardens. In fact, when Cleopatra visited as Caesar's guest, she probably stayed here, most likely near the Villa Farnesina by the Tiber banks. The Janiculum continues to provide a verdant setting as home to Rome's spectacular Botanical Gardens below the Piazza Garibaldi.

Each day a little before noon, Italian soldiers wheel out a howitzer from beneath the Garibaldi Statue and fire a blank shot over Rome to mark the *mezzogiorno* (noon). Those in the know line the terrace, which has breathtaking views of Rome, to watch the splendid military affair. The heart-stopping boom is thrilling. Protect developing ears by keeping small children well away from the cannon's backfiring blast, but older kids can stand on the terrace directly behind the cannon for fullest, hair-blowing effect.

WHAT A BLAST!

For centuries, Romans marked time by ringing church bells, but with so many churches, each keeping its own time, a better system was needed. In 1846 Pius IX began shooting a noon-marking cannon from the terrace of Castel Sant'Angelo over the rooftops of Rome—with real cannonballs! Eventually, the cannon was moved to the Janiculum, and blanks replaced balls.

With refreshments from the carts in leafy Piazza Garibaldi, consider walking a portion of the Passeggiata Gianicolo, the long, garden-like street that leads up to the square from Via Garibaldi on the south side and continues downhill on the north. Two north-side highlights include a monument to Garibaldi's wife, Anita—looking very much like Annie Oakley—and an elegant lighthouse, a gift from Italians living in Argentina. Look closely at Anita in her gun-slinging, multitasking pose: as her horse rears up, she balances a baby on her lap and hoists a gun in the air—the ultimate power mom.

CATACOMBS OF S. CALLISTO *(S. Callixtus), Via Appia Antica, 110. Open 9am-noon and 2:00-5pm. Closed Wednesdays and the month of February. Tel. 06-513-0151. Tickets, € 8 adults. Ages 14 and under, € 5, ages 5 and under, free.*

Labyrinthine catacombs—spooky, dark, and underground—make some kids uncomfortable, but the creepiness factor is soon tempered by the presence of colorful graffiti, a lack of any dead bodies (all have been removed) and captivating stories told by well-versed staff guides. Touring here is an especially welcome respite from late-summer heat because the air below is always clean and cool.

The catacombs were the burial places of Rome's 1st and 2nd-century Christians. Early Christian symbols, fragments of text, and wall pictures are intriguing and fun to figure out. Images such as an anchor were a way for persecuted Christians, unable to show any signs of their faith, to disguise a cross. A lamb or dove signified Christ and peace. What about all the fish you see? The letters of the Greek word for fish—IXΘYE—are an anagram of the first letters from each word in the phrase "Jesus Christ, Son of God, Savior."

San Callisto, the first, largest and hence most-famous Roman catacomb, is sacred for Catholics because it contained two crypts in which five popes were interred between 230 and 283 AD. It also held the body of St. Cecilia, a patron saint of music.

Among the martyred popes buried here was St. Eusebius (309 AD), who held office for only four months before dying under the Emperor Maxentius. On the back of the large marble monument dedicated to him, you'll see, in an ironic twist of fate, that the marble was once a sign for Maxentius. One side, that is, was devoted to the persecutor, and the other to the persecuted.

The crypt of St. Cecilia is striking for its haunting statue, a copy of an original by Maderno, which has been removed to S. Cecilia in Trastevere. The sculpture marks the place where her body was found and recreates the position it was found in, including a cloth that covered her partially-severed head. Her hand positions show signs of her faith: three fingers on one hand represent the Holy Trinity (Father, Son and Holy Spirit) of the Catholic faith while the other holds up one finger, representing belief in only one God.

Cecilia was martyred in 230 AD with an attempted beheading. She clung to life for three days, singing softy in her final hours...for hours, and hours.

CATACOMBS OF PRISCILLA, *Via Salaria, 430. Open 8:30am-noon and 2:30-5pm. Closed Mondays. Tel. 06-862-06272. Tickets € 8 adults. Ages 7-14, € 5, ages 6 and under, free. Web site: catacombepriscilla.com.*

This is an equally fascinating, but more intimate, catacomb than S. Callisto. It's also less crowded. It claims the oldest known fresco image of the Madonna. The catacombs of Priscilla were a donation consisting of the saint's private home and land, so some of these chambers connect to what was once a great Roman villa. Wide aisles, colorful frescoes and more headroom make an otherwise-shadowy business comfortable for squeamish kids or claustrophobic adults.

GALLERIA DORIA PAMPHILJ, *Via del Corso, 305. Open 9am-7pm. Closed Jan. 1, Easter, and Dec. 25. Tel. 06-679-7323. Tickets € 11. Ages 6-26, € 7.50. Web site: dopart.it/roma.*

Note: From the exit on Piazza Collegio Romano, go right and take little Via Lata to get back to the Corso. You can pay a visit to *Il Facchino* (the porter), a fountain depicting a man holding a water barrel from which you can drink. He was the 15th-century head of the Porters' Guild who bottled Roman water and took it to markets, and he is another of Rome's "talking statues."

Once at the gallery, distract kids with scavenger hunts for relics, original servant uniforms and mythological ceiling frescoes. The notable art collection includes a rare double portrait by **Raphael** and Annibale **Carracci's** *Flight into Egypt*, a landmark in the world of landscape definition. The jewel of this Galleria, packed with masterpieces by Tintoretto, Tiziano, Parmigianino, Raphael, **Bernini,** Correggio, Reni and **Caravaggio**, is the extraordinary portrait of the Pamphilj pope **Innocent X** by Diego Velazquez. The family felt the portrait was so powerful that it made any other great painting hanging near it appear mediocre. So, in 1927, they moved it to its own room along with a bust of Innocent crafted by Bernini.

The two portraits of Innocent display very different sides of the same man. Velazquez' painting showed a stern, commanding man with a red face, in a red chair, with a red hat and cloak, in a red room. Everyone thought the pope would be enraged, but he simply remarked that it looked too much like him. Compare it to Bernini's noble bust of the same man, and note the artist's whimsical details. For instance, he carved creases into the pope's frock, or *mozzetta,* so it looks as though it was folded too long or was improperly pressed. And notice, too, that one of the buttons is only half-buttoned, a very human mistake for such a powerful man. Either the pope really looked that way or Bernini had a great sense of humor.

Caravaggio dominates the 1600s room with two, spectacular, side-by-side paintings: *Rest During the Flight into Egypt* and the *Penitent Magdalene.* Caravaggio used the same model for both paintings and even posed them alike, so the face of the saintly Madonna looks just like the sinful Magdalene. What do you think he was trying to imply?

The Galleria offers a charming little café with coffee, tea, sandwiches and other *spuntini* (snacks), where soft drinks are served on silvered coasters. From inside the main entrance, the door to the café is on the left, just before the stairs.

THE JEWISH GHETTO *is on the left bank of the river, roughly bordered by Via Arenula, Via Botteghe Oscure, and the Theater of Marcellus.*

During the period of Jewish containment (begun in 1555 by Pope Paul IV and abolished in 1870), the ghetto was entirely surrounded by

walls. Three gates allowed Jews out in the morning and closed again at dusk. Today, it's a quiet and elegant neighborhood with a gorgeous **Synagogue**, a fitting symbol of the strength of Rome's Jewish community. In addition to the synagogue and its museum, look for the quaint "turtle fountain" in Piazza Mattei, shops and restaurants along historic Via di Portico di Ottavia, and remnants of the portico itself in the shadow of the Theater of Marcellus. Many of the zone's bakeries and restaurants specialize in old Roman-Jewish cuisine, and I urge you to try mouth-watering specialties like crispy fried artichokes (*carciofi Giudia*). See **Where to Eat** listings for details on Gigetto, Piperno, Pompiere and Sora Lella, to name a few.

Nearby Ponte Fabricio was called the Bridge of Jews (Ponte dei Giudie) because it joined Tiberina Island to the Jewish Ghetto. Pair them for efficient exploration.

KNIGHTS OF MALTA KEYHOLE, *Piazza dei Cavalieri di Malta at the far end of Via di Santa Sabina on the Aventine Hill.* Take a cab here if walking uphill is too tiring for young children. Otherwise, from V. S. Maria in Cosmedin (at Piazza Bocca d. Verità), hike up the secret, cobbled, footpath, Clivo Rocca di Savella, and continue right along V. Santa Sabina.

The Aventine is the southernmost hill of Rome's original seven, rising from the valley of the Circus Maximus. The star attraction is the view through the **Keyhole of the Knights of Malta,** but the hill is also home to an enchanting suburban district of rose-clad villas and orange-tree-dotted parks.

People come by the busload to the villa of the Grand Master of the Knights of Malta because it has a view across three countries: the Order of Malta (one of the smallest independent states in the world), Italy, and the Vatican, the smallest of city-states. When you peer through the ornate keyhole, you'll see St. Peter's dome beautifully framed by the immaculate Maltese gardens. Take a photo through the keyhole, rubbed worn by scads of peeping Toms, and a second one a half-inch away. Compare results later.

Also on Via di Santa Sabina is **Parco Savello,** a great place to unwind and enjoy its fabulous Roman skyline while children climb the park's historic orange trees, planted in 1932 to commemorate the first Spanish orange tree brought to this very spot by St. Dominic in 1220.

Next door, the lovely church of **Santa Sabina** (422) is a great example of early Christian architecture and is often outfitted for summer weddings. Inside, the biggest draw is the 5th-century set of main doors that retain a few original cypress panels depicting biblical scenes. Look for the ***black stone*** on a pedestal in the right aisle. Satan supposedly threw it at St. Dominic to distract him from his prayers.

MUSEO DELLA CIVILTA ROMANA *(Museum of Roman Civilization), Piazza G. Agnelli, 10 (in the Roman suburb of EUR). Tues.-Sat., 9am-2pm; Sun., 9am-1:30pm. Tel. 060608. Strollers permitted.*

The star of the show here is the enormous model (1:250 scale) of 4th-century Imperial Rome that you will have no doubt seen on posters all over the city. You can survey Constantine's Rome from above the model, which takes up an entire room. Other models in this splendid museum recreate major monuments at their apex. Display rooms are arranged according to emperors and their respective periods. Don't miss the upclose plaster casts of the topmost panels from Trajan's column.

MUSEO DELLA MURA *(Museum of the Walls), Via di Porta San Sabastiano, 18. Open Tues.-Sun., 9am-2pm. Closed Mondays. Tel. 06-704-75284. Tickets € 5. Ages 6 and under, free. Online tickets: ticketclic.it.* Ring the bell for entrance. For this awkward location, have a cab wait or pair it with a tour of the nearby Appia Antica. The terrace walk often closes for safety concerns, so call ahead to avoid disappointment.

This sleeper of a museum is inside the best-preserved gate of the city's ancient Aurelian Wall, Emperor Aurelian's defensive wall built from 270 AD around all seven hills and a portion of the Janiculum. Called the Porta San Sebastiano, it served as entry gate to the city from Via Appia Antica. The arch in front of it is the Arco di Druso, a remnant of an ancient aqueduct.

What makes this miniscule museum is the chance to traverse the open ramparts. From your post on the huge fortified walls, you can still see a fair amount of countryside as it may have looked to ancient country bumpkins who would have crossed miles of barren scrub and wasteland before coming upon the enclosed city. What might a humble traveler, fresh from his hometown hut, imagine was inside such imposing walls? Back inside, the brief displays consist of a few vestibule-sized rooms, the terrace overlook and some **Medici** and **Barberini** crests.

ORTO BOTANICO *(The Botanic Gardens), Largo Cristina di Svezia, 24. Open Tues.-Sat., 9:30am-6:30pm. Closed Sundays and August. Tel. 06-499-17107. Tickets €8. Ages 6-11, €4, ages 5 and under, free.* The gardens are walking distance from the Ponte Sisto and across the street from Villa Farnesina. With young travelers, take a cab to save their energy for exploration inside.

Rome's botanical gardens are conveniently located in Trastevere, taking up a wedge of land from the bottom of the Janiculum to the top, just under the Garibaldi Statue. They offer a restorative, green break in a day filled with museums, churches and city traffic. The freedom to run and the mystery each path offers delights children while parents love the beauty and rarity of some key species.

Aim for the Japanese Gardens at the top, where a pagoda completes the Far East effect. On the way up, you'll pass enchanting bamboo stands, one of the widest collections of palm trees anywhere, and a lovely central fountain. There's even a scented garden planted especially for the blind.

S. MARIA IN ARACOELI *(say air-a-chelly), Piazza Aracoeli on the Capitoline Hill. Open 9am-12:30pm and 3:30-6:30pm, until 5:30pm in winter.*

Romans are supreme architectural palimpsests, always laying down new architecture atop ancient structures and incorporating traces of the old into the new. This 7th-century Christian church dedicated to the Mother of Christ is built over a pagan temple to the mother of the gods, Juno Moneta. It is made up of old temple columns as well as new materials. A sacred altar within depicts a vision Augustus had of a Virgin and child when the Tiburtine Sibyl, one of the ten female prophets of the ancient world, prophesied to him of the coming of a king who would reign for centuries. The altar marks the spot where he had his vision.

CAN YOU FIND AN EMPEROR, A POPE AND A FARMER?

1. The sacred marble altar with carvings of Augustus and the holy family. (Look left of the main altar, below a freestanding chapel dedicated to St. Helena).

2. An Imperial Column. (On the left, third from the main doors.) It says, *"a cubiculo Augustorum,"* and the column in front has a 15th-century Madonna and child fresco.

3. Lacoohontis. The discoverer of the Laocoön statue, **a farmer,** Felice de Fredis, is commemorated on a wall-plaque near St. Helena. His name is in the first line, and "Lacoohontis" is written in the third.

4. Barberini bees. The spectacular stained glass one above the main doors reminds us that pope **Urban VIII** funded a restoration of this church.

KIDS!

St. Helena was the mother of Constantine, who made Christianity the official religion of Rome. It is fitting that she is honored in this church with both pagan and Christian elements, since she played a significant role in both worlds by being an empress of the old order who searched for pieces of Christ's cross and brought them to Rome. Note the rare porphyry stone on the sarcophagus; porphyry was always used as a mark of distinction. You'll have seen it on the dress of the Capitoline Roma and the columns of the Temple of Romulus in the Forum.

Honor is paid here as well to Felice de Fredis, who found one of the greatest treasures of the ancient world that had been buried under a farm field for centuries: the *Laocoön*, an ancient sculpture grouping of a Trojan priest and his two sons struggling with sea snakes. The twisting bodies and highly defined muscles greatly influenced **Michelangelo** and other artists of the time (see Vatican Museums).

SS. QUATTRO CORONATI, *Via dei Querceti and Via dei Santi Quattro Coronati. Open 9am-noon and 4-6pm. Web site: santiquattrocoronati.org.*
This church, a few blocks from San Clemente, was a fortified abbey in the 4th century. Its belltower—said to be the oldest in Rome—

dates from the 9th century. Go here to find the **Chapel of S. Silvestro,** containing cherished frescoes painted in 1246 that depict scenes from the life of Constantine, the famous ruler who made Christianity the official religion of the empire and ended the persecutions.

This is a choice stop for adults and mature children who will like the secret-agent quality of getting in. Unlock the well-guarded frescoes by locating the convent sign (*Monache*), where you'll find a big barrel and, on the same wall, a small window. When you ring the bell, a nun will open the window. Ask for "San Silvestro," and give her a couple of Euro as a donation. She'll hand you a key, or *chiave* (say "*key-ah-vay*"), and will point to a plain door opposite the window. Unlock the door, give back the key, and the room of frescoes is yours to enjoy.

Inside, see if you can locate these parts of Emperor Constantine's conversion story: stricken with leprosy; being cured by Pope Sylvester I; conferring power on the pope with a tiara. Constantine's conversion allegedly led to his substantial donation of land to the Church, called the "Donation of Constantine." The donation was proved a fabrication in the 15th century, far too late to give back the land!

TRASTEVERE *(literally, "Across the Tiber"), the area west of the Tiber River. We'll focus on the area surrounding the Ponte Sisto and Santa Maria in Trastevere.*

Families who have lived here for many generations are fiercely proud of their *rione*, or district, and many consider themselves distinctly other-than-Roman. The zone has a decidedly more medieval feeling to it than Rome's *centro*. Trastevere's narrow, cobbled, serpentine streets cast a sort of ramshackle charm that can make some visitors uneasy.

Explore the area near the Ponte Sisto and Vicolo del Cinque where you'll find a high concentration of shops, excellent restaurants (see *Where to Eat*), pizza-to-go and a terrific English-language bookstore (**Almost Corner Bookstore** on Via del Moro). Make your way to Santa Maria in Trastevere, one of the oldest major basilicas of Rome, taking in post-card views of laundry-strung streets that send you back a few hundred years with every step. At night, panhandlers and young adults inhabit the main piazzas, but they should not dissuade you from wandering this atmospheric neighborhood.

THE VITTORIO EMANUELE II MONUMENT, *Piazza Venezia. Open 9:30am-6pm; in winter, until 4:30pm. Closed Mondays. Free.* ***Glass Elevator*** *€ 7. Ages 10 and under, € 3.50. Find it on the terrace behind the monument.*

Encourage high-energy kids to climb all 244 steps to the top. The balconies and terraces spilling out along the way beg for exploration. Critics dubbed the massive monument, built in 1911, "the wedding cake," because of its blinding white Brescian marble design, but the scale is about right for an ancient temple. It holds the Tomb of the Unknown Soldier, a fine (free) military museum, several expansive terraces (usually uncrowded), a slick glass elevator ride, and a delightful, little-known café with photo-op views.

The unfortunately-placed Vittoriano is dedicated to Italy's first king after the Unification, which, in brief, united northern and southern Italy by taking over the middle (Rome and the Papal States). Ironically, when this monument to a united Italy was built, along with the Via di Fori Imperiali, it cut the heart of Rome in half by dividing the Roman and Imperial Forums in two. The Sanctuary of the Flags, also called the Altar of the Country *(Altare della Patria)*, on the uppermost terrace, lists cities not yet freed at the time of Italy's liberation.

> The Vittoriano caps the Corso, Rome's most central street. *Corso* means race and, indeed, up until the 18th century, riderless horses were annually raced down this street from Piazza del Popolo at its north end. The horses were stopped in Piazza Venezia by raising large white sheets in front of them. The square is called Piazza Venezia because Pope Paul II, a Venetian, built the first grand Renaissance palace right here (Palazzo Venezia) in 1466 for a commanding view of that cherished event.

Stay to the right to find the café, the *Charlie and the Chocolate Factory* elevators to the panoramic terrace, and the **Museo del Risorgimento** (the 19th-century movement that led to Italy's unification). You'll find swords with Roman symbols on the hilts, some paintings, sculpture, war collectibles, propaganda buttons and hand-made ribbons and pins worn in support of soldiers, along with an impressive display of uniforms and state gifts.

EXTRAS OUTSIDE ROME

OSTIA ANTICA *(4C BC) Viale dei Romagnoli, 717. Open in summer, 8:30am-7:30pm (ticket office closes at 6pm). Closed Mondays. Tel. 06-5635-8001. Tickets €6.50. Scavi Museum open 10am-3pm.*

Twenty minutes by train makes this the closest and easiest day trip from Rome.

Trains depart the Stazione Ostienze every half hour and cost € 1.50 (same ticket for public buses). From the Ostia Antica station, you need only cross a pedestrian bridge and walk about a block to reach the site. The last returning train to Rome departs around 5pm, but check schedules to be sure. Bring plenty of water and snacks just in case the museum's quality cafeteria is closed. Offsite, however, you can easily walk into Ostia Antica's charming town for a meal.

After hectic city touring, unwind in this historic town where mosaics, frescoes, ancient shops, baths, homes, temples, a theater and even the remains of a public lavatory await you. Viewing Ostia Antica is one of the best ways to get an idea of what an ancient Roman city looked like. This one has been in existence as long as Rome has; it was most likely founded by King Ancus Martius in the 6th century BC. As a fortified citadel guarding the mouth of the Tiber, it was an important military and commercial port for Rome until the waters shifted away from its shores. A newer port was built farther up the coast, literally shutting the old town down. Exploring the abandoned city is an experience similar to visiting **Pompeii** or Herculaneum. No one can help peeking around just one more corner in the hopes of finding another fabulously-tiled floor or partially-frescoed wall.

CARPE DIEM!

The oft-repeated phrase means seize the day—a philosophy that's easy to understand when you realize that for most Romans, life was nasty, brutish and short. As Karl Christ points out in *The Romans,* more than 80% of the burial inscriptions at Ostia Antica are for people under the age of 30.

Climb up the stairs of the Terme di Nettuno (Baths of Neptune) on the right side of the main street, *Decumano Massimo,* to survey the whole site and get an upclose view of the Bath's large tile floor depicting Neptune, god of the sea, majestically riding in his watery chariot pulled by four seahorses.

Further on, you'll find the impressive theatre and the Piazzale delle Corporazioni business district. From

the stands of the theatre, you can see the remains of the Temple of Ceres. Walk around the 64-office square where the mosaic inlays of some floors are still intact. The tile floors of each office, or stall, depicted the proprietor's goods or home country (elephants for ivory sellers, for example), so it's fun to guess what was sold or where the goods came from. As is typical of a port town inhabited by foreigners, there's a wide array of symbols from around the world and a variety of religious temples, including a synagogue.

On the left side of the main street, directly across from the theater, you'll find the Horrea dell' Hortensius. The ruined foundation walls of what was once a storage facility have been overgrown by masses of foliage, making it ideal for hide-and-seek or private picnics. (Beware: Bees rule during high summer).

Throngs of freight traffic once crowded the Tiber. Water buffalo harnessed to the freight barges pulled their loads from here to a shipping dock on Tiberina Island. It was a common sight to see long trains of the beasts plodding along the banks of the Tiber.

Continuing down the main road, you will come upon the Capitolium. Walk behind it (on Via Casa di Diana) to find the Thermopolium, a tavern or inn complete with marble countertops, intact flooring and coat hooks for patrons.

Crossing the maze-like city, you'll discover bakeries, cemeteries, homes and warehouse foundations. See if you can find the 2nd-century public bathroom seats.

TIVOLI'S HADRIAN'S VILLA AND THE VILLA D'ESTE.

At half an hour by car, **Tivoli's** two astounding properties, Emperor **Hadrian's** classical villa and a cardinal's Renaissance villa, make delightful additions to a Roman holiday. Each shows elite Roman lifestyles from different eras. They are near each other but not easily within walking distance.

HADRIAN'S VILLA (*Villa Adriana*), *Tivoli. Open daily except holidays, 9am-dusk. Tel. 07-743-82733 or 06-399-67900. Tickets € 8. Audio guides € 5. Online tickets: coopculture.it, service charge is applied. Best reached by cab or private transport. Allow for a minimum of two hours at this phenomenal site. Consider bringing a picnic as the cafeteria is rather light.*

The charm of **Hadrian's** Villa, built in 118 AD, lies in the harmony of the vast natural landscaping around 2nd-century Imperial ruins. Children are in paradise here, running amid the ruins, splashing in fishponds and reflecting pools, and playing games of hide-and-seek amid outdoor sculptures and crumbling, frescoed walls. The look of these wild, overrun ruins is what inspired English Romantics like Keats, Shelley and Byron before Rome's monuments were stripped of their damaging vines and shrubbery. And plenty of Hadrian's Greek-inspired architecture survives. The baths, gardens, pools, library and theater had a remarkably different look from traditional Roman structures. Best of all, it's still possible to find yourselves virtually alone here, enjoying the peace and tranquility of this vast estate while kids bound in and out of ruins, looking for treasures and resident cats.

> *Hadrian was the first emperor to wear a beard. Succeeding emperors always wore one.*

Hadrian's Villa was the largest, richest and most luxurious villa of the Roman Empire. Really more of a small city, it covers some 115 square acres. Current estimations of its original grounds fall somewhere around five times that—

completely in character, given what we know of Hadrian.

The villa and its grounds were so dense with treasures that, even after nearly 2,000 years of plundering, over 300 masterpieces were found on site. Though most of these have been moved to museums around the globe, some are in the Vatican and Capitoline museum collections.

VILLA D'ESTE, *Piazza Trento, 5, Tivoli. Open Tues.-Sun., 8:30am-dusk. Tel. 199-766-166. Tickets € 8. Audio guides €. Web site: villadestetivoli.info. Closed Mondays, Jan. 1, May 1, & Dec. 25.* Allow about an hour and a half to visit not counting the half-hour car trip each way.

In 1550, Cardinal Ippolito II d'Este, a son of the notorious Lucrezia Borgia, transformed this former convent into a fabulous Renaissance villa with a lavish display of Italian-style gardens. D'Este apparently took great delight in the movement of water. More than 500 playful fountains shoot, splash, drip, flow, spray, dribble, cascade and pool on the Cardinal's verdant estate, making it one of the top day trips from Rome.

Though the fountains are the big draw, shady, terraced paths amid garden nymphs and grottoes offer a delightful refuge from the city, and you shouldn't leave without a quick look inside the gorgeous villa with its mannerist frescoes. Kid favorites include the fishponds, the Pegasus, boat fountains, a musical hydraulic water organ and a miniature version of Rome. Many great artists worked on the villa and its gardens, including none other than **Bernini,** who was hired to expand and renovate during the 17th century.

FURTHER AFIELD

POMPEII, *Via Villa dei Misteri, 2, Pompeii, main entrance at Porta Marina. Open in summer, 8:30am-7:30pm (last entrance at 6pm); in winter, 8:30am-5pm (last entrance at 3:30). Closed holidays. Tel. 08-185-75347. Tickets € 11. Audio guides are € 6.50. Guided tours cost an extra € 5 per person and last 1 hour and 40 minutes. Web site: pompeiisites. org.* There are two lines, one for tickets only and a much longer one for tickets/tour. Skip the tours, zip to the ticket-only counter and then rent an audio guide from the central kiosk. Make sure you pick up the excavation map. Painfully slow, guided tours under the hot sun are no fun.

Pompeii is approximately three hours from Rome by car, train (Circumvesuviana train from Naples, Pompeii Scavi stop), or bus. It should be noted that there are several parking lots, but the one closest to the main entrance offers free parking if you eat at its little trattoria.

Though Pompeii is a popular day trip, it is unrealistic to think you'll see everything here in a day, especially with young children who can't handle more than a few hours in the labyrinth of rock and rubble-

strewn streets that provide almost no escape from the summer sun. Consider the far more convenient excavations of Ostia Antica as a great alternative for families who want a similar experience in far less time. However, if a trip to Pompeii is a must for your family, here's how to see the highlights with the needs of a family in mind:

If fascinating Pompeii is considered the king of Roman day trips, the evocative plaster casts of bodies consumed by the catastrophic eruption of Mount Vesuvius, which destroyed the town in 79AD, and the equally striking *Villa dei Misteri* are the top reasons why.

Skip Pompeii's amphitheater at the farthest edge of the grounds, saving loads of time and lots of walking; if you've been to Rome's Colosseum, this is redundant. Instead, begin by exploring the temples and basilica just beyond the Porta Marina entrance. Take a left when you arrive at the **Forum.** It is easily identifiable as a big green patch on the park map.

Proceed to the Granary of the Forum, a long, covered building on its north end, where you'll see a few plaster casts of the fugitives as well as a host of items found in the town. It is certainly more convenient to see these few body casts now than to trek across town to see the larger group in the Garden of the Fugitives.

The focus early in your tour should be the **Villa of the Mysteries** (*Villa dei Misteri*). This major highlight is often missed because tired-out tourists give up. To get there, you must go outside the city gate of Porto Ercolano. At the gate you can view the 3rd-century BC walls of the city. Climb its flight of steps, and walk along the walls like a guard patrolling the city.

Outside the gate, you'll find marks in the tufa walls made by stones shot during a siege on the town by General Silla in 89 BC.

Just like Rome's *Appia Antica*, this outer road was reserved for necropolis tombs, making the walk to Villa of Mysteries an intriguing one.

The Villa is a 2nd-century BC edifice remade several times. Unlike most of Pompeii's structures, this multi-level one still has a roof of sorts, protecting gorgeous wall frescoes. Don't miss the one depicting the marriage ritual. While exploring this empty house's nooks, terraces and crannies, seek out Egyptian motifs, servants' quarters, private rooms and a whimsical grape press with a ram's-head base.

When you're ready, return to town and make your way to other highlights, like the large House of the Faun and the charming House of the Tragic Poet with its famous *Cave Canem*, a "Beware of Dog" sign.

In 73 BC, Spartacus and his band of fellow gladiator-slaves escaped and set up camp on Vesuvius. Spartacus very quickly became a real threat to Rome. So, ruthless General Crassus (of the first Triumvirate—Caesar, Crassus, Pompey) was sent to put him down. Crassus triumphed and then quelled any further thoughts of revolt by lining the road to Rome—the Appian Way—with thousands of crucified rebels.

USEFUL INFORMATION

BOOKS—English Language

Trastevere's **Almost Corner Bookstore** on Via del Moro (No. 45) is steps from the Ponte Sisto (and it's not on a corner). Tel. 06-583-6942. Don't be fooled by its tiny size; books are stashed rafter high, but the tremendous help know where every title is kept. A well-chosen selection of childrens' titles is always present.

Near the Spanish Steps, on Via della Vite (No. 102), is the **Anglo American Book Company**. The roomy interior is stacked with a comprehensive group of titles that includes travel and classics sections and a small selection for children. Tel. 06-679-5222. Web site: *AAB.it.*

Don't miss Caroline Lawrence's series of mysteries set in Ancient Rome (for middle-school readers).

For a huge selection, especially in travel and classics, try **Feltrinelli International,** Via Vittorio Emanuele Orlando, 84, near Piazza della Repubblica. Tel. 06-482-7878.

CINEMA—in English

Going to the movies is a good rainy-day activity in any country. Film houses that show English-language films: Nuovo Olimpia, Via in Lucina, 16; and Multisala Barberini, Piazza Barberini, 24/26 (Web site: *cinemadiroma.it)* for what's showing.

Films playing in their original language have "(v.o.)" after the title. Or look in the Cinema Lingua Originale section for listings of film being shown in their original (often English) language.

COMPUTERS AND INTERNET CAFÉS

These days most hotels and inns have wireless Internet service, making Internet cafés and computer centers less in demand, but there are still plenty where you can surf the net, make phone calls and check e-mail. Attendants show you to a computer, and you pay when you are finished. Among the many restaurants and cafés that let you surf the web, you may find the café at Bramante's Cloister (Santa Maria della Pace), off Piazza Navona to be beautiful and fairly quiet (Via Arco della Pace, 5), while the new Internet café at Tazza D'Oro (Pantheon), provides individual workspaces and legendary coffee (Via dei Pastini, 2). A few others in the center:

INTERNET POINT, Via Corso Vittorio Emanuele II, 129. Conveniently located at the corner of Corso Vittorio and Corso Rinascimente this bright facility is cut above the average dimly lit cave.

MAIL BOXES ETC., Via del Gesù, 91. You can access the Internet, and ship packages home from this shop near the Pantheon.

MAIL

Stamps (*francobolli*) are available at post offices and most *tabacchi* shops (with a "T" on their signs). Popular opinion holds that the Vatican post is faster than the Italian State service, but you may not post Vatican-stamped mail in Italian State boxes (and vice versa).

THE CENTRAL POST OFFICE, Piazza San Silvestro, 19, off the Corso. Open Mon.-Thurs., 9am-noon and 3-6pm; Fri., 9am-noon.

MAIL BOXES, ETC. has many locations in the city, from Via del Gesù (Pantheon) to Via Leonina (Colosseo). See their Web site, mbe.it, for all locations. They can pack and ship most package sizes. Fax, overnight deliveries and other business services also available. Open 9:30am-7pm.

VATICAN POST OFFICE, Piazza San Pietro. Open Mon.-Fri.; 9:30am-7pm; Sat., 8:30am-6pm. Closed Sundays and during papal ceremonies. Another office is inside the Vatican museums.

SHOPS

Two major fashion zones cater to a variety of styles and pocketbooks: **Piazza di Spagna** and **Via del Corso.** Most shops close midday between 1-3:30pm; department stores stay open all day.

The bulk of tourist-choked streets around the Spanish Steps are devoted to luxury institutions: Via Condotti alone plays host to Armani, Cartier, Gucci and Prada. The Corso, running from Piazza del Popolo to Piazza Venezia, has a wider range that appeals to all generations and budgets.

Teens and young adults will find edgy stores on the Corso and along more charming **Via Giubbonari**, just off Campo dei Fiori. Giubbonari's pedestrian-only streets are neatly packed with a wide variety of quality goods and fun merchandise. Trendy, high-end men's stores like Empressa make you feel like you're in SoHo while glitzy bargain shops entice teenage girls. For less atmosphere but moderate prices, walk **Via Nazionale** from Piazza Venezia to Piazza della Repubblica or **Via Cola di Rienzo** from the Vatican to the Tiber.

If you're in need of essentials, Rome's largest department stores are **Coin** at Piazzale Appio and **La Rinascente**, which is located in the beautiful Galleria Sordi, along with several other high-end stores. Find it on Via del Corso, across from Piazza Colonna.

For religious artifacts, you can't do better than to stroll down the old Roman **Borgo Pio,** a colorful, pedestrian-only street from Castel Sant'Angelo to the Vatican. The western end is a hub of religious goods and souvenirs while the remaining five blocks are dotted with restaurants, cafés, markets and small shops.

TRANSPORT

BUSES

Buy bus tickets (*biglietti,* say "bill-yet-ee") at *tabacchi* shops, bars or newsstands and validate them in the machine on the bus. Orange public buses, and the green electric (116 and 117) minibuses that thread through town, use the same tickets and work on an honor system. Currently, a ticket (BIT) costs €1.50 and is good for unlimited rides within 100 minutes from the time it is first stamped; one-day €6 BIG passes expire at midnight; and a three-day pass runs €16.50. Ages 9 and under ride free. Most places that sell tickets also sell bus route maps. The same tickets can be used for the metro; simply validate in station machines before you board.

Expired cards will beep at validation. The fine for riding without a ticket is a minimum €100, payable immediately or at the police station where you will be taken if you do not have cash.

Get to know the green electric minibuses. The 116 serpentines the city center from Piazza Farnese, past the Pantheon and up the Via Veneto to Villa Borghese. The 117 minibus runs in a north-south direction from Piazza del Popolo, down the Corso to the Colosseum and S. John Lateran.

STOP-N-GO BUS TOURS

Archeobus: Valid for 48 hours: € 12 adults. Ages 9 and under, free. Family rate (2 adults + 2 kids aged 10-17), € 40. 9am-10pm daily, every hour on the hour from San Marco on Piazza Venezia.

110 City Tour: Valid for 1 day: € 18 adults, € 15 kids 10-17. Ages 9 and under, free. Runs every 20 minutes from Piazza dei Cinquecento (Termini Station). Purchase tickets on board. Tel. 06-4695-2252. Web site: *trambusopen.com.*

The Archeobus and the 110 City Tour are air-conditioned buses that let you hop on and off when the mood strikes. Archeobus hits major archeological sites like the Via Appia Antica, the Museum of the Walls and Catacombs; the 110 double-deckers make a city loop. A round-trip ride takes about 1 hour and 45 minutes. Regardless of timelines, however, the buses can be far and few between, leaving you to abandon the service once you get off and find yourselves waiting for the next one to show up.

LIMOUSINES

Romeshuttlelimousine.com Tel. 06-619-69084. This company takes groups (up to 14) on day trips to places like Naples, Pompeii and Sorrrento, but they also have reasonable rates between airports and the city center.
Romecabs. Tel. 39-339-352-5028. Web site: *romecabs.com.* Approximately € 45 for 2 in a private limo from FCO airport to the city. Romecabs also offers tours, daytrips, and custom itineraries. English-speaking drivers on request, and online booking is easy.

TAXIS

Taxis are found at marked stands. Alternatively, call **Radio Taxi Service:** 06-3570, 06-4994 or 06-6645. Operators take your address, even a street corner, and send a taxi for a small additional fee. For your safety, enter only official white or yellow taxis with the SPQR symbol and Commune di Roma sign on their license plates. Your taxi should have a meter and a sign on the left back seat door with the license number. Fares between the city center and airports are fixed at € 48 for Fiumicino and € 30 for Ciampino. Other fares vary by time of day, day of the week, location and number of bags, but generally begin at around € 2.80 daytime and € 4.91 at night.

SCOOTERS AND BICYCLES

Rome is not a place to learn how to ride a scooter; the chaotic tangle of one-way streets is overwhelming to newcomers. The scooter-savvy with a valid driver's license, however, will find rental places dotting the city. Expect to pay €50-70 a day, including helmets.

Biking picturesque, cobbled roads is nearly as challenging. It's easy to become separated by crowds. For older kids, the best places to bike are Villa Borghese's vast grounds or Via Appia Antica on Sunday mornings (see *Extras in Rome*).

Rental stands can be found on the Corso, in Borghese Park and at Piazza del Popolo, to name a few. Today, you'll even run across Segway rentals and bike share stands. Other options:

Bici & Baci, Via del Viminale, 5 (near Termini train station). Tel. 06-482-8443. Web site: *bicibaci.com*. Open daily. This is the cream-of-the-crop bike and scooter company, where you can even book a guided tour via vintage scooters or Fiat 500s! Expect to pay €4 per hour/€11 per day.

Collalti Bici, Via del Pellegrino, 82. Tel. 06-688-01084. Open Tues.-Sat., 9am-1pm and 3:30-7:30pm; Sun., 9am-7pm. Closed Mondays. Bicycles only.

On Road, Corso Vittorio Emanuele II, 204 (near Piazza Navona). Tel. 06-688-01966. Open Mon.-Sat., 9am. Closed Sundays. This scooter rental company even offers GPS devices and will deliver to your hotel. Insurance and a tank of gas are included. Their Web site lets you choose your scooter and book online: *scooterhire.it*.

Roma Rent, Via di San Paolo alla Regola, 33 (near Campo de' Fiori). Tel. 380-643-2278. Open daily, 8:30am-7p.m. Includes helmets, locks and a map of Rome. These vintage-looking bikes even offer baby seats and child extension bikes, and they can deliver to your hotel.

Top Bike Rentals and Tours, Via Carlo Botta, 11. Tel. 06-488-2893. Web site: *topbikerental.com*. Open daily. This company has high-quality bikes, including extra seats for young riders, baby seats, helmets, lights, locks, and even a free cycling map and holder. They also offer tours by bike. Find them between the Colosseum and the train station.

WHERE TO STAY

The focus here is on hotels, B&Bs and apartments particularly suitable for families, convenient location and room configurations being more desirable than a host of amenities far from the action. Central (Pantheon, Navona) areas allow families to return to their lodgings throughout the day and put many sights and restaurants within walking distance. In Italy, most hotels offer a variety of discounts dependent on children's ages and will often add an additional bed upon request, for a minimal fee.

Two popular Web sites for accommodations in Rome are *Booking.com* and *Venere.com*. When searching for a hotel, be aware that the rating system in Italy is different from that of the United States. Stars are based on amenities, which can be misleading. Thus a modest hotel with all the right features—a restaurant and fitness room for example—may garner 4 stars, while a gorgeous B&B in a great location may only be given 3. These listings use the American system.

CAMPO DEI FIORI AREA

Four stars

HOSIANUM PALACE, Via dei Polacchi, 23. Tel. 06-697-191. Web site: *hosianum.com*. A 16th-century cardinal's palace on a quiet street near Piazza Venezia has provides a light breakfast (served from its terrace in summer), plasma SAT TVs, Wi-Fi and 4-star decor.

Doubles, triples and a few quads can be assembled with twin beds. The rooms are spacious for families, but the wardrobes are a tight squeeze.

HOTEL LUNETTA, Pza. Paradiso, 68. Tel. 06-683-95056. Web site: *hotellunetta.com*. Newly renovated, Lunetta, has a choice location between Campo dei Fiori and Piazza Navona. Its family suite offers 2 adjoining rooms and 2 baths. Among the usual SAT TV, Wi-Fi, and A/C, you'll find soundproofed windows, a charming rooftop terrace, a modern spa in its ancient basement, and a large breakfast buffet with hot foods.

HOTEL PONTE SISTO, Via dei Pettinari, 64. Tel. 06-686-310. Web site: *hotelpontesisto.it*. Perhaps just shy of a 4-star but every bit of a top 3-star, families flock to the Ponte Sisto for its pleasant interior courtyard, prime location, SAT TV, pay movies and adjoining double rooms (a rarity in Rome). Unite two doubles or a double and a triple or, if your kids are small, take the fourth-floor suite with a private terrace. It has a double bedroom and a living room with a pullout sofa.

Three stars

HOTEL CAMPO DE' FIORI, Via del Biscione, 6. Tel. 06-688-068650. Web site: *hotelcampodefiori.com*. Note that staying this close to the charming square is central and convenient, but it can be loud, especially in summer when populated with barhoppers. That aside, this little jewel offers a terrific terrace, some private terraces, and several nearby apartments, making it very family friendly indeed. Wi-Fi is free, and soundproofed rooms have A/C, a bar, flat screen TVs, and pay-per-view.

HOTEL DELLA TORRE ARGENTINA, Via Corso Vittorio Emanuele II, 102. Tel. 06-683-3886. Web site: *dellatorreargentina.com*. This 18th century palace retains plenty of its charm, like pretty, exposed brick interior arches. Spacious, family-sized, two-bedroom suites can accommodate up to 5 people, and some have terraces. All rooms have A/C, SAT TV, and Wi-Fi. The perfectly central location puts you in walking distance to sights, restaurants, and transportation (there's a bus stop right out front), but it is on a busy street.

RESIDENZA FARNESE, Via del Mascherone, 59. Tel. 06-682-10980. Web site: *residenzafarneseroma.it*. These simple, yet charming (and smallish) rooms are in a very desirable location. Formerly a 14th-century monastery, this well-run hotel has some doubles with a pullout twin, and all rooms come with A/C, SAT TV and Internet. A gorgeous cappuccino and space for kids to play are right outside your door in Piazza Farnese.

Two stars

HOTEL TEATRO DI POMPEO, Largo del Pallaro, 8. Tel. 06-683-00170. Web site: *hotelteatrodipompeo.it*. Now a Hôtel de Charme and reaching for three stars, this well-known hotel has all the basics in super convenient location. The third floor of its annex (on Via Chiavare) has only two rooms, so if you take them both, your family will have a wonderful, economical suite. Rooms have A/C, a fridge, and SAT TV.

Rezidenza Giubbonari

Apartment rentals

RESIDENZA GIUBBONARI, Via dei Giubbonari. Tel. 06-686-4568. Web site: *residenzagiubbonari.com*. If you book early, you might be able to catch one of these moderately priced apartments in a lovely building near colorful Campo dei Fiori. Its pedestrian-only street, lined with fun shops, is a hub of activity by day but quiets down at night. Each apartment sleeps 4-6 people with 2-3 bedrooms, two baths, kitchens, A/C, wireless internet, SAT TV, and its own washer and dryer—a real perk. The top floor apartment has three bedrooms and two terraces.

COLOSSEUM, FORUMS AREA

Five stars

THE INN AT THE ROMAN FORUM, Via degli Ibernesi, 30. Tel. 06-691-90970. Web site: *theinnattheromanforum.com*. This luxury town home is one of the exclusive, Small Hotels of the World collection. The richly dressed Master Garden Suite sleeps five people and comes with a private patio and access to the property's walled roof garden, a real bonus with kids. Many of the rooms have fireplaces and some have sitting areas. The Inn is well appointed: from plasma TVs to I-pod amplifiers. You don't even have to leave the Inn to visit ancient Rome; its basement boasts a 2,000 year-old cryptoporticus from Trajan's era.

HOTEL PALAZZO MANFREDI, Via Labicana, 125. Tel. 06-7759-1380. Web site: *palazzomanfredi.com*. Views of the Colosseum and the Gladiator's barracks (*Ludus Magnus*) from this classically inspired hotel are terrific. The street is busy and a bit far from the center, but transportation is plentiful, and the rooms and terrace are lovely. The fine family rooms have two doubles. Or, choose one of their nearby apartments, which hold up to five guests and share all of the hotel's services, such as daily linen change and 24-hour concierge.

Four stars

HOTEL COSMOPOLITA, Via Santa Eufemia, 5. Tel. 06-99-7071. Web site: *hotelcosmopolita.com*. This pretty hotel at Trajan's Column is very central and only just off larger streets. Family rooms are available on request with discounts for kids under 12 years of age.

Three stars

CAESAR HOUSE RESIDENZE ROMANE, Via Cavour, 310. Tel. 06-679-2674. Web site: *caesarhouse.com*. Close to a 4-star with its elegant rooms, Internet access, A/C, SAT TVs, mini-bars, little gym, and limited room service, this small hotel—six rooms total—may very well be taken up by your entire group. The Colosseo Suite has two bedrooms and two baths, a living room, kitchen ADSL and a view of the ruins.

HOTEL LANCELOT, Via Capo D'Africa, 47. Tel. 06-7045-0615. Web site: *lancelothotel.com*. Affordable, no-frills, family accommodations in quad rooms (sleeps four) with breakfast included near the Colosseum and S. Clemente, but far enough from other sights that you lose the convenience of returning to your rooms easily for breaks. Some rooms have balconies; all have A/C and other niceties.

Bed and Breakfasts

NICOLAS INN, Via Cavour, 295, Scala A, Int. 1. Tel. 06-976-18483. Web site: *nicolasinn.com*. Children under five are not accepted, but families with teens and large groups may find this nicely located B&B an affordable alternative to hotels. The four modest rooms are spare but large (by Italian standards) and have pretty iron beds. All are outfitted with Wi-Fi, TV's, private baths, minibars and king-size beds, some of which can be reconfigured as twins. One room is a triple. What they lack in hotel polish, they make up for in attentiveness. Unlike most B&Bs, which leave you without a staff, the affable English-speaking owners are always available during the day and happy to answer any questions—a real rarity in its class.

PANTHEON, NAVONA AREA

Five stars

GRAND HOTEL DE LA MINERVA, Piazza della Minerva, 69. Tel. 06-695-201. Web site: *grandhoteldelaminerve.com*. The impressive location on a pretty square behind the Pantheon is in walking distance to just about everything. The rich rooms are fairly large (some have balconies), and the service is great. It's expensive, but maybe the mini-gym, 24-hour room service, and striking roof garden will soften the blow. There are some triple rooms on offer. Internet access is available.

Pretty sitting room in one of Albergo del Senato's suites

Four stars

ALBERGO DEL SENATO, Piazza della Rotonda, 73. Tel. 06-678-4343. Web site: *albergodelsenato.it*. This long-established, excellent hotel is long on charm and really caters to families. It's got a great location—a lovely 19th-century building on the Pantheon square. It pays to reserve by phone here, because the various-sized rooms can be selected to best fit your group. Many deliver knockout views of the Pantheon and its bustling piazza. The hotel also offers a mini-apartment and a larger apartment, both good choices for families. Room 602 is a suite that sleeps four, consisting of a bedroom, a living room with a pullout sofa for two and a choice private terrace. The communal terrace faces the Pantheon and has an outdoor bar (5:30-11pm). All rooms have Wi-Fi, A/C, soundproof windows, SAT TV, minibars, hairdryers and an ample include the ample breakfast.

HOTEL NAZIONALE, Piazza Montecitorio, 131. Tel. 06-695-(Web site: *nazionaleroma.it*. In a historic, 18th-century palace that shares a landmark square with the Sundial of Augustus, this grand old hotel is a bit inconsistent, with some rooms that are quite tired, but many are gracious in size and style and, despite the central location, remarkably quiet. Such large and stately hotels like this one are usually located further away from the action, making the Nazionale a rare gem indeed.

Three stars

ALBERGO CESARI, Via dei Pietra, 89a. Tel. 06-674-9701. Web site: *albergocesari.it*. For over two hundred years, this hotel has been serving travelers who want a choice location near the Pantheon without paying too much for the privilege. As a bonus, it offers triple and quad rooms consisting of real twin bed—not sofa beds. All rooms have A/C, Internet, Pay-per-view, and soundproofed windows, which is a good thing since pedestrians, en route between the Trevi and the Pantheon, do file by until late. Some of the rooms overlook the pretty, ancient stock exchange, which shares its piazza. The breakfast is sufficient, and the roof top terrace is a delight.

HOTEL REGNO, Via del Corso, 330. Tel. 06-697-6361. Web site: *hotelregno.com*. Regno has a very central location, but it's on one of Rome's high-traffic streets. Ask for a room off the Corso, and you're set. Many rooms are recently renovated, and all come with A/C, SAT TV, wireless Internet, and minibars. Some rooms have terraces, and the family room sleeps four (but it's small). The lovely breakfast buffet, snack and coffee bars, and room service provide more than most 3-stars.

Bed & Breakfasts

CANALI AI CORONARI, Via dei Tre Archi, 13. Tel. 06-683-09541. Web site: *residenzacanali.com*. This charming 18th-century palace holds court on a quaint pedestrian-only street filled with antiques dealers. Rooms are equipped with A/C, hairdryers, SAT TV, minibars, daily maid service and private baths. The location is central, yet removed on a quiet street. The suite can accommodate up to four people, and top-floor rooms have terraces.

NAVONA GARDEN SUITES, Via del Governo Vecchio, 73. Tel. 06-682-10863. Web site: *navonagardensuites.com*. As the name implies, two of these suites occupy the garden level of what was once the stables for this picture-perfect, 15th century palace. The reasonably-priced rooms are in the back of the property, not on the street, so they are peaceful, yet the shops, stores, and action of the enchanting Navona neighborhood lay just beyond the palace's massive front doors. The "DaVinci" suites share the garden and each sleeps up to four people in king and queen beds; the Raphael suite is off-site and has less charm, so be careful which you book. All suites have mini-bars, A/C, and Internet access.

NAVONA GOVERNO VECCHIO, Via del Governo Vecchio, 118. Tel. 06-454-29400. Web site: *navonagovernovecchio.com*. This pretty medieval palace offers a fairytale setting but with modern conveniences like A/C, mini-bars, and flat screen TVs. The street is one of our favorites: pedestrian only and lined with homey restaurants and charming shops. Book early here, as there are only five rooms total. One room has twin beds, and the quad consists of two double beds. Children under 4 stay free.

Apartment rentals   *Twin Room at Palazzo Olivia*

PALAZZO OLIVIA, Via dei Leutari, 15. Tel. 06-682-16986. Web site: *palazzo-olivia.it*. Renting an apartment in Rome can be a daunting experience. You can rent rooms or apartments in this pretty, historic palace with confidence. Choose from one or two bedrooms, or take one of each on the same floor for a large group. All the essentials are there: A/C, SAT TV, kitchenette. The best part is you'll be steps from Piazza Navona with twice the space of a hotel room—at a fraction of the price.

SPANISH STEPS/TREVI AREA

Five stars

HOTEL DE RUSSIE, Via del Babuino, 9. Tel. 06-328-881. Web site: *hotelderussie.it*. Without question, this is the coolest hotel in the *centro*. The de Russie has it all: glamour, understated style and a lovely spa. Once you hit your gorgeous room, you'll forget all about the sky-high price and the congested di Spagna streets.

Four stars

HOTEL DEI BORGOGNONI, Via del Bufalo, 126. Tel. 06-699-41505. Web site: *hotelborgognoni.com*. Pretty, modern, tranquil and yet right in the thick of it, this hotel is an excellent choice for those wanting to be between the Spanish Steps and the Trevi, but out of the tourist-choked streets surrounding them. The ample and elegant doubles (which can be made triples with an extra bed), room service and bicycles are all family-pleasers.

INN AT THE SPANISH STEPS, Via Condotti, 85. Tel. 06-699-25657. Web site: *atspanishsteps.com*. Sitting squarely in the center of the crowd-packed, high-end shopping zone usually means loud rooms, but this is a tranquil place with an inner courtyard and a garden terrace sporting lemon and olive trees. There are some connecting rooms and family rooms; if you really want to break the bank, the 5-star penthouse suite in their sister building, called The View, sleeps eight. Fabulous.

Three stars

APARTHOTEL CONDOTTI PALACE, Via della Croce, 15. Tel. 06-679-4661. Web site: *condottipalace.com*. (Note: check-in is around the corner in the main Hotel Condotti, Via Mario de Fiori, 37). Condotti Palace is a relatively new addition to the Hotel Condotti Group, and it's the star of the show, with stylish rooms in a lovely palazzo near the Spanish Steps—at reasonable prices! Family rooms have a double bed, either 2 singles or a pull-out sofa, and 1-1/2 baths. Junior suites can also sleep four. A/C, Wi-Fi, SAT TV, mini bars, and a communal roof garden complete the picture.

HOTEL MADRID, Via Mario de'Fiori, 93-95. Tel. 06-699-1510. Web site: *hotelmadridroma.com*. A reasonably-priced, boutique hotel in this swanky zone may seem too good to be true, but the Madrid is a solid choice. Simple, family-friendly suites can accommodate up to five people in two rooms with one bath (shower only). Taking breakfast on the roof top terrace is a treat.

HOTEL SAN CARLO, Via delle Carrozze, 92-93. Tel. 06-678-4548. Web site: *hotelsancarloroma.com*. This little jewel is steps from "The Steps." The unique family quad has a queen bed and a loft with two twins, so it's a little less private than two separated rooms, but still more private than four beds in the same room. The deal-maker is its own private terrace. All rooms have A/C and SAT TV, but there is a jump in style from the standard to the superior rooms. Superior triple and quads are also available; all have free Wi-Fi and some have small private terraces.

Bed and Breakfasts

DOMUS BORGOGNONA, Via Borgognona, 12. Tel. 06-699-22361. Web site: *domusborgognona.com*. This handful of choice and attractive rooms, all on the fourth floor of a well-positioned apartment building. Each room has a different color theme, with rich coordinating fabrics on the walls and draperies, and they are all outfitted with A/C, plasma TVs, and mini bars. The quad is comprised of two bedrooms (one double bed and one set of twins) and one bath (shower only). There is also a small breakfast room.

Apartment rentals and suites

INTERNAZIONALE DOMUS, Piazza di Spagna, 20. Tel. 06-691-90237. Web site: *internazionaledomus.com*. Situated on the 3rd floor of an 18th century palace, these amazing apartments are unique because they are run much like a hotel, offering limited room service, fine linens, daily cleaning on demand, and a front desk (staffed until 10pm). Some rooms have marble fireplaces, terraces, and frescoed ceilings, and many are spacious. By combining two units, you could accommodate as many as ten people.

SUITES ROME, Via della Croce, 67. Tel. 06-678-5749. Web site: *suitesrome.com*. Not a hotel, apartment, nor B&B, lovely Suites Rome is just that: 4 perfect suites. Right in the thick of the Spanish Steps action, two of these charmers sleep four in style. All have SAT TV, Internet, Minibars and A/C. Though no staff are on-site, they assist as you request. Gorgeous.

TRASTEVERE AREA

Three stars

HOTEL SANTA MARIA, Vicolo del Piede, 2. Tel. 06-589-4626. Web site: *htlsantamaria.com*. If the quiet, medieval zone of Trastevere is your cup of tea, then this popular hotel might be the best spot for your family. Very basic but spotless, charming and well-run, it deserves a look for its triples, family suites (accommodating up to six) and close proximity to pretty Santa Maria in Trastevere and the Ponte Sisto bridge, which you'll be crossing every day to see the sights.

CASA SAN GIUSEPPE, Vicolo Moroni, 22. Tel. 06-583-33490. Web site: *casasangiuseppe.it*. Three stars may be a reach for this spartan-but-spacious former convent, but you can't argue the terrific location, on a quiet, charming street just across the Ponte Sisto, or the bargain prices. All the basics are there: A/C, mini-bar, TV, Wi-Fi Internet station, breakfast, and even a pleasant, internal courtyard.

RELAIS LE CLARISSE, Via Cardinale Merry Del Val, 20. Tel. 06583-34437. Web site: *leclarisse.com*. This great charming, former cloister offers spacious rooms and a lovely communal outdoor terrace. The Family suite holds 2-5 people with 1 large bed and a double sofa bed, while the mini apartment gives you 2 bathrooms a little kitchen and the option of a sofa bed and 2 large beds or 4 twins. All rooms come with Wi-Fi, A/C, SAT TV, and buffet breakfast.

VATICAN, CASTEL SANT'ANGELO AREA

Four stars

HOTEL DEI MELLINI, Via Muzio Clementi, 81. Tel. 06-324-771. Web site: *hotelmellini.com*. Located on the right bank of the Tiber across from Augustus' Mausoleum, this superior hotel is walking distance to lots of sights without fighting the Spanish Steps crowds just across the river. Pick up buses in nearby Piazza Cavour, or cross the Ponte Umberto to be at Piazza Navona in minutes. A rooftop terrace, and a modern gym add to the usual amenities. Some triples available.

VIA VENETO AREA

The Via Veneto is pretty, but its location is slightly inconvenient for families who want to return to their hotel throughout the day. Here is where you'll find legendary 5-star hotels like the Majestic, the Bernini Bristol and the St. Regis. Since this book focuses on family convenience, we only suggest our favorite among them.

Five stars

REGINA BAGLIONI, Via Vittorio Veneto, 72. Tel. 06-421-111. Web site: *baglionihotels.com*. Of the many grande dames on the Via Veneto, the Regina makes the list for its understated grace and generous room sizes. If space allows, they will book two double rooms that share a common outer hallway door, giving you a "suite" of sorts. It is within walking distance to Piazza di Spagna, the Borghese Gardens and Triton's Fountain. The Baglioni is a great choice if you need more space for young children. Internet access is available. The substantial breakfast buffet is a treat, and they just may have the best hot chocolate in Rome.

BEYOND THE CENTRO

Five stars

GRAND HOTEL PARCO DEI PRINCIPI, Via G. Frescobaldi, 5 (Villa Borghese). Tel. 06-854-421. Web site: *parcodeiprincipi.com*. This stylish hotel is away from the center; but if you absolutely must have quiet or one of the best pools (unheated) in Rome, this is your place. The spacious and opulent rooms literally drip with gilt. You will be within walking distance of the zoo and Villa Borghese.

VACATION APARTMENTS

Vacation apartments are cost-effective and spacious alternatives for families, and Rome has many from which to choose. You lose the services of a concierge, but you gain lots of space, separate bedrooms, a kitchen and, often, a terrace and a washing machine. With kids, a fridge full of drinks and snacks fresh from one of Rome's open-air markets is a real plus.

Two-bedroom apartments can double your space at half the cost of hotels, but you get what you pay for, so be wary of unproven Internet sources. Some of the most reliable: the knowledgeable staff of *Italyperfect. com,* the U.S.-based offices of incredibly helpful *Papaverorentals.com,* the intimate and affordable units from *Residenza Giubbonari* and *Palazzo Olivia* (latter two listed above).

WHERE TO EAT

Restaurants and trattorie are open during meal hours (lunch and dinner) only. Cafés, also called bars, are open all day. Though the lines of distinction are beginning to blur, consider restaurants more formal than the casual trattorie, which tend to serve typical, homey, Roman fare. It is important to note that, in Rome, most restaurants do not open for dinner until after 7pm, as a rule. You may want to bridge the gap between lunch and dinner with snacks in the late afternoon, especially with young kids who are used to eating much earlier in the evening.

Look for *servizio incluso,* which means tip is included in the price. *Servizio non incluso* means, of course, the tip is not included. *Pane e coperto* is a bread-and-cover charge some establishments use as a base charge. Effort has been made to avoid touristy establishments often written about in a plethora of guidebooks.

> In Italy, the word *bar* refers to coffee and light, all-day dining. You pay the cashier first; bring the receipt to the counter for service, then stand at the counter to consume your purchases. If you prefer to sit at a table, do not pay first. A waiter will take your order, but you pay more for this service—often double.

APPIA ANTICA—Restaurants

HOSTARIA ANTICA ROMA, Via Appia Antica, 87. Tel. 06-513-2888. Web site: *anticaroma.it.* Tues.-Sun.. Lunch and dinner. This is a quality choice on the rather barren Appia Antica. The romantic interior courtyard, lit with candles at night, was an ancient *columbarium,* or storage for cinerary urns containing the ashes of high-ranking Roman freed men of the Augustan age. After exploring nearby catacombs, lunch in sunshine is a treat. Fresh fish and an extensive wine list are the specialties, but the ample menu pleases most palates. Try the pork and potatoes, lasagna with swordfish or other Mediterranean-based dishes. Tuesday and Thursday evenings the menu includes recipes from an Imperial-age chef.

CAPITOLINE HILL—Restaurants

ENOTECA CORSI, Via del Gesù, 87/88. Tel. 06-679-0821. Lunch only. Closed Sundays and the month of August. An *enoteca* is predominantly a wine bar with small meals to accompany tasting, but this place has a full-on lunch that locals love. Good Italian homecooking in a humble environment. Moderate.

LA TAVERNA DEGLI AMICI, Piazza Margana, 37. Tel. 06-699-20637. Web site: *Latavernadegliamici.net*. Lunch and dinner. Closed Mondays. The right note of casual elegance is struck at this white tablecloth restaurant with a tasty menu in a picturesque, secluded square just west of the Capitoline hill. Refined, yet kid-pleasing dishes like pasta *amatriciana* (with bacon) and spaghetti *cacio e pepe* (pecorino cheese and pepper) are offered alongside beautifully prepared dishes such as shrimp and apple salad, filet mignon and gratin zucchine tarte. Moderate.

RISTORANTE ALVARO, Via dei Cerchi, 53. Tel. 06-678-6112. Lunch and dinner. Closed Sunday dinner and Mondays. This family-owned restaurant sits in the shadow of the *Palatine Hill* and *Circus Maximus*. It's a quick two-block walk from the famous *Mouth of Truth*, too. Expect typical Italian fare in a warm setting. Moderate.

VECCHIA ROMA, Piazza Campitelli, 18. Tel. 06-686-4604. Closed Wednesdays. Web site: *ristorantevecchiaroma.com*. With its pretty setting and upscale Italian dishes, you may want to save this spot for your last night in Rome. Or, book the fountain room for a parents' night out (it has only one table). Reserve for dinner, and specify an outside table if you desire one. Expensive.

CAPITOLINE HILL—Cafés, cut pizza and gelato

CAFFETERIA CAPITOLINA, Piazza Caffarelli, 4. Tel. 06-361-2325. Enter from behind or inside the museum. Take a break while enjoying one of the nicest panoramas of Rome. This is not a good place for lunch, but it's perfect for a light snack and refreshing juices and coffees.

VITTORIANO CAFÉ, Victor Emanuele II Monument terrace. Get there by climbing up the monument's right side and following café signs, or from the Capitoline Piazza in back (easier) by taking the stairs left of the Senate building, then turning right inside the doors where a long corridor leads to the terrace, café and views, views, views.

CAMPO DEI FIORI—Restaurants

AI BALESTRARI, Via dei Balestrari, 41. Tel. 06-686-5377. Lunch from noon and dinner from 7pm. Closed Mondays. No-frills local favorite Balestrari slings excellent *forno* (wood-burning oven) pizza supported by only-average pastas. Pizza cooked in this manner comes out crisp and quick, giving it the unmistakable flavor of Italian pizza. Inexpensive.

CAMPONESCHI, Piazza Farnese, 50. Tel. 06-687-4927. Dinner only from 8pm. Closed Sundays. Web site: *ristorantecamponeschi.it*. Leading fish restaurant on a par with La Rosetta. Elegant, glamorous and best for adults and refined teens. Expensive.

FILETTI DI BACCALÀ, Via Giubbonari at Largo dei Librari, 88. Tel. 06-686-4018. Opens around 6pm nightly. Closed Sundays. Walk right in, head straight to the back kitchen and ask for a *filetto, porta via* (to take away). Wait as the chef dips a fresh cod fillet in special batter and deep-fries it, pronto. There are tables for sit-down dining if you prefer, but kids love to grab and go. No frills and no credit cards. Inexpensive.

OSTERIA AR GALLETTO, Vicolo del Gallo, 1; Piazza Farnese, 102. Tel. 06-686-1714. Lunch and dinner. Closed Sundays. On a tiny side street off Piazza Farnese, this pleasant restaurant has seating on the Piazza, so kids can run around the square while you wait for your meal. Inside, you'll find Lazio soccer team memorabilia and a warm, inviting space. Moderate.

PIERLUIGI, Via d. Monserrato at Piazza dei Ricci, 144, north of the Campo. Tel. 06-686-1302. Web site: *pierluigi.it*. Lunch and dinner. Closed Mondays. This sophisticated steak-and-seafood restaurant has a large, outdoor seating area. Its lovely location in old Rome is convenient, but not touristy. Specialties like *scalopine* (of veal) *al limone*, *piccatina al limone* and *bistecca* (steak) *di manzo* are a good bet. The seafood selection includes lobster, snapper, scampi and even ravioli with seafood. Most kids like the little, ear-shaped *orecchiete con broccoletti* (with broccoli bits). For desert, try the *torta di cioccolato* (chocolate tart with cream) or the *torta di ricotta*. Moderate.

RISTORANTE DA PANCRAZIO, Piazza del Biscione, 92/94. Tel. 06-686-1246. Web site: *dapancrazio.it*. Lunch and dinner. Closed Wednesdays. The basement dining room is carved out of the ruins of the Theater of Pompey, but outside tables in this great location in a quiet square just off the Campo are reason enough to come. Try the *bucatini* (fat spaghetti) *all'amatriciana* or the artichoke ravioli for a taste of authentic Roman fare. Ask permission to view the exposed theater ruins. Moderate.

CAMPO DEI FIORI—Cafés, cut pizza and gelato

ARISTO CAMPO, Piazza Campo dei Fiori, 30. The piazza is home to one of Rome's most beloved outdoor markets by day, and it's a meeting ground for barhoppers by night. This sandwich shop is perfect for grabbing a quick sandwich or fixing a picnic for later. The pork sandwich is a Roman classic, especially popular in winter.

CAFFÈ FARNESE, Piazza Farnese, 106. Tel. 06-688-02125. An excellent location and respectable coffees keep this hotspot filled with locals and tourists alike. Stand at the bar and swill down a drink with a pastry in hand, or sit at one of the in-demand outdoor tables. Primarily, expert barristas make beautiful and delicious drinks, but there are also pastries, sandwiches and gelato.

Roscioli Forno

FORNO CAMPO DEI FIORI, (No. 22 on the piazza). Tel. 06-688-06662. Web site: *fornocampodeifiori.com*. Open Mon.-Fri., 7am-2pm and 5-8pm; Sat., 7am-2pm. Closed Sundays. A local institution, Forno recently expanded its tiny quarters to include a space across the street. The original serves up famous *pizza rossa* (red) and *pizza bianca* (white), the reasons Romans and tourists alike brave the lines here. The new space stocks freshly baked cookies and delicious sandwiches. The aromas alone are worth the trip. Go for breakfast or for a late lunch of hot breads, sandwiches, fresh cookies and muffins.

IL FORNAIO, Via dei Baullari, 4, at Corso Vittorio Emanuele II. A bakery and traditional deli located between Navona and the Campo.

ROSCIOLI FORNO, Via dei Chiavari, 34, off Via Giubbonari. The Roscioli dynasty continues to deliver exceptional breads, baked goods, and cut pizza from this location. Open all day. Closed Sundays.

COLOSSEUM—Restaurants

ALLE CARRETTE, Vicolo delle Carrette, 14 (a tiny street off Via Cavour, just past Via Tor di. Conti). There is also a backdoor entrance at Madonna dei Monte, 95. Tel. 06-679-2770. Dinner only. Tasty, wood-fired pizzas with a wide variety of toppings are served from this tiny, hole-in-the-wall joint, steps from the Forums. Both Via Fori Imperiali and Via Cavour are large, hectic streets, yet this little antique alley is remarkably charming. A line forms as the night wears on. Inexpensive.

HOSTARIA DA NERONE, Via delle Terme di Tito, 96. Tel. 06-481-7952. Closed Sundays and the month of August. To find this quaint, mid-priced restaurant on the Oppian Hill, take the steps right of the Metro stop across from the Colosseum. At the top, go right to the first street. Delicious *saltimbocca alla Romana* (thin-sliced veal wrapped in razor-thin prociutto) and *vitella con limone* (veal with lemon) are prized. Reserve dinner in advance. Moderate.

LA NAUMACHIA, Via Celimontana, 7. Tel. 06-700-2764. Web site: *naumachiaroma.com*. Everyone loves this reliable pizza place a few blocks from the Colosseo because it also has great salads, risotto, and pasta, and at very affordable prices. You'll find it just south of Via di S. Giovanni in Laterano. Moderate.

LI RIONI, Via dei S. Quattro Coronati, 24. Tel. 06-704-50605. Closed Tuesdays. Dinner only. The excellent pizza dominates the menu in this fun neighborhood pizzeria with interior walls dressed to look like street scenes.

LUZZI, Via di S. Giovanni in Laterano, 88 (at Via Celimontana). Tel. 06-709-6332. Closed Wednesdays. This family-friendly trattoria with a wood-burning oven is a few blocks from the Colosseum. Moderate.

COLOSSEUM—Cafés, cut pizza and gelato

CAFÉ CAFÉ, Via dei Santi Quattro Coronari, 44. Tel. 06-700-8743. Open from 10am. Sunday brunch buffet, 11:30am-4pm. Not a bar but a tearoom with lunch, dinner and all-day dining. The large tea selection is accompanied by soups, salads, light meals, smoothies and pastries.

CAFFÉ SAN CLEMENTE, Via S. Giovanni in Laterano, 124. Take a break at this simple café just across from San Clemente.

L'ANTICA CORNETTERIA di Enzo e Valter, Via Labicana, 78. Tel. 06-7045-4084. These guys know pastry, and they're open nonstop for those with a late-night sweet tooth. Find them east of S. Clemente.

JEWISH GHETTO—Restaurants

AL POMPIERE, Via Santa Maria dei Calderari, 38. Tel. 06-686-8377. Web site: *alpompieriroma.com*. Closed Sundays. Coffered ceilings, whitewashed walls and grand old palace rooms make this huge second-floor restaurant a wonderful spot for family dining. *Pompiere* means fireman, as you'll deduce from the logo: a fireman dousing a roasted chicken with a bottle of wine. Off-hand sophistication with numerous wait staff in cummerbunds and starched shirts is tempered by worn green velvet curtains. This is a pleasant choice in the heart of the characteristic Ghetto where you will find traditional Roman fare such as gnocchi, penne *arrabbiata* (spicy sauce) and plenty of lamb, beef and fish. Moderate.

GIGGETTO, Via del Portico d'Ottavia, 21/A. Closed Mondays. Tel. 06-686-1105. Web site: *giggetto.it*. Lunch and dinner. Rome's Jewish Ghetto, now a posh neighborhood, is home to a unique cuisine that preserves the recipes of old Jewish Rome. The decidedly dressed-down Giggetto, run by third-generation family owners, is a good fit for families. Try the famous trio of fried artichokes (*carciofi alla* *giudia)*, zucchini flowers *(fiori di zucca)* and cod fillets *(baccalà)* that are hallmarks of this fare. Roman classics like cannelloni, spaghetti with clams and *bucatini al'amatriciana* (pasta with a tomato-bacon sauce) make solid seconds. The picturesque location beside the ruins of the Portico of Ottavia and the Theater of Marcellus beckons you to an enjoyable after-dinner walk. Moderate.

LA SORA LELLA, Via Ponte Quattro Capi, 16 (Tiberina Island). Tel. 06-686-1601. Web site: *soralella.com*. Lunch and dinner. Though a bit more formal than it used to be (no shorts—even at lunch), this terrific restaurant still carefully preserves the true tastes of authentic Roman fare that it has been known for since 1943. Reservations recommended. Dress for dinner. Moderate.

PIPERNO, Monte Dei Cenci, 9. Tel. 06-688-06629. Closed Sunday night, Mondays and the month of August. Web site: *ristorantepiperno. com*. This hotspot serves upscale traditional fare in a uniquely Roman atmosphere. Piperno claims the distinction of being the oldest restaurant in the Ghetto. They are famous for crispy fried artichokes in the Jewish style and homemade dishes like ravioli and pasta *fagioli* (with beans). As you dine in this beautiful piazza alongside the notorious Palazzo Cenci, recall the story of Beatrice Cenci who was executed at Castel Sant'Angelo for contracting her abusive father's murder. Reservations recommended. Expensive.

JEWISH GHETTO—Cafés, cut pizza and gelato

LA DOLCE ROMA, Via Portico d'Ottavia, 20b. Tel. 06-454-70303. Closed Sunday afternoons and Mondays. If you're craving a chocolate chip cookie, American-style carrot cake or brownies, step inside this tiny storefront bakery.

PASTICCERIA "Boccione" LIMENTANI, Via Portico d'Ottavia, 1. Tel. 06-687-8637. Open Sun.-Thurs., 7:30am-9pm; Fri., 7:30am-3:30pm. Closed Saturdays. Follow your nose to this famous Jewish bakery on the edge of the Ghetto.

PANTHEON/NAVONA—Restaurants

ARMANDO AL PANTHEON, Salita de' Crescenzi, 30/31. Tel. 06-688-03034. Web site: *armandoalpantheon.it*. Lunch and dinner. Closed Saturday nights and Sundays, and the month of August. Just west of the Pantheon, Armando's has been serving authentic Roman dishes since

1961. They have the distinction of *Cucina Romana*, the city's stamp of approval that their recipes preserve old Roman cuisine. The tastes may not necessarily appeal to kids, but these usually do the trick: *saltimbocca* (thinly pounded veal wrapped in prociutto), ravioli *all'Armando*, and spaghetti *aglio e olio* (with a little olive oil). To find traditional Roman cuisine, look for the *Cucina Romana* symbol in restaurant windows. Moderate.

CICCIA BOMBA, Via del Governo Vecchio, 76. Tel. 06-688-02108. Lunch and dinner. Closed Wednesdays. Pizza is the main attraction, though a nice selection of Italian dishes supports it here. After dinner, walk off your meal by wandering this funky, pedestrian-only street full of shops. Inexpensive.

DA ALFREDO E ADA, Via dei Banchi Nuovi, 14. Tel. 06-687-8842. Closed Sundays and Mondays. The charm of this modest place with a couple of tables is two-fold: tasty comfort food since 1945 and the rustic locale off the beaten path between Castel Sant'Angelo and Piazza Navona. Moderate.

DA BAFFETTO, Via del Governo Vecchio, 114. Tel. 06-686-1617. Dinner only at this jam-packed pizzeria dominated by its forno oven. People line up to eat here, though the quality can be questionable and the menu is limited. Try the paper-thin pizza *piacere*, "any way you like." Inexpensive. No credit cards.

DA FRANCESCO, Piazza del Fico, 29. Tel. 06-686-4009. Lunch and dinner. Closed Tuesdays. Francesco's only gets more crowded as the night wears on because it produces some of the best pizza in Rome and because it sits in a trendy, ivy-covered piazza. A large supporting menu pleases anyone not having pizza, and adults will love the antipasti, which can be a meal in itself. Like many places, Francesco's only serves pizza at dinner; unlike many, they open for dinner early, at 7pm. A bonus when kids are used to eating earlier than Romans.Inexpensive.

DA TONINO, Via del Governo Vecchio, 18. Tel. 06-687-7002. Lunch and dinner. Closed Sundays. Usually no menu, just authentic Roman dishes by the Bassetti family. The pastas, salads and meats here are delivered with a decidedly low-key vibe. The waiter seats you at a paper-covered table and simply asks what you want. Try pasta with tasty sauces like *pomodoro* (plain tomato), *amatriciana* (with bacon), *bolognese* or *carbonara* (bacon and cheese, no tomato). Dessert is also traditional, like the moist *Torta delle Nonna* (grandmother's cake) or *fragole e limone* (tiny strawberries in lemon juice). Dining here is inexpensive and always delicious, so the place fills up fast—go early. Cash only.

FORTUNATO AL PANTHEON, Via Pantheon, 55. Tel. 06-679-2788. Web site: *ristorantefortunato.it*. Lunch and dinner. Fortunato has built a loyal old-school following on its superior treatment of traditional Italian dishes, especially among die-hard politicians. Business-casual dress code is expected. Moderate.

HOSTARIA DELL'ORSO, Via dei Soldati 25c. Tel. 06-683-01192. Web site: *hdo.it*. Dinner only. Closed Sundays. Gorgeous, romantic and historic, dell'Orso is supremely located at the bank of the Tiber River in a medieval building protected by the city. The building served as a hostelry in the 14th century, and as a 16th-century hotel it hosted Romantic travelers such as Goethe and Montaigne. As a 20th-century hotspot, it has seen jetsetters from Gable to Onassis. Chef Gualtiero Marchesi delivers his own signature dishes, such as risotto with saffron and gold leaf; as beautiful to look at as they are to eat. Not appropriate for rambunctious kids. Expensive.

IL CORALLO, Via del Corallo, 11. Open lunch through dinner. Pizza lovers, craving ultra thin, wood-fired pizza should head here lunch or dinner.

LA MONTECARLO, Vicolo Savelli, 13 (off Corso Vittorio Emanuele II, a few blocks from Piazza Navona). Tel. 06-686-1877. Web site: *lamontecarlo.it*. Lunch and dinner. Closed Mondays. This bustling pizza place is famous for its delicious pizza, huge portions, and a friendly wait staff. The casual style is suitable for families. The pizza is superior; the pastas are mediocre but kid pleasing—as is having the order arrive on a huge silver platter, à la medieval times. The pastas and salads are large enough to share, and they are reasonably priced at 8-10 Euros. Don't worry if there's a line; they can seat a lot of people, and they serve them almost as fast as they order.

LA ROSETTA, Via della Rosetta, 8. Tel. 06-686-1002. Lunch and dinner. Closed Sundays. Web site: *larosetta.com*. Massimo Riccioli's swanky, top-rated seafood restaurant at the Pantheon is considered by many to be the finest in town. Reservations are essential for dinner. Expensive.

LA SAGRESTIA, Via del Seminario, 89. Tel. 06-679-7581. Closed Wednesdays. Family-run casual trattoria with spaghetti, pizza and other Italian favorites, set in the shadow of the Pantheon. Moderate.

MACCHERONI, Piazza delle Coppelle, 44. Tel. 06-683-07895. Web site: *ristorantemaccheroni.com*. The fun 40's décor and young crowds make this simple but lively restaurant a perfect choice for families. Moderate.

PIZZICO, Piazza Maddelena, 8. Neapolitan pizza (soft and thicker) is served from this pleasant indoor/outdoor pizzeria a few doors north of the Pantheon. Families appreciate the airy casual interior as much as the view of pretty S. Maria Maddelena in front. Since the place is large, there's often little or no wait. Inexpensive.

PONTE E PARIONE, Via S. Maria dell'Anima, 62. Tel. 06-681-92278. Lunch and dinner. This solid ristorante/pizzeria on the street west of Navona has a good selection of veal, pasta, salads, pizza and tasty gnocchi. Moderate.

RISTORANTE ARCHIMEDE S. EUSTACHIO, Piazza dei Caprettari, 63. Tel. 06-686-1616. Web site: *archimedesanteustachio.it* Refined dining in a quiet pocket only a block west of the Pantheon is hard to beat. Pretty Piazza San Eustachio's adjoining square is where you'll find this exceptional restaurant with classic dishes such as the *vitello al limone* (veal with lemon) and *saltimbocca* ("jump in your mouth" veal). Moderate.

TRATTORIA DA GINO E PIETRO, Via del Governo Vecchio, 106, (at Vicolo Savelli). Tel. 06-686-1576. Closed Thursdays. This warm and amiable restaurant west of Navona has lots of space for families, and it can accommodate most walk-in groups. The large selection of tasty home-cooking means everyone will be happy. Moderate.

TRINITY COLLEGE MUSIC BAR, Via del Collegio Romano, 6. Tel. 06-678-6472. Web site: *trinity-rome.com*. Opens at noon. You can scarcely get more casual and clubby than an Irish pub, no matter which country it's in. Comfort foods like steak, burgers and salads make the menu. Brunch is served on weekends, for which reservations are advised. Trinity is just off the Corso.

PANTHEON/NAVONA—Cafés, cut pizza and gelato

ANTICA SALUMERIA PANE E PIZZA, Piazza della Rotunda (Pantheon), 4. Stop in for a deli lunch of sandwiches and fruit.

CAFFÈ SANT'EUSTACHIO, Piazza Sant'Eustachio, 82. Tel. 06-688-02048. Web site: *santeustachioilcaffe.it*. Open daily, 8:30am. Always at the top of the list for good reason: they roast their own beans and the shop is lovely.

FRIGIDARIUM GELATERIA, Via Governo Vecchio, 112. Web site: *frigidarium-gelateria.com*. On the path between Castel Sant'Angelo and Piazza Navona, you'll come across this sparkling new gelateria just when you need fuel.

GELATERIA DEL TEATRO, Via Coronari, 65-66. Probably the best gelato in Rome is served from this gorgeous location on a pedestrian-only street. Kids can watch the gelato maker through the large glass street window, then run inside to try the fresh, creamy, creations. Divine.

GIOLITTI, Via Uffici dei Vicario, 40. Tel. 06-699-1243. Web site: *giolitti.it*. Open until midnight. Sparkling 30's decor makes Giolitti's average-quality ice cream taste all the better. In its heyday, this was top drawer. Presently, the quality has dropped, but the crowds keep coming.

LO ZOZZONE, Via del Teatro Pace, 32. Tel. 06-688-08575. Open 9am-9pm; weekends, from 10am. This well-established sandwich counter makes fresh Pizza Bianca, halves it and stuffs it with your choice of ingredients like lunchmeats, cheeses or veggies. A medium is huge and runs about €2.50.

PASTICCERIA CINQUE LUNE, Corso Rinascimento, 89. The alluring scents of fresh baked goods will help you find this small bakery between Piazza Navona and the Pantheon.

TAZZA D'ORO, Via degli Orfani, 84. Tel. 06-678-9792. Closed Sundays. Perhaps the most well-known coffee bar in Rome, but often packed with tourists. Brave the crowds to experience the rich creations that keep them at the top of café culture. Try the iced coffee, called *granita,* for a special treat.

ZAZÀ, Piazza Sant'Eustachio, 49. Tel. 06-688-01357. Open 9am-11pm. Web site: *pizzazaza.it*. Mod storefront selling only cut pizza. Find it just across from famous Café Sant'Eustachio.

ALFREDO RISTORANTE L'ORIGINALE, Piazza Augusto Imperatore, 30. Tel. 06-687-8734. Web site: *alfredo-roma.it*. Closed for lunch on Mondays. Creator of *Fettuccine Alfredo* and former home to Hollywood movie stars of the silver screen. Moderate.

DA SETTIMIO ALL'ARANCIO, Via dell'Arancio, 50-52. Tel. 06-687-6119. Lunch and dinner. Closed Sundays. Widely popular, slightly more grand classics are served in a clubby setting that manages to stick to Roman cuisine. Regulars come for the hearty steaks and homemade breads at affordable prices. Can be quite crowded even at lunch. Moderate.

GINA EAT & DRINK, Via S. Sebastianello, 7a. Tel. 06.678-0251. Web site: *ginaroma.com*. This soup and sandwich shop on the street left of the Steps is a fashion 'do.' All-day dining and custom picnic baskets (including thermos of coffee) are available from the stylish restaurant with a menu carrying dishes like *pasta e fagioli* (bean soup), salad with pear, cheese and pine nuts and sandwiches that range from turkey to ham and Brie. Pre-order a basket and head up to the Pincio.

IL MARGUTTA RISTORARTE, Via Margutta, 118. Tel. 06-326-50577. Web site: *ilmarguttavegetariano.it*. The daily brunch buffet at this crisp, modern restaurant is a draw for everyone looking for beautiful, fresh, tasty food—and not just vegetarians. The wide variety of dishes assures most everyone will be pleased. Dinner is perhaps more upscale than small kids may like, but adults will appreciate the gourmet fare that looks as good as it tastes. They call themselves a "ristor-arte," because they display art by up and coming artists.

OSTERIA MARGUTTA, Via Margutta, 82. Tel. 06-323-1025. Lunch and dinner. Closed Sundays. Margutta is known as the street of the artists because many have occupied it over the years. Gregory Peck's character lived here (No. 51) in the movie *Roman Holiday*. Pretty, ivy-clad Margutta is a romantic restaurant that presents linguine with prawns, tortelloni and other homemade pasta dishes along with a nice selection of fish and meats. Moderate.

OTELLO ALLA CONCORDIA, Via della Croce, 81. Tel. 06-679-1178. Lunch and dinner. Closed Sundays. Web site: *otello-alla-concordia. it*. Otello's secret courtyard makes a welcome oasis from di Spagna crowds. Tourists and locals both flock to it so come early or prepare to wait. Moderate.

RISTORANTE RE DEGLI AMICI, Via della Croce, 33B. Tel. 06-679-5380. Web site: *ristoranteredegliamici.com*. Lunch and dinner. This popular restaurant offers a few outside tables that fill up quickly, but more tables lie within. Kids like the campy, decorative elements on the walls and ceiling where they can pick out the Mouth of Truth, the she-wolf with twins Romulus and Remus and other Roman icons. The food is of average quality, but the prices are fair.

SPANISH STEPS—Cafés, cut pizza and gelato

CASINA VALADIER, Piazza Bucarest, (Viale del Belvedere) Pincio Hill. Tel. 06-699-22090. Web site: *casinavaladier.it*. Lunch and dinner daily. Closed Mondays. Gorgeous and historic Casino Valadier recently reopened after years of restoration. You can't get better views or a better location to hang out with your kids. Marvel at the Pincio's panorama (Piazza del Popolo and St. Peter's), and enjoy its leafy gardens while you lunch on the terrace where there's even a children's menu.

CAFFÈ CIAMPINI, Viale Trinità dei Monti, 1. Tel. 06-678-5678. Web site: *caffeciampini.com*. Opens at 8am for all-day dining until 1am. Closed Wednesdays. Lunch and dinner are served in the greenhouse; a separate coffee-bar entrance is on the uphill side. A very pretty view and a charming, glass-enclosed terrace make for a pleasant stop on the path between the Pincio and Piazza di Spagna.

CIAMPINI, Piazza S. Lorenzo in Lucina, 29. Tel. 06-687-6606. Web site: *ciampini.com*. Open 7:30am-9pm. Closed Sundays. This is one of the best gelato shops in Rome. A full café menu supports the sweets nicely. Find it on an attractive square west of the Corso.

FATAMORGANA GELATO, Via Laurina, 10, steps from Piazza del Popolo. Web site: *gelateriafatamorgana.com*. One of Rome's finest gelaterie now has a chain of storefronts dotting the city. Like all of the best gelato, no thickeners, preservatives, or food coloring are added. With a focus on health, many flavors are gluten-free, low-calorie, lactose-free and even sugar-free.

TRASTEVERE—Restaurants

DA AUGUSTO, Piazza de' Renzi, 15. Tel. 06-580-3798. Lunch and dinner. Closed Sundays. Within this medieval zone with characteristic cobbles and line-strung laundry, Augusto is a laid-back restaurant tucked into one of the picturesque side streets between the Ponte Sisto and Santa Maria in Trastevere. Moderate.

IL DUCA, Vicolo del Cinque, 56. Tel. 06-581-7706. Lunch and dinner. Closed Mondays. A standout on a street full of primarily English-owned pubs and trattorie, Duca slings wood-fired pizza and traditional pastas in a convivial, red-checkered-cloth atmosphere that puts kids at ease. Inexpensive.

PARIS, Piazza San Calisto 7/a (near S. Maria in Trastevere). Tel. 06-581-5378. Web site: *ristoranteparis.it.* Closed Sunday nights and Mondays. Paris is always fashionable, and this restaurant is no exception. But don't expect French food here, just Roman fish, meat and pasta classics like fettuccine, ravioli and fried cod. Moderate.

PIZZERIA PANATTONI, *Ai Marmi*, Viale Trastevere, 53-59. Tel. 06-580-0919. Dinner only. Closed Wednesdays and the month of August. Ask a local for great pizza, and they'll probably steer you here. Fans have nicknamed it the morgue, *l'orbitorio,* for its tables topped with slabs of marble. The big draw is the giant, wood-burning oven that three pizza chefs work at the same time. Impossibly, their long, wooden-handled pizza paddles never get tangled. Packed and bristling with activity, young people love it; old people want more space between the tables. Inexpensive. No credit cards.

ROMOLO NEL GIARDINO DI RAFFAELLO E DELLA FORNARINA, Via di Porta Settimiana, 8. Tel. 06-581-8284. Web site: *ristoranteromolo.it.* Lovely Romolo is situated in the garden of Raphael's beloved girlfriend *the fornarina,* or baker's daughter. The interior courtyard allows you to dine outside but protected from street traffic. Delicious authentic flavors are at home in this historic building where Raphael and Michelangelo often lunched. The slightly high prices are in line with the gorgeous location, where many locals come to celebrate special occasions.

SURYA MAHAL, Via di Ponte Sisto, 67. Tel. 06-589-4554. Web site: *ristorantesuryamahal.com.* Dinner only. Closed Mondays. Delicious Indian food served in an ultra-cool location atop the little hill in Piazza Trilussa. The large restaurant feels like a secret garden because it can't be seen from the street, making it fun to find, too. Face the piazza's fountain, and take the steps up (on the right). White-tented outdoor seating with patio heating takes the chill out of cool nights. Moderate.

TRASTEVERE—Cafés, cut pizza and gelato

ANTICO CAFFÈ DELL'ISOLA, Via Ponte Quattro Capi on Tiberina Island. This old café has been quenching thirsts of travelers since 1925. In summer, the *spremuta di limonata* (fresh squeezed lemonade) is some of the best.

FATAMORGANA GELATO, Via Roma Libera, 11 (Piazza S. Cosimato). A secondary location for this famed gelateria.

TREVI—Restaurants

AL MORO, Vicolo Bollette, 13. Tel. 06-678-3495. Closed Sundays. Good Italian food can be found steps from the Trevi throngs at this slightly upscale restaurant. Moderate.

BACCANO BISTROT, Via delle Muratte, 23. Tel: 06-6994-1166. Web site: *baccanoroma.com.* This fresh, Parisian take on old classics serves bistrot burgers and fare all day long, from 10am to 2am. It's a good, safe bet in this otherwise, heavy tourist zone.

TREVI—Cafés

IL GELATO DI SAN CRISPINO, Via della Panetteria, 42. Tel. 06-679-3924. Web site: *ilgelatodisancrispino.com.* Closed Tuesdays. Two brothers run this top gelato shop, and they are known for their high standards, smooth gelato and sorbet and unique palate-pleasing flavors (around 20) like honey, ginger/cinnamon and pistachio. The grapefruit is from India, the coffee is Illy, and the honey is from a nature preserve in Sardinia. Today, San Crispino has branched out, with several locations around Rome, including Terminal A at the Fiumicino airport, and at the Pantheon, in Piazza della Maddalena, 3. But this remains their first store front. No chemicals, preservatives or false aromas are used.

VATICAN/CASTEL SANT'ANGELO—Restaurants

CAFFÈ MELONI, Via Vittorio Emanuele II, 298/300. Tel. 06-686-9722. This real, working-Rome café provides lightning-fast service in close proximity to Castel Sant'Angelo. Friendly barristas hop all day long; but show up in the morning when the whole place smells of fresh baked *cornetti*, a moist Italian version of croissants, and you'll be hooked. To get a hot one here, ask for a *cornetto della casa* (of the house).

DAL TOSCANO, Via Germanico, 58/60. Tel. 06-3972-5717. Web site: ristorantedaltoscano.it. Lunch and dinner. Closed Mondays. T-bone steak joint with a nice selection of soups, salads and pastas, too. Moderate.

IL PAPALINO, Via Borgo Pio, 172. Tel. 06-686-5539. Web site: *ilpapalino.com*. Closed Mondays. With its large menu and delicious pasta sauces, a variety of taste buds are pleased in this fine trattoria, a notch above most casual places in this zone. Al fresco tables exist, but the inside tables, usually filled with Italian families, are equally pleasant. Try the homemade ravioli and tortelloni. Moderate.

L'INSALATA RICCA, Piazza Risorgimento, 4-5. Chain offering a large menu of salads, antipasti, pastas and pizzas at inexpensive prices.

LA VERANDA DELL'HOTEL COLUMBUS, Via della Conciliazione, 33 or enter at Borgo San Spirito, 73. Tel. 06-687-2973. Web site: *hotelcolumbus.net*. Reservations are essential (you can book in advance online and even pick your table) at this romantic, torch-lit courtyard steps from St. Peters. The interior hall of this old della Rovere family palace is equally impressive, but be sure to specify which space you prefer. You will be treated to excellent cuisine, such as risotto with lamb, pasta with saffron and artichoke, or broccoli and ginger and a lovely, ample selection of fine meats and fish. Expensive.

PIAZZA DELL'UNITÀ MARKET, Piazza dell'Unità 7-14, on Via Cola di Rienzo. Open 7am-8pm, closed Sundays. Pick up fruit and vegetables to go at this amazing and vast covered market. Have the kids look for the S.P.Q.R. above its enormous arched entrance.

TAVERNA ANGELICA, Piazza Amerigo Capponi, 6. Tel. 06-687-4514. Web site: *tavernaangelica.it*. Dinner nightly; lunch on Sundays. One of the few above-average restaurants within walking distance of the Vatican museums, this one serves tasty Mediterranean dishes. Reservations recommended. Moderate.

TRATTORIA DINO, Via Tacito, 80. Lunch and dinner. West of Castel Sant'Angelo in a tiny joint filled mostly with locals that enjoy traditional, Italian fare. Moderate.

TRE PUPAZZI, Via Borgo Pio, 183. Tel. 06-688-03220. Closed Sundays. Make reservations or go early to this popular restaurant, especially at dinner when the pedestrian-only medieval street becomes even more enchanting. Moderate.

VATICAN/CASTEL SANT'ANGELO—Cafés, cut pizza and gelato

BAR CONCILIAZIONE, Via Borgo Pio, 162. Homey coffee bar and diner where you can get soups, salads, sandwiches and a few pastas of the day. Families like the extra-large booths and air-conditioning.

DOLCE BORGO, Via Borgo Pio, 142. This is a tiny, top-quality bakery with fresh treats located on the St. Peter's side of the Borgo Pio.

GRAN CAFFÈ BORGO, Via Borgo Pio, 170. Coffee, baked goods and café fare are served here, midway between St. Peter's and Castel S. Angelo.

HEDERA, Borgo Pio, 179. Tel. 39-06-6832971. Web site: *hederaroma. it.* Stop in this fresh gelato and sweets shop for modern flavors, slushy granite, and creamy sorbets.

OLD BRIDGE, Via Bastioni Michelangelo, 5. Long-favored Vatican gelateria at the southern end of Via Leone IV.

VIA VENETO/QUIRINALE—Restaurants

COLLINE EMILIANE, Via degli Avignonesi, 22 (near Triton's Fountain). Tel. 06-481-7538. Lunch and dinner. Closed Mondays. It's clear how lovingly cared-for this award-winning, family-run trattoria is from the moment you enter into the gentle hum of its pleasant front room. Handmade, classic Bolognese cuisine is prepared and served with a casual sophistication. Gorgeous veal, pounded paper thin, squash-filled tortelloni and fettuccine with Bolognese sauce are standouts. Save room for the sumptuous desserts, also made in-house. Reservations are essential. Moderate.

DA TULLIO, Via di San Nicola da Tolentino, 26 (off Piazza Barberini). Tel. 06-474-5560. Lunch and dinner. Closed Sundays. As a high-end, top-quality Tuscan steak house, Tullio is a meat-and-potatoes place. A star reputation makes it crowded, but once you're in, try the aged prime beef roasted over an open fire and dressed with fresh Parmesan and basil. Reservations are essential. Expensive.

HARD ROCK CAFÉ, Via Vittorio Veneto, 62 A. Tel. 06-420-3051. Web site: *hardrock.com*. American-style burgers and loud rock-and-roll bring comfort to homesick kids. Moderate.

IL BOSCAIOLO, Via degli Artisti, 37. Tel. 06-488-4023. Closed Mondays; Sat-Sun, dinner only; Tue-Fri lunch and dinner. Little ambiance but excellent pizza can be found at this pizzeria with an expanded menu that lends itself to casual family dining. Side dishes such as spinach, grilled vegetables and white beans provide a daily dose of vegetables. Inexpensive.

L'HAMBURGHERIA DI EATALY, Via Veneto, 11. Eataly's popular new hamburger place may have an American theme, but the burgers, hotdogs, and even french fries are all created with locally-grown products. Eataly is a proponent of the Slow Food movement. Kids don't care. Just get them the goods.

L'OLIMPO, roof garden of the Bernini Bristol Hotel, Piazza Barberini, 23. Tel. 06-420-10469. Web site: *berninibristol.com*. Monday-Saturday, lunch and dinner; Sunday, noon-3pm, jazz brunch, reservations are a must. Brunch is a foreign concept for Romans and, of those on offer in the city, few resemble an American affair. L'Olimpo has one of the best, and every seat offers a view over Rome. The lovely terraces boast 360° views. Expensive.

VIA VENETO/QUIRINALE—Cafés, cut pizza and gelato

CAFÉ DE PARIS, Via Vittorio Veneto, 90. Tel. 06-420-12257. Lovely deserts, panini and toasts (think an elegant toasted ham and cheese) are at the ready in this sparkling, classic café, which serves espresso and cappuccino all day from two separate locations on the Veneto.

FORNO CERULLI, Via di S. Nicola da Tolentino 53. Tel: 06 488 2627. Web site: *fornocerulli1937.it*. This long-time bakery has expanded, for the better. They have been baking up pizza and baked goods since 1937. Today's menu includes pizza, pastas, salads, and sandwiches made with their fresh breads.

ROME ON THE WEB–internet resources

060608.IT The Comune di Roma hosts this great site loaded with information. You can research events, shows, and cultural activities and explore everything from public transportation to laundry service.

ACCESSIBLEITALY.COM Loads of information for traveling with any kind of disability, including information on equipment rental and delivery—from oxygen to wheelchairs.

ATAC.ROMA.IT The public bus site with route maps and trip planning tools.

BABYRIDERS.IT This wonderful service rents baby equipment such as strollers, beds, car seats and such to make your stay in Roma even easier, and they deliver! Easy online ordering makes it a breeze, and you can leave your heavy equipment at home.

CAPITOLIUM.ORG Devoted to the Forum with live Web-cams you can control.

COOPCULTURE.IT Cultural info and online tickets to sights such as the Forum/Palatine/Colosseum, Hadrian's Villa, and Nero's Golden House. Here, you may buy and print your Colosseo tickets to avoid standing in line.

ENIT.IT Official site of the Italian State Tourism Board.

ITALIARAIL.COM North American site for booking European train tickets.

RAILEUROPE.COM North American distributor for Eurostar Italia (ES).

ROMAPASS.IT These cards are available from any Tourist Information kiosk. €34 buys 3 days unlimited public transportation, free admission to 2 museums and reduced rates to others. Ages 5 and under, free. Use it to skip admission lines and head directly to pre-reserved ticket windows. A great value.

SANTASUSANNA.ORG The American church has a host of information and services, including papal audience booking.

TICKETCLIC.IT Very useful online booking site for a variety of museums and exhibitions in Rome and beyond.

TICKETERIA.IT (tosc.it) Online tickets to sights that include Galleria Borghese, Palazzo Barberini, Palazzo Spada and Castel Sant'Angelo.

TRAMBUSOPEN.COM Information on the **110 bus city tour** and the **Archeobus** route.

TRENITALIA.COM Italian site for all trains.

TURISMOROMA.IT The English-language version gives news, cultural listings, sports events, historical information and more. Test your Rome knowledge with the Roma Fanzine quiz.

QUESTIONS?

CHIAMAROMA—*Dial* 060608.
From Rome, call this hotline for English-speaking assistance.
Otherwise, Comune di Roma tourism info: 06-3600-4399.

Tourist Information Booths in Rome open every day:
Castel Sant'Angelo—Piazza Pia
Imperial Forums—Piazza del Tempio della Pace
Piazza Navona—Piazza delle Cinque Lune
Piazza San Giovanni in Laterano
Santa Maria Maggiore—Via dell'Olmata
Termini train station—Piazza dei Cinquecento
Trastevere—Piazza Sonnino
Trevi Fountain—Via Minghetti
Via del Corso—Largo Goldoni
Via Nazionale—Palazzo delle Esposizioni

SOURCES

Blunt, Anthony. *Borromini*. London, 2001.
Boatwright, Mary Taliaferro. *Hadrian and the City of Rome*. New Jersey, 1987.
Carandini, Maria Antonelli, ed. *Roma Vostra*. Roma, 2003.
Champlin, Edward. *Nero*. London, 2003.
Futura Edizioni. *The Popes*. Roma, 1997.
Harrison, Barbara Grizzuti. *Italian Days*. New York, 1989.
Hibbard, Howard. *Bernini*. New York, 1990.
King, Ross. *Michelangelo and the Pope's Ceiling*. New York, 2003.
Kirwin, W. Chandler. *Powers Matchless: The Pontificate of Urban VIII, the Baldachin and Gian Lorenzo Bernini*. New York, 1997.
Macadam, Alta. *Blue Guide Rome*. New York, 2003.
Majanlahti, Anthony. *The Families Who Made Rome*. London, 2005.
Masson, Georgina. *The Companion Guide to Rome*. New York, 2003.
Ovid. *Metamorphoses*. Indiana, 1955. Trans. Rolfe Humphries.
Puglisi, Catherine. *Caravaggio*. London, 1998.
Scribner III, Charles. *Bernini*. New York, 1991.
Soprintendenza Archeologica di Roma. *The Roman Forum*. Milan, 1998.
Suetonius. *The Twelve Caesars*. London, 1989. Trans. Robert Graves.
Tripp, Edward. *The Meridian Handbook of Classical Mythology*. New York, 1970.
Vasari, Giorgio. *The Lives of the Artists*. Oxford, 1991.
Virgil, *The Aeneid. New York, 1981*. Trans. Allen Mandelbaum.

INDEX

A

Accomodations (Where to Stay), 202
Acqua Vergine, 108, 117
Aeneas, 29, 34, 41, 44, 121, 135-136, 167, 172
Aeneid, 15, 135, 167, 172, 233
Aesculapius, legend, 68, 69
Agrippa, Marcus, 15, 87,108-109
Alexander VII, Pope, 149
Antony, Marc, 14, 35, 87, 109
Apollo Belvedere, 164, 171
Apollo and Daphne myth, 134
Apollodorus of Damascus, 49-50
Appia Antica, The, 179-181, 185, 195, 199, 213, 200
Ara Pacis Augustae (Altar of Peace), 15, 121
Arch of Constantine, 54, 168
Arch of Septimius Severus, 35-38, 42, 47
Arch of Titus, 27, 36, 44, 52-54
Augustus, 14-16, 28-29, 38, 41, 48, 50, 55-57, 65-67, 87, 107, 109-110, 121, 135, 187
    Mausoleum of, 50, 67, 121
    Sundial, 67, 106-107, 109-110
Aurelian Wall, 185
Aurelius, Marcus, 17, 32-33, 42, 46, 107-110
Aventine Hill, 25, 62, 65, 68, 184

B

Baldacchino, of St. Peter's, 20, 86, 91, 117, 146-147, 154-155, 158
Barberini, Pope Urban VIII, 19-21, 46, 48, 76, 86, 91, 110, 117, 125-128, 153, 156-158, 167, 187, 233

National Gallery of Classical Art, 19, 127-128, 177-178
Basilica Aemilia, 35
Basilica Giulia, 37, 39, 41
Basilica St. Pietro in Vaticano, (See St. Peter's)
Baths of Caracalla, 37, 80, 178
Belly Button of Rome, 38
Bernini, Gian Lorenzo, 19-22, 46, 66, 85-86, 88-89, 91-93, 97, 110, 112, 128-129, 132-137, 146-147, 149-158, 160, 167, 177-178, 183, 233
Bernini, Pietro (father of Gian Lorenzo), 116, 132, 154
Bike rentals, 114, 179, 200
Bioparco Zoologico di Roma (zoo), 130, 137
Bocca della Verità, 62, 63, 68, 184
Bonaparte family, 132-133
Bone Church (S. Maria della Concezione), 124-127
Bookstores, 95, 111, 166, 189, 196
Borghese, Cardinal Scipione, 21, 131, 137
Borghese Galleria, 18, 21, 127, 130-137
Borgia, Lucrezia, 76, 193
Borgo Pio, 44, 146, 158, 161, 173-174, 175, 198
Borromini, Francesco, 78, 81-82, 85-86, 89, 116, 128, 153, 177-178, 233
Botanical Gardens (Orto Botanico), 186
Bramante, Donato, 18, 78, 89, 153, 165, 168-169
Bridges
    Michelangelo's Bridge, 80
    Ponte Fabricio, 68, 184
    Ponte Palatino, 65
    Ponte Rotto (Broken Bridge), 65, 68

Ponte S. Angelo (Bridge of Angels),
160
Ponte Sisto, 81, 83, 186, 188-189,
196
Bruno, Giordano, 79
Buses, 198-199

C

Caesar, Julius, 14, 28-29, 41-42, 77, 99,
180, 233
Campidoglio, 17-18, 27-30, 35, 170
Campo dei Fiori, 26, 73-79, 198
Cannon on the Janiculum Hill, the, 180
Canova, Antonio, 132
Capitoline Hill, 17, 25-34, 42-46, 67, 97, 186
Capitoline Museums, 27, 30, 32-33,
44-46
Capuchin Cemetery, 81, 120, 124, 127
Caracalla, 37-38, 80, 178, 179
Caravaggio, Michelangelo Merisi da,
18-19, 30, 76, 84, 90, 120, 132, 136,
177-178, 183, 233
Carracci, Annibale, 78, 91, 94, 128, 154,
177, 183
Casina di Raffaello, 130-131, 138
Castel Sant'Angelo, 16, 87, 91, 95, 110,
118, 121, 143, 145-147, 157-158,
160-161, 173, 178, 181, 198
Castor and Pollux (Dioscuri), 28, 32, 41,
112
Catacombs
Of Priscilla, 182
Of St. Callisto, 181-182
Cenci, Beatrice, 178
Changing of the Guard (President's
Palace), 112
Chigi Chapel, 120
Chigi, Agostino story, 80
Christina (Cristina) of Sweden, Queen,
118, 120
Churches and Basilicas
Gesú, 94, 96, 97
S. Agnese in Agone, 21, 82, 85-86,
89, 129
S. Andrea al Quirinale, 129
S. Carlo alle Quattro Fontane
(St. Carlino), 128-129
S. Clemente, 51, 57-58
S. Cosma and Damiano, 43, 47
S. Giovanni in Laterano, 17, 67-76
S. Ignazio di Loyola, 94, 97
S. Luigi dei Francesi, 18, 84, 90

S. Maria del Popolo, 18, 113, 115,
119-120
S. Maria della Concezione,
124-125, 127
S. Maria dell'Orazione e Morte, 80
S. Maria della Pace, 170
S. Maria in Aracoeli, 30, 43, 48, 67,
97, 186
S. Maria in Cosmedin, 62-65, 68,
184
S. Maria in Trastevere, 189
S. Maria sopra Minerva, 67, 93
S. Pietro in Carcere, 47
S. Pietro in Montorio, 153
S. Pietro in Vaticano (St. Peter's),
17-21, 73, 76, 83, 85-86, 91,
116-117, 136, 143, 145-147, 149-
157, 162-165, 167-168, 170, 184
S. Pietro in Vincoli, 60, 171
S. Quattro Coronati, 58, 187
S. Susanna, 162, 234
Cicero, 35, 55
Cinemas, 196
Circus Maximus, 55-56, 62, 63-68, 89,
115, 184
City of Water (Città dell'Acqua), 111
Cloaca Maxima, 28, 37, 63
Collegio di Propaganda Fide, 85, 116
Colosseum, 16, 27-30, 35, 37, 42, 44,
51-54, 57, 60-61
Columns
of Marcus Aurelius, 42, 107-109
of Phocas, 40, 87
of Trajan, 48-50, 108, 110, 185
Computers and Internet Cafes, 95, 197
Constantine, Emperor, 30, 33, 54, 146,
151, 166, 188
Cordonata, of Michelangelo, 17, 31-32

D

David, The, 133, 136, 178
D'Este, Villa, 192-193
Day Trips and More, 177
Delle Rovere, Pope Julius II, 17, 22, 60,
81, 146, 165, 171
Domitian's Stadium, 84
Domus Aurea, 16, 52, 59

E

Egyptian Museum (Vatican), 164,
170-171

Egyptian Obelisks, 65-66, 112, 118, 149
Egyptian Cat, the, 94
Elephant statue, the , 66, 93
Extras In Rome, 177
Extras Outside Rome, 190
EUR, 185

F

Facchino (the porter), 34, 183
Farnese, Pope Paul III, 16-17, 32-33,
  76-77, 97, 115, 147, 156, 170
  Palazzo, 18, 75, 77, 80-83, 94, 154
Filarete, Antonio, 150
Films, 12, 63, 125, 196
Flavian Ampitheatre (see Colosseum)
Forum,
  Imperial, 15, 29, 48-50, 108
  Roman, 15-19, 25, 27-28, 30, 35,
    37-46, 51-52, 57, 63, 87
  Trajan's, 29, 48-50, 108, 185
Fountains, 16, 19-22, 46, 54, 66, 79-80,
  85-86, 88-89, 107-109, 116, 118-119,
  124-126, 128, 130, 149, 168, 183-184,
  193-194
  Fontana dei Quattro Fiumi (Four
    Rivers), 21, 66, 85-86, 88
  Fontana della Barcaccia, 116
  Fontana delle Api, 126
  Fontana delle Tartarughe (Turtle
    Fountain), 184
  Fontana di Trevi, 107-109, 117
  Fontana di Tritone, 124-125, 126,
    140
  Fontanella del Facchino, 34, 183
  Fountain of the Moor, 88

G

Galileo, Gallilei, 19, 79, 118, 155, 170
Galleria Borghese, 18, 21, 127, 130-137
Galleria Doria Pamphilj, 20, 46, 182
Galleria Nazionale d'Arte Antica, 128,
  177
Galleria Spada, 75, 78
Garibaldi, Anita, 181
Garibaldi, the statue and piazza, 180-181,
  186
Gesù, Il, 94, 96-97
Ghetto, the, 183-184
Gianicolo (Janiculum) Hill, 153, 180-181
Giardino degli Aranci (Parco Savello),
  68, 185

Glass Elevator (Victor Emanuele II
  Monument), 45, 50, 189
Golden House (see Domus Aurea), 16,
  52-53, 57, 59, 77, 171
Golden Milestone, the, 38-39

H

Hadrian, 16, 44, 49-50, 67, 87, 92, 109,
  121, 147-148, 158-160, 192-193
Hadrian's Villa (Tivoli), 192-193
Hotels and accommodations, 202-212
House of Monsters, 118, 123
House of Romulus, 55-57
House of the Vestal Virgins, 36, 41

I

Imperial Forums, 15, 29, 48-50, 108
Innocent X Pamphilj, Pope, 20, 46, 66,
  86, 127, 153, 183
Internet Cafes, 197
Internet Sources, 231
Isola Tiberina (see Tiberina Island), 65,
  68-69, 184, 192

J

Janiculum (Gianicolo) Hill, 153, 180-181
Jewish Ghetto, 69-70, 183-184, 219-220
Julius Caesar, 14, 28-29, 41-42, 77, 99,
  180, 233
Julius II, Pope, 17, 22, 60, 81, 146, 165,
  167-168, 171

K

Keats, 122, 179, 193
Knights of Malta Keyhole, 68, 184

L

Lacus Curtius, the, 40, 132
Laocoön, the, 59-60, 169, 171-172, 187
Lapis Niger, 35, 37
Last Judgment, the, 17-18, 170
Limousines and car service, 199
Leo X, Medici Pope, 22, 89, 93, 159,
  165, 167
Lucrezia, Madama, 76, 193
Ludus Magnus, 57
Lupa Capitolina (Capitoline she-wolf),
  30, 34, 46

M

Maderno, Carlo, 85, 125, 177, 182
Mail, 197
Mamertine Prison, 47
Maps
    Ancient Rome, 26
    Capitoline Hill, 32
    Medieval/Renaissance Rome, 74
    Modern Rome, 106
    Palatine Hill, 56
    Papal Rome (Vaticano), 144
    Roman Forum, 36
    St. Peter's Floor Plan, 152
Marforio, 32-33, 87
Markets of Trajan, 49, 50
Mausoleum of Augustus, 121, 126, 211
Mausoleum of Hadrian, 16, 91, 121,
    145-147, 158-160
Medici, Pope Leo X, 22, 89, 93, 159,
    165, 167
Meta Sudans, 54
Michelangelo Buonarroti, 17-18, 29, 31,
    32, 41, 59-60, 78, 80, 83, 87, 93, 147,
    152-154, 159-160, 165-171, 187, 233
Mithraic Temple, 58
Moses (Statue of), 18, 60, 171
Mouth of Truth (see Bocca della Verita)
Museums and Art Galleries
    Capella Sistina (see Sistine Chapel),
      17-18, 146, 163-170
    Capitoline Museums, 27, 30, 32-33,
      44-46
    Palazzo dei Conservatori, 27, 33
    Egyptian Museum (Vatican), 164,
      170-171
    Galleria Borghese, 18, 21, 127,
      130-137
    Galleria Doria Pamphilj, 20, 46 182
    Galleria Nazionale d'Arte Antica,
      128, 177
    Galleria Spada, 75, 78
    Museo della Civiltà Romana, 185
    Museo della Mura, 185
    Museo Nazionale di Castel S.
      Angelo, 16, 87, 91, 95, 110, 118,
      121, 143, 145-147, 157-158, 160-
      161, 173, 178, 181, 198
    Museo Palatino, 52, 54, 56
    Museo Pio Clementino (Vatican),
      164-165, 191
    Sistine Chapel, 17-18, 146, 163-170

Vatican Museums, 145-146,
    163-172, 187

N

Necropolis di S. Pietro (Scavi), 157, 162
Nero, 15-16, 47, 52-54, 57, 59, 65, 77,
    111, 120, 146, 150, 171, 233
Nero's Golden House (see Domus
    Aurea), 16, 52-53, 57, 59, 77, 171
Nero and the Theater of Pompey story, 77

O

Obelisks, 65-67, 88-89, 91-92, 109-110,
    112-113, 115, 118-119, 128-129,
    147-149
Orto Botanico, (Botanical Gardens), 186
Ostia Antica, 190, 191, 195

P

Palaces
    Palazzo Barberini, 94, 128
    Palazzo dei Conservatori, 27, 33
    Palazzo della Cancelleria, 83
    Palazzo Falconieri, 81-82
    Palazzo Farnese, 75, 77, 80, 83, 94,
      154
    Palazzo Madama, 89
    Palazzo Nuovo, 32
    Palazzo del Quirinale, 112
    Palazzo Senatorio, 27, 30, 34
    Palazzo Spada, 75, 78, 82
    Palazzo di Venezia, 53, 55
    Palazzo Valentini (Roman Houses),
      47
Palatine Antiquarium, 56
Palatine Bridge, 65
Palatine Hill, 26-28, 35-36, 44, 51-52,
    54-56, 62, 64
Pamphilj, Pope Innocent X, 20, 46, 66,
    86, 127, 153, 183
Pantheon, 15-16, 20, 26, 40, 67, 73-74,
    84-87, 89-92, 107-110, 146, 160
Papal Audiences, 145, 162
Parco di Castel Sant'Angelo, 145-147, 161
Parco Savello (the Orange Tree Park), 68,
    185
Pasquino, 34, 74, 87, 95
Passetto, the Papal Wall, 159
Paul III Farnese, Pope, 16-17, 32-33,
    76-77, 97, 115, 147, 156, 159, 170
Perugino, 128, 167-168, 177

Phaedra and Hipploytus myth, 58
Piazzas
    Piazza Barberini, 19, 21, 124-128
    Piazza dei Campo dei Fiori, 75-79
    Piazza del Campidoglio, 17-18, 27, 30
    Piazza del Popolo, 65-67, 113, 114-115, 118-120, 190, 198-200
    Piazza del Quirinale, 67, 112, 128
    Piazza della Bocca della Verità, 26, 62, 63
    Piazza della Repubblica, 196, 198
    Piazza di Montecitorio, 67, 107, 109-110
    Piazza di Spagna, 85, 113, 114, 116, 151, 198
    Piazza Farnese, 18, 75, 77, 80-83, 94, 154
    Piazza Garibaldi, 180-181
    Piazza Mattei, 184
    Piazza Minerva, 66, 93
    Piazza Navona, 20-21, 66, 73-75, 82, 84-89, 92, 108, 110, 119-120, 129, 170, 233
    Piazza Risorgimento, 173-174
    Piazza San Pietro, 67, 148, 158, 197
    Piazza Santa Maria in Trastevere, 188-189
    Piazza Venezia, 26, 50, 97, 122, 189-190, 198-199
Pietà, the, 17, 60, 147, 152-153
Pietro da Cortona, 94, 178
Pincio Gardens, 67, 113, 114, 118, 119, 130, 131
Pluto and Persephone myth, 135
Pompeii, 12, 191, 194, 195, 199
Popes
    Pope Innocent X Pamphilj, 20, 46, 66, 86, 127, 153, 183
    Pope Julius II Della Rovere, 17, 22, 60, 81, 146, 165, 167-168, 171
    Pope Leo X Medici, 22, 89, 93, 159, 165, 167
    Pope Paul III Farnese, 16-17, 32-33, 76-77, 97, 115, 147, 156, 159, 170
    Pope Urban VIII Barberini, 19-21, 46, 48, 76, 86, 91-92, 110, 117, 125-128, 153, 156-158, 167, 187, 233
Portico di Ottavia, 184
Pozzo, Fra Andrea, 94, 96-97
President's Palace (Quirinal Hill), 67, 112, 139, 177

Q

Quirinal Hill, 49, 67, 111, 112, 128

R

Raphael (Raffaello Sanzio), 29, 46, 59, 73, 76, 80-81, 89, 91, 120, 128, 132, 156, 164-170, 177, 183
Raphael Rooms (Stanze), 164-167
Reni, Guido, 20, 94, 127, 178
Restaurants (Where to Eat), 14, 69-71, 98-103, 139-141, 173-175, 213-230
Roma, the goddess, 34, 43, 44
Roman Forum, 15-19, 25, 27-28, 30, 35, 37-46, 51-52, 57, 63, 87
Roman Houses (Palazzo Valentini), 47
Romulus and Remus, 34, 46, 63, 172
Rooms of St. Ignatius, 94, 96-97

S

Sacra Via, 42, 44, 54
Salvi, Niccolo, 107-109
Scavi Tour, excavations under St. Peter's, 157, 162
Scooters and Bicycles, 200-201
Shelly, Percy Bysshe, 178-179, 193
She-wolf, the, 30, 34, 45, 46, 63
Shops and shopping, 76, 83, 87, 95, 109, 111, 120-122, 161-162, 189, 197-198, 221
Sistine Chapel, 17-18, 146, 163-170
Skull Church (S. Maria dell-Orazione e Morte), 80, 120, 127
Spanish Steps, 19, 21, 23, 26, 67, 74, 105-107, 113-118, 196, 198
Spartacus story, 12, 196
St. Peter's Basilica, 17-21, 60, 66-67, 73, 76, 83, 85-86, 91, 116-117, 136, 143, 145-147, 149-157, 162, 164-165, 167-168, 170, 184
Stories, Myths and Legends
    Apollo and Daphne, 134
    Artistic Admiration (Raphael), 170
    Artistic Envy (Bramante), 169
    Beware of Greeks Bearing Gifts (Laocoön), 172
    Born to Build (Bernini), 154
    Chain Reaction (S. Peter), 61
    Double Take (Bernini & Borghese), 137
    Ego Trips (Michelangelo), 60
    Ghosts In the Trees (Nero), 120

Give and Take (Nero), 53
Girl Power (Hadrian), 44
Growing Up Vestal, 41
Heavenly Healing (Castel Sant'Angelo), 158
If You Can't Say Something Nice... (Trajan), 50
More Bernini (Navona), 88
Legend of Aesculapius (Tiberina Island), 68-69
Legend of Romulus & Remus, 34, 63
Nero and the Theater of Pompey, 77
One Bad Apple (Venus & the Golden Apple), 133
Phaedra and Hippolytus (S. Clemente), 58, 187
Point of No Return (Caesar), 99
Raphael Was Here (Domus Aurea), 59
The Cenci, 69, 178
Throw Your Food (Villa Farnesina), 80
Valor of Marcus Curtius, 40
What a Blast! (Janiculum Cannon), 181
Streets
Via Appia Antica, 179, 181, 185, 196, 199-200
Via Cola di Rienzo, 173, 175, 198
Via Condotti, 122, 198
Via dei Fori Imperiali, 26-29, 35-36, 42, 48
Via del Coronari, 95
Via del Corso, 106-107, 109, 111, 122, 190, 197, 198, 200, 233
Via de' Giubbonari, 74, 76, 83, 198
Via del Babuino, 106, 121-122, 198
Via del Governo Vecchio, 74, 95
Via delle Quattro Fontane, 128, 177
Via Giulia, 74, 80-82, 144
Via Nazionale, 26, 198, 233
Via Portico d'Ottavia, 26, 184
Via Sacra, 36, 42, 44, 54, 56
Via Veneto, 76, 105-106, 124-127
Sundial of Augustus, 67, 74, 106-107, 109-110
Synagogue, the, 184, 192

T
Tabularium, 27, 30, 32, 36, 45
Talking Statues
Facchino, 34, 183
Lucrezia, 34
Marforio, 34, 74, 87
Pasquino, 34, 74, 87
Taxis, 199
Temples
Temple of Antoninus and Faustina, 36, 42-43
Temple of Castor and Pollux, 28, 32, 36, 41, 112
Temple of Hercules, 65
Temple of Isis, 66-67, 91-92, 94
Temple of Julius Caesar, 15, 41
Temple of Romulus, 28, 43, 47, 187
Temple of Saturn, 35, 38-39
Temple of Venus and Roma, 16, 44-54
Temple of Vesta, 36, 41, 65
Temple of Veiovis, 45
Theater of Marcellus, 15, 183-184
Theater of Pompey, 77, 99, 216
Tiberina Island, 65, 68-70, 184, 192
Tivoli (Hadrian's Villa and Villa d'Este), 192-193
Trains (metro), 198, 232
Trajan's Column, 48-50, 108, 110, 185
Trajan's Markets, 48, 50
Transport, 198-199
Trastevere, 26, 68, 74, 80, 83, 182, 186, 188-189, 196, 233
Trevi Fountain, 107-109, 117, 233
Triton's Fountain, 19, 21, 107, 124-126

U
Umbilicus Urbis (see Belly Button of Rome), 38
Urban VIII Barberini, Pope , 19, 21, 45, 48, 76, 86, 91-92, 110, 117, 125-128, 153, 156-159, 167, 187, 233

V
Valadier, Giuseppe, 115, 119
Vasari, Giorgio, 18, 83, 170, 233
Vatican City, 144-172
Vatican Museums, 59, 60, 143, 146, 152, 156, 163-172, 184, 187
Victor Emanuel (Vittorio Emanuele) II Monument, 45, 50, 115, 189-190, 215

Villas
Villa Adriana (Hadrian's Villa), 16,
192-193
Villa Borghese park and gardens,
18, 21, 106, 113-115, 127, 130-138,
200
Villa d'Este, 193-194
Villa Farnesina, 80, 180, 186
Villa Medici, 19, 106, 118-120, 139,
171
Villa of the Mysteries, Pompeii, 195
Vittoriano (see Victor Emanuel II
Monument)
Virgil, 15, 34, 135, 167, 172, 235
Vulcanal (see Lapis Niger), 37

Z

Zoo (Bioparco Giardino Zoologico), 130,
137

Notes

Notes

Notes

Notes

Notes